kept 7/19

D1410051

SAM STERN
VIRGIN TO VETERAN
— HOW TO —
GET COOKING
WITH CONFIDENCE

LP

LYONS PRESS
Guilford, Connecticut
An imprint of Globe Pequot Press

photography by
Chris Terry

Cooking has to be one of the greatest pleasures of all time; it's creative, it's fun, it's relaxing, and it's social. It's the ideal excuse for getting mates and family around. It's also an ideal activity on purely selfish grounds. Cooking for yourself means you get to make informed choices about what you eat. When you're feeling greedy you can indulge (but in a good way). When you're training for a marathon or just want to get yourself fit you can cook and eat to take greater care of yourself. It saves loads of time: yes, a great home cooked meal can be thrown together from scratch in less time than it takes to take delivery of a pizza. And those long slow cook recipes are the perfect opportunity to do something chilling while your roast is sizzling away in a very low oven. But if you're just starting out of course it can feel daunting. So think of *Virgin to Veteran* as a personal masterclass. I'm not a professional chef but I've been a passionate cook since I can remember. I've cooked in all kinds of kitchens (at home, at college, all over the place) and I cook every meal from scratch as I totally believe that you are what you eat and that every meal you eat has to earn its place on your plate. So I've structured the book to be relevant, (only foods you'd really want to eat), comprehensive (I've pulled together loads of key information in the introductions to each chapter), and easy to follow. You'll find each recipe moves logically through every step you'll need to take. It encourages you to be creative. And it starts with a guide to setting up a workable kitchen—a place where you can bang on the music and get into cooking with confidence.

SAM

THE VIRGIN KITCHEN SETUP

THE KNIFE SET Knives are like an extension of your arm: you need them close to your board. I'm right handed so that's where I put my knife block. Use the appropriate one for the job (p9). Don't store them in the drawer—it ruins the blades and it's dangerous. Keep them in a block or on a wall-mounted magnetic strip, or in a chef's roll instead.

SEASONINGS Sometimes I'll put these on a tray, sometimes they'll be grouped together. Clear a space to put any appropriate oils, vinegars, spices, dried herbs, a lemon, salt, and pepper.

THE TIMER Check you've got a reliable timer available: bang it on the counter where you can't miss it, set the timing function on your oven, or set your cell phone; if you're wandering off when something tasty's cooking you don't want to forget it.

SETTING UP YOUR BASE KITCHEN

Go into any kitchen store and there are thousands of bits of equipment begging "buy me." Who needs them? You don't. What you do need is an organized space, the right bits for the job, a workable refrigerator, and smartly stocked shelves and cupboards. Get this lot sorted and get yourself cooking...

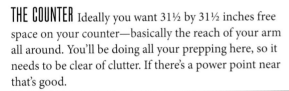

THE COUNTER Ideally you want 31½ by 31½ inches free space on your counter—basically the reach of your arm all around. You'll be doing all your prepping here, so it needs to be clear of clutter. If there's a power point near that's good.

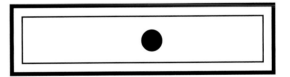

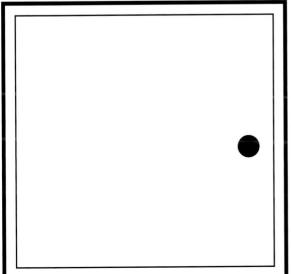

THE CUTTING BOARD It's not glamorous but a good board anchors your cooking. It'll help you master fast, precise cutting and won't ruin your knives (cheap plastic ones do). Get two. A tight grained wooden one (1–2 inches thick) for all your vegetable work and a plastic one to use for prepping raw fish and meat.

KITCHEN SCALES For me these have to be digital, but it's your choice (p8). Have them handy—especially for baking where you will be needing to measure absolutely everything.

TOOLS OF THE TRADE

HARDWARE ESSENTIALS

These are the hand tools I find myself using all the time. Get them cheap from any specialist kitchen store. Rather than lose them in drawers, I stick them in pots and sit them by my board then shift them across to the stove when I'm working there.

WOODEN SPOONS For turning/beating/creaming/mixing. Long cool handles won't burn your hands and the ends won't melt. Hand-wash.

METAL SPOONS For measuring and baking. Don't use them in pans, they'll scratch.

LONG METAL SKEWER For testing steak/roasts/chops for doneness. Cheap and it works.

SLOTTED SPOON For draining and lifting food out of oil/liquids/stir-fries.

BALLOON WHISK For whipping cream/meringue/egg whites, etc. Helps make the smoothest of sauces.

TONGS For quick and easy turning, shifting meat, and other slippery things in and out of hot pans or lifting spaghetti onto dishes. A key tool in your arsenal.

SPATULA Use to turn food. Made in metal and nylon (for nonstick pans) their wide, slotted head and off-set angle is ideal for turning and shifting.

FISH SLICE Designed to slide easily under a whole bit of fish so you can turn it neatly (the solid head helps). Use for wide food like chicken schnitzel or small roasts.

THIN SPATULA Slide under cookies to release from the pan or use to frost cakes. It's long, narrow, and very thin, so perfect for lifting food like steaks to check for doneness.

RUBBER SPATULA Has flexibility and at least one rounded tip to retrieve all the batter from the cake bowl/sauce from the pan.

POTATO RICER A giant garlic press for potatoes. Inexpensive. Makes the best, driest mashed potato.

LADLE For moving soups and other liquids (eg. crepe mix/eggs for omelet) into or out of the pan.

PEELER Use to peel potatoes and other veg. Cuts carrots/zucchini/cucumber into ribbons; makes chocolate curls/Parmesan shavings.

MICROPLANE GRATER For fine grating hard cheese/citrus zest.

GARLIC CRUSHER What it suggests. Does it fast. Alternatively, use a chef's knife (p9).

SILICONE BRUSH Nifty. Use to brush eggwash/glaze on pie dough; grease pans/dishes/soufflé dishes; brush oil onto food; re-apply a marinade.

HARDWARE DRAWER

Some gear here you could improvise...

ROLLING PIN For rolling out pie dough/thinning meats, and crushing dry ingredients (or use a clean wine bottle instead).

TWEEZERS For nipping bones out of fish (if using eyebrow tweezers sterilize them).

COOKIE CUTTERS For cookies/scones/big ravioli (or use a paring knife/thin glass). Can also be used as cook's rings.

PIE WEIGHTS For baking tarts blind (or use ceramic baking beans or dried lima beans/rice).

APPLE CORER Neat and fast (or cut around the core with a paring knife).

COOK'S RINGS Shape rice/salad/rosti other cheap eats to create height. Looks impressive.

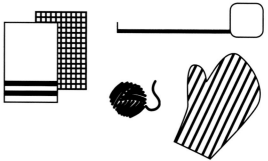

SOFTWARE DRAWER

Bits you'll take for granted but are so useful (often essential). I always keep a dish towel handy for shifting things fast, hanging onto small or slippery dishes that oven mitts won't hold, protecting my hands against hot handles, and mopping spills.

DISH TOWELS For blotting salad greens/covering dough; wiping hands; protecting.

OVEN MITTS Get them thick enough and check your hands can move in them.

PAPER TOWELS Draining fried food/French fries; drying veg and salad; wiping pans out.

TAPE MEASURE For measuring the bottom of cake and tart pans for accurate baking.

WAX PAPER/BAKING PARCHMENT For lining pans; cooking food in paper.

PLASTIC WRAP Covering and wrapping: thinning meats; perfect shaped poached eggs.

STRING Measuring pans; tying a bouquet garni, cuffing chicken legs.

FOIL For protecting food during cooking; wrapping; protecting a resting roast; cooking food in foil packages.

FREEZER BAGS Come in all sizes. Get labels for freezer and use a freezer pen.

CHEESECLOTH Cheap cloth used to make cheese; fine straining liquid for jellies.

PASTRY BAG For decorating cakes; shaping meringue; piping mash.

ON THE SHELF (or in the cupboard)

Some of your hardest working items, bowls especially.

MIXING BOWLS 1 x 4 quart and 3 smaller for stacking: Pyrex is less likely to scratch than plastic (essential if using to whisk egg whites) or to absorb smells: use it for mixing/freezing/reheating/melting chocolate/making sauces over hot water.

MEASURING CUPS AND PITCHERS For measuring/mixing liquids, controlled pouring for sauces/mayo.

COLANDER For draining anything. Use as a fruit bowl or over pan as a steamer.

SIFT For sifting flours, etc. for baking/draining vegetables. Use to puree fruit.

BOX GRATER For grating cheese/vegetables, etc.

MORTAR AND PESTLE For bashing marinades/smashing spices.

GRINDER For grinding your own meat. Makes a radical difference.

PASTA MACHINE Reasonably cheap and gives impressive results.

POTS AND PANS

Poor pans won't do your techniques proud: if you're buying new you want a good surface, a weight to suit your hand, and metal handles so you can fry and bake. Thick bottoms mean your food is less likely to burn and you'll keep in control. Nonstick are easier to use but don't last as long.

LIDDED SAUTÉ PAN For sautés (high-heat frying/tossing food) and stews/sauces.

GRIDDLE PAN Pan-grills fast and healthier than frying. Like an indoor barbecue.

OVENPROOF SKILLET Metal handled. For fry-bake recipes and standard fry.

PASTA PAN Needs to be big. Convert to a steamer/use for stocks.

MEDIUM SAUCEPAN For making soups/sauces, boiling potatoes.

SMALL SAUCEPAN For cooking eggs, small amounts of vegetables or heating milk.

WOK For stir-fries, also good for deep-frying but it'll need a flat bottom.

CRÊPE PAN Easy in and out for pancakes and good for flatbread.

OMELET PAN Neat 6-inch pan: just the right size and multitasks.

DISHES

Don't go mad: see how few you can get away with: raid prokitchen stores for value.

CASSEROLE DISH Get the size to suit your needs. I like using wider ones.

LARGE SHALLOW BAKING DISH For bakes/lasagna/roasting vegetables.

RAMEKINS For prep storage/desserts/soufflés/baked eggs.

MUGS, CUPS, PLATES, AND BOWLS Use your usual stuff for mixing, prepping, and serving.

GET HOOKED
hang your pots and pans for space, time, accessibility.

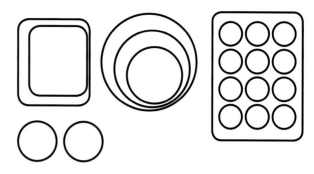

PLUG-INS

You can do pretty much everything in the kitchen by hand but there are times when it's good to get a machine to share the effort...

KETTLE For tea/boiling up water to pour into pan for vegetables/making up stock.

STICK BLENDER Blends soups/hummus/bread crumbs/sauces.

ELECTRIC HAND MIXER For mixing and whisking cakes/eggs/sauces.

FREESTANDING MIXER Brilliant for mixing bread/pizza dough/cake batters.

PROCESSOR Does a bit of everything. Best for mixing pie dough.

BLENDER Fast and very efficient. Cool food a bit before using and never overfill.

DEEP-FAT FRYER A safer way to deal with deep-fry.

ICE-CREAM MACHINE Opens up the world of homemade ice cream. I love mine.

PANS AND THINGS

No rules here, except get a roasting pan that's thick enough to use on your stove and thick baking sheets which don't buckle in the heat for pizza.

ROASTING PANS Get one big enough to take a chicken plus vegetables and a smaller one.

YORKSHIRE PUDDING PAN 4 individual holes, or use a muffin pan or smaller roasting pan.

TART PANS Get bigger (9 inches) and individual (4 inches) for sweet and savory tarts/quiche.

LOAF PANS For bread/loaf-shaped cake/teabreads. Get a 1-pound or 2-pound one.

BAKING SHEETS For pizza/cookies/scones/finishing/reheating food/catching drips.

CAKE PANS Get 1 x 8½-inch round pan for proper cakes, 2 x 7 inches for sponge cakes.

SPRINGFORM CHEESECAKE PAN Springform means the cake is easily released.

WIRE RACK Avoid the bottom of new baking getting damp: get a higher one or elevate what you've got.

GETTING THE MEASURE

Accurate measuring gives you a confident base to work from when you're starting out. It's about getting the balance of ingredients right. Having a carrot-heavy casserole for example is not a disaster, but exact measurement is more crucial in baking. If the amount of raising agent's wrong or the egg/fat/flour ratio is out your cake may not be as light as it could be. Use imperial/metric, cups, spoons, US cup measurements, old-school scales with weights, electronic jobs with loads of extras like thermometer, timer, whatever—as long as it's easy to read, fits into your space, and is above all accurate. Once you're fully into it, you'll find you can start to judge your measurements by eye. Recipes are written in a mix of measurements: check online for conversions for dry weight and liquid volumes, or use an app or an oven magnet instead.

✚ EMERGENCY ROOM

FIRE BLANKET Keep one handy just in case; throw over a burning pan if it's safe (never use water and don't try to pick the pan up and run with it).

CELL PHONE Call for help if there's a real problem; better safe than sorry.

PLASTERS For small nicks; happens to the best of us but take care.

COLD WATER For very minor burns; hold under cold running water. For worse; call for help.

CUTTING THINGS

A good-quality knife makes all the difference in the kitchen. It should be balanced in your hand, not too heavy, razor sharp, and with a good grip. Don't think you need to be getting the most expensive: some Japanese handmade beauties are highly desirable but maybe something to work up to. A reasonably priced stainless steel knife with a fully forged reinforced blade is easily found in kitchen stores.

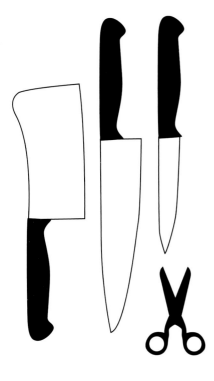

THE ONES FOR THE JOB

CHEF'S KNIFE A multi-purpose broad blade. Good for precision cutting/dicing/slicing/chopping/cubing/light butchery.

PARING KNIFE A small short-handled blade useful for smaller jobs. Use to trim and prepare vegetables/fruit/cheese.

BREAD KNIFE A serrated blade for doing the obvious effortlessly. Also good for cutting butternut squash/pineapple/eggplants.

CARVING KNIFE A long, thin blade perfect for carving neat, wafer-thin slices of meat.

FILLETING KNIFE A long, thin, flexible blade. The give in the blade lets you work cleanly to lift raw fish off the bone.

BONING KNIFE A long, narrow slightly curved blade with a sharp tip. Only used for boning meat, so only needed if you're into butchery.

CLEAVER A big, heavy knife with a very broad blade. Use for heavy jobs (e.g. chopping through ribs/bone) which would damage other blades.

SCISSORS Endlessly useful. Use to clean and trim fish; butterfly small chicken; snip string/chives/bacon. Get a good strong pair from a specialist kitchen store.

BLUNT KITCHEN KNIFE Use to run around the edge of pans to loosen your baking.

CUTTING RULES

• Check your knife is sharp enough—treat it to the steel if not.

• Check your hand and the knife handle aren't greasy.

• Always chop on your board.

• If doing a lot of knife work, sit a damp dish towel under your board to keep it steady.

• Grip the knife well: put it comfortably in your hand; sit your thumb to the side of the handle, never on top of it.

• Wash knives by hand and dry immediately.

KNIFE SHARPENING

Keep your blades in best shape and your knives will last: more importantly you'll get maximum performance out of them and they'll be safer (blunt knives slip). Use a steel—a rod of high-carbon steel on a handle—on all non-serrated blades for longevity, safety, and sharp techniques. Do it every time you use your knife so it never blunts in the first place. If in doubt, ask your friendly butcher for an impromptu lesson.

1 Hold the steel comfortably in one hand. Point it up and away from you. Check your hand is safely behind the guard.

2 Take the knife in your other hand and cross the steel and blade just above their respective handles.

3 Firmly slide the knife at a 20-degree angle along the steel so its edge is honed from its base to tip. Repeat the process on the other side. Do it a few times until you're happy with the outcome. Wash the knife before using.

HEATING THINGS

THE OVEN

It's your best friend for baking, roasting, pan-baking, simple reheating; so, get to know it and then work with it. Fact is, every one is different. Gas, electric, or convection? That's just the start of it. Work out what sort of beast yours is and then work with it.

THE BROILER

An under-rated part of your arsenal: use for cooking steaks, chops, whole fish and fillets, kebabs, finishing omelets, gratins, cooking bacon. Slide the broiler pan and rack to the right position for high, medium, or slow-cook. Preheat to high; reduce to a temperature you judge appropriate. Brush prepped food lightly with oil (too much oil or a heavy marinade may flare up, so take care). Use oven mitts to slide the tray in and out. Broil food both sides until done: turn kebabs a few times. Broiling sends oil out into the atmosphere so use the extractor fan, open window, or consider griddling food then oven baking. Pros: broiling is healthy, the fat drains away. It can taste delicious (think in-door BBQ). Cons: food can dry out so watch it.

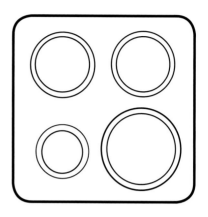

THE STOVE

The fast action station where you'll be developing your fundamental skills: griddling, frying, browning to seal and develop flavor, sautéing, reducing, stirring, whisking, adding, adjusting, seasoning, tasting things: cooking. So, keep tools, seasonings, oils, ingredients close by; get comfortable with using the right ring on the stove for the job and the pan; learn to adjust the heat through a recipe to get best results. Try switching between stove, broiler, and oven to achieve different results: pan-fry quickly then bake finish: start the omelet in the pan and finish under the broiler: mix and match.

OVEN *Rules*

USE THE TOP SHELF for quicker cooking/higher temperature dishes, middle for medium, and bottom for lower temperature/slower cooking dishes.

SET THE RACKS before you preheat.

ALWAYS PREHEAT THE OVEN at the right stage of your recipe.

CHECK THE TEMPERATURE IS REACHED before you put the food in.

If you're using a convection oven, **SET IT FOR 25°F LESS** than specified.

DON'T USE CONVECTION FOR BREAD (it disturbs the dough).

DON'T OPEN THE DOOR during cooking unless you have to.

CHECK FOR DONENESS if you need to toward the end of cooking.

OPEN AND CLOSE THE OVEN DOOR SLOWLY and gently to avoid air disturbance.

USE THE TIMER but don't trust it; it's only a machine.

Temperatures

Knowing how to shift from one temperature system to another means you can interpret any recipe with confidence. The recipes here give fahrenheit measures—for other systems check online.

COOLING THINGS

REFRIGERATOR ETIQUETTE
• Check the temperature: just below 41°F is safe.
• Don't overfill it: it'll stop the airflow and alter the temperature.
• Sit smaller packs at the front so you can see to the back.
• Use old stuff before new: First In–First Out is the rule.
• Cool hot food down before storing it.
• Wrap things well to store: use storage boxes for stacking.
• Don't be a slave to sell-by dates: smell, touch, use your judgment.
• Dishes such as curry/stews/casseroles benefit from chilling for a day or two.
• Save time: rise dough in the refrigerator overnight: chill batter for breakfast pancakes.
• Wash it with soapy water: sprays taint flavors.
• Check individual chapters for refrigerator rules on specific ingredients.
• Defrost frozen food in the refrigerator overnight.

SHELF LIFE—*what goes where...*

TOP SHELVES: soft cheese, yogurt, cooked meats, cream, butter, hummus, etc.

MIDDLE SHELF: covered leftovers

LOWER MIDDLE SHELF: covered and in-pack raw meats and fish

BOTTOM SHELF: Well-covered and in-pack raw poultry on plates

SALAD DRAWERS: Veg/salad greens and hard cheeses

DOORS: relishes, pickles, sauces, ketchup, juices, milk, white wine

THE FREEZER

Something interesting happens when you start to cook: you get to love bits of equipment you've previously frozen out. Your freezer becomes less a graveyard for peas and ice cream, more an addictive resource; time-saver; cash-cow. Freeze the following things and all's good: homemade ready-meals like chili, casseroles, stews, meat and vegetable burgers, pies, pasta dishes, soups, tomato and meat sauces, pizza bases. Store by-products of your efforts like stocks, pie dough, leftover egg whites and wine in ice-cube trays. Bang in frozen vegetables, berries, frozen fish, and shrimp; freeze a whole emergency chicken: freeze bits of the bird (thighs, legs, breasts, wings) a steak, and a chop or two; homemade ice cream.

HOW TO Freeze stuff

• Check your items to freeze are properly cold.
• Set freezer to fast freeze: a quicker freeze means better results.
• Wrap food to be frozen up well in plastic wrap to protect against the arctic cold.
• Label the bags or boxes before you fill them.
• Freestanding bags are easy to pour/spoon food into.
• Freeze small bits of leftover sauce/gravy in ice-cube trays.
• Don't overfill freezer bags/boxes: two-thirds full is good.
• Fish is hard to freeze at home: best to buy already frozen.
• For easy access later, individually wrap steaks/burgers/chops in plastic wrap before putting in freezer bags.
• Freeze cakes and scones cooked (reheat the scones): freeze fruit pies uncooked and reheat.
• Don't freeze anything that's been frozen then thawed out.
• Don't cook raw food from frozen.

STORING THINGS

THE PANTRY

A revelation: when testing recipes for this book I was spending ages looking for the right dried herb. I've got dozens of pots and, eventually, I organized them alphabetically. I reckon it saved me minutes every day. It's an extreme example, but fact is when you can see what you've got you're going to use it; a storage space isn't just a load of shelves full of random things: looking at it should inspire you.

OILS Have a huge influence on your cooking. Some add positive flavor (olive, sesame, walnut); some are healthy (olive, canola), some are brilliant for frying and using at higher temperatures (peanut/sunflower/vegetable). Use the right one for the job but other than that it's down to taste. Store in a cooler, darker place in your pantry as oils do go off.

VINEGAR Not just for fries. Use white, red, cider, balsamic, and malt. Their acidity can make or break a salad dressing, add depth to a stew or sauce; raspberry adds a fruity note, tarragon is chic, Chinese wine lifts things.

SEASONINGS Sea salt is brilliant as it gives texture and bursts of flavor; grind it into cooking for even distribution, just keep it off the table. Black pepper is best freshly ground. Use lemon, lime, vinegars.

SPICES AND DRIED HERBS I keep a good few in as they're the fastest and easiest way to transform basic ingredients. Use in rubs and marinades, and sprinkle in different combinations; see what suits.

STOCK CUBES Keep good ones in for emergencies. Bear in mind the stock will be saltier than homemade, so adjust seasoning.

FLAVORINGS AND TOP SAUCES Keep English and Dijon mustard for dressings/sauces/mash; Worcestershire and anchovy sauces for a beefy touch to meat dishes; oyster, soy, hoisin, red bean paste, sweet chili, Thai fish sauce, for Chinese/Thai; harrisa paste for a spicy kick to marinades: mint jelly/sauce for lamb; horseradish, ketchup, brown sauce, passata, tamarind paste, and lime juice for the rest.

CANS AND JARS No kitchen's complete without tomatoes, chickpeas, lima beans, kidney beans, cannellini beans, corn, coconut milk, olives, capers, anchovies, jalapenos and sundried tomatoes.

DRIED BREAD CRUMBS Panko are best. Make your own (p201) or buy from Chinese stores.

DRIED PASTA Throw spaghetti, linguine, and penne in the pantry and dinner's always in.

SWEET THINGS Keep in thin honey for balancing sweet/sour in a sauce or stew, adding to marinades/yogurt, drizzling over ice cream, cake glazing; red currant jelly for sweetening meat jus with citrus for an instant gravy; dark corn and maple syrup, blackstrap molasses, raspberry jam, and fig relish for the rest.

BAKING My baking cupboard features dried yeast, baking powder, baking soda, all-purpose and self-rising flour, bread flour (white and whole wheat), cornstarch, cocoa, oats, dried fruits, nuts, seeds, cocoa, 70% chocolate, crystallized ginger, custard powder, leaf gelatin for setting jellies, superfine/granulated/raw brown sugar, and vanilla. See p198–199 for more details.

TEA BAGS AND COFFEE For cooking and drinking.

HARD CIDER AND RED AND WHITE WINE (Sauvignon's good).

STORE LORE

- Use up old stuff before you buy new.
- Keep jars labeled and labels facing forward.
- Keep shorter things to the front of shelves.
- Organize ingredients to type: so, baking things in one area, oils and vinegars together, spices and dried herbs, pastas, noodles, rice, and other grains together, cans together, etc. Make it geographic.

COOKING THINGS

And so it begins: we've sorted out the kitchen, now for the recipes. Just a few points to remember...

 Make sure to **READ EACH RECIPE THROUGH** before you start so you won't miss a vital step like "the day before" or a key ingredient.

 Consider **"MISE EN PLACE"** as part of your prep.

 DON'T WORRY IF YOU MAKE A MISTAKE: some of the best discoveries happen when you're going wrong; getting around it is half the fun.

 Once you've got the techniques sorted **EXPERIMENT** with a dish.

 Expect that **THE SAME DISH WILL TASTE DIFFERENT EVERY TIME** you cook it even if you've followed the recipe to the letter; that's the joy of it.

 It's probably **BETTER NOT TO TRY SOMETHING FOR THE FIRST TIME** when you've got a load of people around, unless you're learning together.

 Think about how you can **SAVE ENERGY** (and cash) as you cook: cover pans with lids; boil a kettle, and pour into the pan for your green vegetables; cook enough for more than one meal—it costs less to reheat the second one than cook another.

 If you're cooking for loads of people, **TRY PREPPING AND EVEN COOKING MUCH OF IT AHEAD**, so you can enjoy yourself.

 Don't forget you can **RECYCLE THINGS**: roast up potato peelings in oil and salt; turn stale bread into bread crumbs; defrosted frozen egg whites are better than standard for whisking/holding air for meringues and soufflés: grate up any dried cheese bits for a sauce: turn excess pasta into a bake, or throw it into a frittata; fry cooked noodles up like a pancake.

 Don't just throw them into a pan, **ENGAGE WITH YOUR INGREDIENTS** at each stage of the process; smell when something's ready; see how raw or cooked through it is: touch it for doneness; listen to its water simmering or boiling; the oil sizzling or spluttering; it's all telling you something a book can't.

 TASTE ... Have a few teaspoons handy so you can dig in and judge the balance in a dish; it's key to seasoning and building your palate.

 KEEP IT BALANCED on the plate: you are what you eat.

 MAKE IT LOOK BEAUTIFUL, even if it's only a snack.

ENJOY—you're in it for a lifetime.

MISE EN PLACE

means "everything in its place." It involves getting out all the ingredients needed for your dish/dishes and the equipment and organizing it around your counter; doing all the preliminary work such as slicing, beating, sifting, or whatever and putting all the individual elements into neat containers ready for cooking.

Vegetables AND SALAD

The Vegetable (salad and otherwise); source of essential nutrition and magnificent eating. My own special relationship with these guys began back in the day when I saw what they meant to my vegetarian sisters. But let's get this straight, vegetables and salads aren't just for vegetarians—they're an essential part of your cooking repertoire. Here's where the knives come in to play: plenty of chopping and slicing required. Seasoning needs to be just so to bring out the best in a veg, especially when you're aiming for beautiful simplicity. It's all about enhancing their textures and flavors, learning not to mask them. On the other hand there are times when you need your veg present in a purely secondary role—subtly flavoring a rich chicken stock, punching some sort of character into a sauce, or sorting out the base for a lovely casserole. Get down with the skill-set in this chapter and you're equipped for most of your savory recipes. Enjoy....

FRESH, FRESH, FRESH
WHAT TO LOOK FOR

POTATOES Should be firm, plump, unblemished, dry: don't cook or buy any with green patches (they're toxic) or shoots ("eyes"): check bags aren't sweaty or smell fishy.
CARROTS, PARSNIPS, TURNIPS, RUTABAGA, BEET, CELERY ROOT Get firm, plump root vegetables without shriveling, spots, or signs of damage.
GREEN BEANS/PEAS Look for bright green, firm snappy pods free of browning.
LEAFY GREENS Avoid any with yellowing leaves/heads (on broccoli) or dried stalks.
MUSHROOMS Good ones have a bloom, smell fresh, and look typical to variety.
CELERY, CHICORY, ASPARAGUS Should smell fresh, be firm, have tightly packed heads.
TOMATOES, PEPPERS, AVOCADOS, EGGPLANTS Buy firm, shiny, heavy examples. Odd shapes are fine but no bruising.
ONIONS, SHALLOTS, GARLIC Go for firm, plump fresh smelling characters.
SALAD GREENS Fresh look just picked, packed with life and brightly colored (no wilting).

WHERE TO BUY
Getting your hands dirty

LOCAL MARKET You can touch, smell to check quality; buy loose in amounts to suit; check which days your stall of choice is there; establish a relationship.

VEGETABLE STORE Find a route home which passes a good one with a fast turnover.

SPECIALTY VEGETABLES Find exotic and unusual veg at good prices in Chinese, Caribbean, and Middle-Eastern stores.

HEALTH AND ORGANIC STORES You can pay extra for organic food (no pesticides) and it can be healthier but check for food-miles—a complex issue. Local is good if fresh.

SUPERMARKET Essentials through to organics available. Loose foods are usually cheaper and you can touch/smell them. Always use the fresh test. Check air miles.

VEG STORAGE

OUT OF THE FRIDGE

Potatoes: remove plastic packaging and store in a cool, dark place. Mealy varieties can last months in a sack/paper bag; waxy types need using in a few days.

Onions: last for months kept in a cool, dry place.

Tomatoes: store in the kitchen at room temperature.

Chiles: store in the kitchen or freeze and use from frozen.

Garlic: can last for six months. Keep away from other foods.

Cress: in the plastic box it comes in: water it.

● ● ● ● ● ● ● ● ● ● ● ● ● ● ● ●

Nuisance Neighbors

If your veg are going off before they should it could be that they are ethylene sensitive (most veg and leaves are). This natural gas is created by tomatoes, pears, melons (and more) so keep them apart.

● ● ● ● ● ● ● ● ● ● ● ● ● ● ● ●

IN THE REFRIGERATOR

Mushrooms: store in a paper bag in the warmest bit of the refrigerator to avoid freezing.

Spinach: store in a plastic bag away from the back; it freezes easily.

Cucumber: store in warmest part of the refrigerator or in the kitchen

Beet: put fresh roots unwrapped in the salad drawer: chilled vac-packs last ages.

Beans/Cabbage: store in plastic bags.

Carrots: last a few weeks without losing nutrients. Store in plastic bags.

Leaves: highly perishable. Store in plastic bags in the salad drawer for a week.

Asparagus: wrap damp paper towels around roots or stand in a jar with a little water in the refrigerator; lasts a few days.

Watercress: store bunches in a jar as above: or in plastic pack.

JUST TENDER ... VEGETABLE COOKING TIMES

Use your eye and a sharp knife. It's hard to be accurate as there are so many variables—use your judgment.

MAKE VEGETABLE STOCK

Wash and chop the following: 2 large onions, 1 celery stalk, 1 large leek, 3 carrots, some fresh parsley or cilantro if you have any, 3 cloves garlic. Dump into a pan with 2.3 litres water, 1 teaspoon salt, a few black peppercorns, a piece of scrubbed lemon peel, and juice. Bring to a boil. Reduce the heat. Simmer, half covered for at least 30 minutes or until reduced by a third. Strain through a strainer. Use or chill.

VEGETABLE AND SALAD NUTRITION

Never under-estimate a vegetable —it's a powerhouse of nutrients. **ANTI-OXIDANTS** ARE UNIQUE TO PLANTS, mopping up harmful free radicals which could otherwise cause diabetes, certain cancers, cardiovascular disease, or a weakened immune system. VEGETABLES CONTAIN SOLUBLE → **FIBER** key to maintaining a healthy digestive system. Eating them raw/steamed (in particular cabbage/leafy greens/broccoli) helps fight diabetes, reduces cholesterol, and makes you look and feel sharper. VEGETABLES ARE A GREAT SOURCE OF ESSENTIAL COMPLEX **CARBOHYDRATES** which convert to glucose and provide us with energy. LEAFY GREENS, SPINACH, AND BROCCOLI ARE RICH IN **IRON** athletes benefit from the *Chromium* IN POTATOES AND GREENS AND THE **POTASSIUM** in asparagus and tomatoes. **VITAMINS** are present in different strengths and combinations, so mix and match and you're getting everything you need.

THE VEG PLOT
What's on offer?

●●●●●●●●●●●●●●●●●●

ASPARAGUS Grassy, sexy, extravagant. Trim the woody stem; steam/griddle/boil: eat with butter/Parmesan/hollandaise, or dunk in a boiled egg. It's delicious, nutritious, and packed with folate.

AVOCADO Buttery, creamy flesh. Blitz it up for guacamole; slice and chop it into salads. Rich in vitamin E (good for skin and hair).

●●●●●●● **HOW TO...** ●●●●●●●
Degorge eggplant
Sprinkle slices with fine salt: let weep for 30 minutes. Rinse under a cold faucet. Dry thoroughly.

BEANS The long thin ones (green and string) and the plump podded ones (fava beans) are all fast to cook and can be teamed with just about anything. Briefly boil/steam and toss in fast flavorings: chopped tomatoes/oil/garlic/chile/a bit of butter, sour cream. Fling into salads, curry, Middle-Eastern dishes.

BEET Earthy sweetness in a hard root. Roast whole or in chunks or boil: adds a chic note to risottos, salads. Get it vacuum-packed to save time. It's a superfood.

BROCCOLI Robust, mustardy taste. Cook briefly (stir-fry or fast boil/steam); eat raw dipped in oil or hummus; bang into cheese sauce; roast in oil/garlic/cumin.

BUTTERNUT SQUASH Sweet and versatile. Roast with oil and garlic; steam/boil/griddle then mash as a side or puree for soups/risottos; add to pies, stews, casseroles.

CABBAGE Sexy when cooked for crispness. Shred, blanch then stir-fry with oyster/soy sauce; lightly toss shredded red/white in dressing or mayonnaise for salads.

CARROTS Sweet, cheap glorious superfood. Best raw in strips with dips/grated into salads; cut into ribbons or thin sticks for stir-fries; boiled/steamed for crushing, mashing; in soups, stews, curries, roast and casseroles for fullest flavor.

CAULIFLOWER Star of cauliflower cheese. Bang into curries/stews; make soups; roast; break into florets and steam/boil briefly; fry in tempura batter. Roast in oil, garlic, chile, and cumin.

CELERY ROOT Knobbly root tasting of celery. Add to standard/parsnip mash.

CELERY Gives a raw, slightly earthy crunch to accompany cheese/dips/hummus. A star in caponata and adds a useful, anonymous note to stocks, stew, and sauces.

CHICORY Chic, crisp, slightly bitter leaves. Good for salads; dipped and scooped into hummus; roasted around a chicken; wrapped in ham and baked in cheese sauce.

CHILES Spicy goodness all the way. Green are usually hotter than red, smaller fiercer than large. Use in curries, stir-fries, soup, salad, and marinades. Wash your hands after handling.

CORN Sweet: strip silks and leaves. Boil until tender. Treat it to butter/spices/lemon/chile; slice the kernels for relish.

●●●●●●● **HOW TO...** ●●●●●●●
Seed chiles
Capsaicin (the heat in chiles) is mostly found in the seeds and membrane. If you like fire on your tongue, just slice or dice. To remove the seeds and leave the membrane: cut off the stem, roll the chile vigorously between your palms and shake the loosened seeds out. To remove both: cut the chile lengthwise, trim the end, and scrape out with the tip of a knife or spoon.

CUCUMBER Deliciously cool and all about texture. Grate for dips and fritters; slice thinly for sweet and sour pickle; chop into half-moons for stir-fries.

EGGPLANT SDecadent, smoky, silky, almost meaty when cooked. Bake/griddle and use in curries, stir-fries, pasta, Middle-Eastern dishes. It drinks oil. Degorge to remove the bitter juices and reduce oil absorption.

GARLIC Like culinary highlighter it opens other flavors up. Use liberally across your repertoire but in measured amounts for each individual dish.

GINGER Unglamorous root with a chic lemon tang. Peel and grate for marinades and sauces; blitz for curry paste; slice into thin sticks for stir-fries; slice it for stocks.

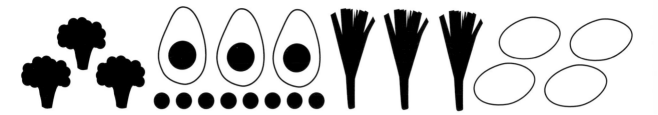

HOW TO...
Crush garlic

Break as many cloves as needed off the head. Lay them flat on a board. Lay the flat of a chef's/other large knife on top. Press down to crush. Remove the skin. Cut out any green shoot. Crush to a paste with the tip of the knife and add a bit of fine salt.

LEEKS Sweet onion-light taste and soft texture; wash to remove grit. Slice to melt into stews/soups/tarts/pies. Cut into julienne strips to cook slowly in butter as a side.

MUSHROOMS Earthy to bland with a variety of textures; griddle or stuff whole portobello mushrooms. Slice, sauté or stir-fry white/cremini mushrooms. Exotic, wild, and Asian mushrooms are more expensive but you don't need as many. Add to stews/soups.

ONIONS Kitchen workhorses. Use shallots (delicate and sweet) for dressings/sautés/raw/salads; red (refreshing) for salsas/dips/salads/onion jam/roasting; white (sweet) for risotto/tarts/stuffing/baking; brown (stronger) for regular cooking; whole baby in casseroles; scallions in salads/stir-fries/champ.

PAK CHOI/BOK CHOY Sweet and nutty with a faintly bitter edge. Strip down, slice, and stir-fry in sesame oil with garlic/soy; steam whole; slice into soups. Ridiculously nutritious.

PARSNIPS Earthy sweetness which caramelizes when roasted. Boil and bang into mashed potato; fling into stews/soups/casseroles.

PEAS Like quick-cook candies with a grassy edge. Boil fast or steam. Team with mint and butter. Use for soups. Add to stir-fries, risottos; toss raw into salads.

PEPPERS Color coded for ripeness—green taste grassier, yellow/orange/red move to sweetness. Eat raw; roast for salads; stuff and roast.

POTATOES Choose your type. Firm, waxy jobs (Jersey Royals, Charlottes) are brilliant for potato salad/curry; mealy (Maris Pipers, King Edwards) are perfect for fries/mashing/roasts/frying/baking.

HOW TO...
Roast peppers for salad

Preheat the oven to 450°F. Sit whole bell peppers on foil in a roasting pan. Roast for 30 to 40 minutes, turning once, or until soft and blistered. Chuck into a freezer bag. After 20 minutes, remove. Strip the skin off; remove seeds: slice flesh. Add oil.

RADISH Chic, crisp, and peppery. Slice into salads; dip in oil/salt; eat with sashimi.

SPINACH Healthy with an iron tang. Baby leaves give an edge to salads; wilt large leaves and toss in lemon/garlic/butter or use in classic pasta dishes/with eggs or fish/on pizza. It reduces alarmingly.

SPROUTS Can taste good. Trim, shred, and stir-fry with garlic; boil briefly and finish in butter with garlic and bacon/chopped chestnuts/slivered almonds.

RUTABAGA Warm, comforting, and sweet. Boil and mash and sex up with cream and spices; roast; dice for a Cornish pasty.

SWEET POTATOES Rich, sweet, and nutritious. Peel and make into soup; bake whole; mash; throw into curries or stews; roast or griddle in chunks. Make tasty wedges.

TOMATOES Don't get ripped off—too many perfect looking tomatoes are tasteless! Buy loose and sniff (look for a peppery whiff from the vine). Use cherry and vine tomatoes for salads; beefsteak for slicing and stuffing; canned for cooking.

TURNIPS Sophisticated tasting white golf balls. Slice for stir-fries/stews; eat raw.

HOW TO...
Skin a tomato

Cut a cross into the base of each fruit with a sharp knife. Bang them into a bowl and submerge in boiling water for a minute. Drain and cover immediately in cold water. Peel the skin off with your fingers, starting from the cross where it's loosened.

WATERCRESS Superfood with a tart taste. Strip any tough stems and use in soups/tarts/sauces/salads/egg sandwiches or as garnish.

ZUCCHINI Can be bland, but that's the challenge. Contrast with chile or garlic; use in a rich tomato sauce or ratatouille; get crisp on a BBQ/griddle.

VEG CUTTER
KNIFE TECHNIQUE

Do this on a strong board using a sharp knife. Using a pivot action, raise the knife over your chosen vegetable and slice down, working across the vegetable and holding it down on your board with the other hand.

CHOP Cut simply into fine/large pieces as your recipe needs.

STRIPS (JULIENNE) Cut into thin slices. Stack a few of these up, then cut into thin strips.

DICE Cut into even slices. Stack a few; cut lengthwise into sticks and across again into even dice.

CIRCLES Cut across your chosen veg to make thick, round slices.

HANGING ONTO THE GOOD BITS *(and flavor)* HERE'S HOW

—leave the peel on your potatoes & carrots as it's home to fiber and vitamins—nutrients fade with age so buy small amounts of veg a time and use immediately—cut with a sharp knife as a blunt one damages cells—cook as soon as your veg are prepped—don't soak veg—the nutrients leak out—steam if appropriate—cook for the minimum amount of time possible—use minimal water—serve immediately—

Salad Rules

■ Salad greens bruise easily: treat them gently.

■ Wash them well in cold water: check for grit and living things.

■ Blot them softly to dry: wet leaves won't hold dressing.

■ Use a salad spinner if you've got the room: they're cheap.

■ Chill leaves for 30 minutes before eating to crisp up.

■ Create a dressing to suit your style of leaf.

■ Crisp leaves (Romaine hearts, Cos, iceberg) carry creamy and oily dressings.

■ Soft leaves work best with oil-based dressing.

■ Leaves have character: bitter, sweet, mild, spiky, soft, explosive—check them out.

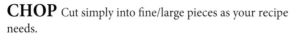

THE LETTUCE LIST

BUTTERHEAD: soft loose leaves with a sweet delicate taste. Easy eating.

CRESS: tiny, peppery, and nutritious. Keep on the windowsill (and trim the roots).

ROMAINE/COS/ LITTLE GEM: crisp, fresh, long leaves. Use for Caesar salad.

CORN SALAD: Mild and delicate. Mix for contrast; good for neat heaping.

RED OAK: Big, sweet loose red-edged leaves. Likes a bold dressing.

LOLLO ROSSO: red, bold leaves (no heart) with a nutty taste.

PEA SHOOTS: sweet, good-lookin, and moist. A good edible garnish.

ICEBERG: Fresh, mild, crisp lettuce with tight, structured leaves. Tear or shred just before using in sandwiches/burgers/ salads/tortillas, or use to wrap hot/cold fillings.

ARUGULA: dark green and peppery leaves. Staple of Italian cooking and side salads.

*A sweet way to radically alter
flavor and transform a dish.*

STORAGE Store big bunches of herbs from the market in cups or jars. Potted herbs need watering regularly. Packages of fresh herbs (expensive) should be stored in the refrigerator.

PREPPING Fresh herbs: Tear leafy herbs or shred them with a knife. Finely chop the leaves of coarse herbs. Snip chives with scissors. Bashing in a mortar and pestle strengthens taste. Dried herbs: are stronger. Use 1 teaspoon of dried herb to every 2 teaspoons of fresh.

BASIL Spicy yet fresh and a bit grassy—think subdued mint. Make pesto (p172), add to tomatoes/pizza (at the end of cooking if you can). Grow in a pot. Never used dried.

BAY Deep, dark, and aromatic. Use whole fresh or dried sparingly in a bouquet garni to flavor a stew, pie, casserole, or bread sauce. Keep a bay tree.

CHIVES Sweet hint of onion. Snip with scissors and use in fast cooking or add at the end. A tasty garnish.

CILANTRO Bright, fresh, and warm with a hint of citrus. Use the leaves, stems, and roots to liven up marinades/dull meats/curries/stir-fries/tex-mex/chili.

DILL Grassy and sharp feathery stalk. Use with fish/eggs/potato, adding at the end of cooking.

LEMONGRASS Lemony and bright. Bash to bruise well then chop very finely. Use for curries. Ready-chopped frozen stalks are a good fast option.

MINT Bright and lively—think chewing gum. Use with lamb/peas/potatoes or cover with boiling water to make into tea.

OREGANO Woody. Use fresh or dice judiciously and add to pizzas/zucchini/marinades.

PARSLEY Grassy, fresh, flat-leafed, or curly. Chop finely over potatoes; works with other herbs, white fish, and over most things. Always use fresh.

ROSEMARY Woody: good for lamb/pork/beef/chicken/BBQ foods. Shove whole sprigs up a roast chicken; chop finely and add to bread dough. Use fresh only.

SAGE Dark woodsy: best with pork, sausages, duck, darker meats, stuffing, cheese, pasta.

TARRAGON Hints of anise; brilliantly enhances chicken/mushrooms/egg/fish dishes; works in sauces/butters/tarts/soups. Use French tarragon only.

THYME Bittersweet and beautiful. Use with meats/pizza/pasta.

MAKE A BOUQUET GARNI
Sit a sprig of rosemary, 10 peppercorns, and 10 crushed cardamom pods on a piece of cheesecloth. Pull it up and tie a bit of stringaround it tightly.

FRIENDS

GREENS
BROCCOLI: ANCHOVY, BEEF, OYSTER SAUCE, SOY, CHEESE, CHILE, CUMIN, GARLIC, **SPINACH:** CHEESE, EGGS, PASTA, NUTMEG, TOMATO **CABBAGE:** BACON, BLACK PEPPER, GARLIC, GINGER, HAM, LEMON, PORK, POTATO

ROOTS
POTATOES: BEET, BUTTER, GARLIC, HARD AND BLUE CHEESES, FISH, LEMON, MEAT, MUSTARD, NUTMEG, ONION, PARSLEY, ROSEMARY **BEET:** BLUE CHEESE, EGG, FETA, GOAT CHEESE, HARD CHEESE, OILY FISH, ORANGE, WALNUTS **PARSNIP:** CURRY POWDER, HONEY, LEMON, NUTMEG, PORK, POTATO **CARROT:** BUTTER, CARDAMOM, LEMON, ORANGE, STAR ANISE

MUSHROOMS
BACON, BLUE CHEESE, EGG, CREAM, GARLIC, PARMESAN, POTATO, TARRAGON

BEANS AND PEAS
BEANS: BUTTER, CUMIN, GARLIC, TOMATO SAUCE **PEAS:** BACON, BEEF, BUTTER, CHICKEN, CHILE, EGGS, LAMB, MINT, PARMESAN, PORK, RICE, WHITE FISH

PEA CHILI, AND MINT SOUP

 HEALTHY FAST FEEDS 2

This super-smooth soup makes for a simple punchy lunch or a couch cuppa soup—the mix of salty and sweet does it. If you're not a bacon fan, make croutons (p29).

INGREDIENTS

4 shallots
1 green chile
2 garlic cloves, peeled
3 tablespoons butter
salt and pepper
2 cups chicken/vegetable stock
    (p49/p15)
3½ cups frozen peas
½ teaspoon granulated sugar
10 small mint leaves
    (or quantity to taste)
4 American bacon slices (optional)
2 tablespoons light cream/yogurt
    (optional)

········· TIME SAVER ·········

This recipe's fast to make but if time's a real issue make it the night before. Cool, cover with plastic wrap, and chill until needed.

PREP Peel and finely dice the shallots on a board using a chef's, paring, or filleting knife. Seed and finely dice the chile. Crush the garlic.

Put a large pan onto heat. Add the butter. Once it foams, add the shallot, garlic, chile, and a tiny pinch of salt. Stir and reduce the heat to low. Pop the lid onto the pan and let the mix sweat very gently without coloring until it softens up. It'll take at least 5 minutes. Don't rush—if you burn the mix it'll get bitter and you'll need to start again.

Meantime, pour the stock into another pan and put it on the stove to heat. Once the shallots have sweated down, add the hot stock and stir well. Add the peas and sugar and season lightly with salt and pepper. Bring the mix to a boil, then reduce the heat and simmer gently for 5 to 6 minutes.

COOK Remove from the heat and add the mint. Now either tip the soup carefully into a food processor and whiz until really smooth, or blitz everything together in the pan using a stick blender. If it's not absolutely smooth, put the soup through a fine strainer (texture matters with this one). Taste and adjust the seasoning. Keep warm.

If you want bacon with your soup, set the broiler to high. Lay the bacon slices on the rack and cook for 2 to 3 minutes per side, until crispy. Rest on paper towels.

PLATE Pour the soup into a warm bowl or mug. Crumble the bacon on top if using, swirl over a bit of cream or yogurt if you like, or leave plain. Enjoy with bread and butter.

CARROT SOUP

HEALTHY

FEEDS 4

INGREDIENTS

1 medium onion
1½ pounds carrots
7 ounces mealy potatoes
1 ounce piece of fresh ginger
2 garlic cloves
1 tablespoon olive oil
½ tablespoon butter
salt and pepper
1 star anise
juice of ½ a lime
4 cups vegetable stock (p15)
a good handful of cilantro

——— BONUS BITE———
LEEK AND CHEESE SOUP

Wash and thinly slice 1½ pounds leeks. Add them to the sweated onion and potato base as before and cook very slowly under a cartouche for 10 minutes. (Leeks turn bitter if browned at all so keep the heat low). Add a handful of torn Italian parsley, 4 cups vegetable/chicken stock, and 2 teaspoons mustard. Simmer for 30 minutes. Cool then blitz in batches with a handful of grated Cheddar. Stir in 3 tablespoons milk. Serve with crumbled bacon bits and/or croutons (p29).

Subtle Asian flavors make this a bit of a soup hero. Sweat the vegetables slowly to release their potential and don't let them brown up. This recipe demonstrates a vegetable soup formula by the way. Use onion/potato/other vegetables/stock in these proportions to create your own variations depending on what's in season.

PREP Slice the onion in two. Peel and chop it with a sharp chef's knife. Wash, dry, and trim the ends away from the carrots. Peel with a knife or peeler and slice into 1-inch rounds. Peel the potatoes over a sink using a peeler or knife. Dunk under the cold faucet as you go to wash surface dirt away. Dry and chop into small pieces.

Peel the ginger with a sharp knife. Grate it finely. Peel and crush the garlic.

COOK Put a large pan on to heat. Heat the oil and butter. Add the onion and a pinch of salt. Sweat gently on low for 5 to 10 minutes until soft not colored, stirring occasionally.

Add the ginger and star anise. Stir and cook for 2 minutes. Add the carrot and potatoes, stirring, and cook over very low heat for 10 minutes with the lid on. If you've got a bit of wax paper or a butter wrapper, lay it directly onto the vegetables and put the lid back on (this paper, or "cartouche" helps retain moisture as the mix cooks). Don't let the vegetables catch or brown up.

Remove the paper. Stir. Add the lime juice and pour in the stock. Tear in most of the cilantro—reserving a few leaves for garnish—and season to taste. Bring to a boil. Reduce and simmer on very low heat for 30 to 40 minutes, or until the carrots are soft (test with a knife).

Cool for 5 minutes. Fish out the star anise. Blitz until smooth with a stick blender in the pan, or let cool for 5 minutes before blitzing in a blender/processor in batches. Taste and adjust the seasoning, by adding a bit more lime juice if it needs a lift.

PLATE Pour the soup into warmed bowls and top with torn cilantro. Serve with croutons (p29) and small wedges of lime for squeezing.

MUSHROOM AND TARRAGON SOUP

FAST

FEEDS 4

Using specific herbs can transform ingredients; here tarragon works its magic to create a soup that's earthy with a twist of anise.

INGREDIENTS

*12 ounces mix of portobello
   and cremini mushrooms*
3 shallots, peeled
2 garlic cloves, peeled
1 tablespoon butter
a splash of olive oil
a few fresh tarragon leaves
*3¾ cups chicken/vegetable stock
   (p49/p15)*
salt and pepper
*3–4 tablespoons heavy cream/crème
   fraîche*

—— CHANGE IT UP ——

Replace the tarragon with Italian parsley and
add a pinch of nutmeg before serving.

PREP Rub the mushrooms with a bit of barely damp paper towels to clean. Don't wash them. Chop or tear them roughly. Dice the shallots and crush the garlic.

COOK Melt the butter and oil in a large pan on low heat. Fry the shallots gently for 5 minutes, stirring with a wooden spoon, until soft and colorless. Add the garlic, most of the tarragon, and all the mushrooms and stir well. Cook gently for 10 minutes with the pan covered, checking and stirring the mix occasionally.

Add the stock. Increase the heat to boil then reduce to simmer on gentle heat in the covered pan for 15 minutes. Season with salt and pepper and add the remaining tarragon.

Let cool for 5 minutes. Add a tablespoon or two of cream or crème fraîche. Pour the soup into a blender in batches and blitz until smooth. Taste and adjust the seasoning to suit your palate, adding more cream/crème fraîche if you like.

PLATE Reheat the soup very gently. Pour it into bowls and enjoy with some good buttery toast, cut into thin slices for dipping.

BONUS BITE

BLITZED SPICED CAULIFLOWER SOUP
Break a medium-size cauliflower into florets. Fry off a chopped large onion with 1 crushed garlic clove, ½ teaspoon each of cumin, turmeric, garam masala, and red pepper flakes in a little oil. Stir in the florets and sweat under a cartouche for 10 minutes, or until soft without coloring. Add scant 1¼ cups ground almonds, 4 cups vegetable/chicken stock, and season to taste. Simmer for 15 minutes. Cool. Add a little lemon juice, taste and adjust the seasoning if necessary. Blitz in batches. Top with torn basil leaves and slivered almonds.

BRUSCHETTA

   FEEDS 2

Italian for great-tasting stuff on toast. Here are three sweet toppings which work whether you're cooking for yourself or the masses. Check out the carpaccio toppings on p83—they also work really well here.

INGREDIENTS

1 garlic clove
4 x 1-inch thick bread slices
(ciabatta/French stick/country loaf)
a little olive oil

PREP Cut the garlic clove in half widthwise. Make your topping of choice (see below).

COOK Put a griddle pan onto high heat. Brush the bread lightly with oil. Griddle for a minute or two on each side until crisp and marked up.

PLATE Rub each bit of bread with the cut garlic clove before spooning over your chosen topping.

—— BONUS BITES ——

MUSHROOM AND TARRAGON TARTS
Make up the mushroom topping (see opposite) adding a pinch of dried or chopped tarragon. Spread on a base of thinly rolled store-bought all-butter puff pastry cut into large circles or as you like. Bake for 20 minutes at 400°F or until the base is crisp.

—— CHANGE IT UP ——

Try rubbing the bread with a lemon or fresh rosemary/basil leaves instead of garlic.

—— TOPPINGS ——

1 FAVA BEAN AND CHEDDAR

Put a pan of water on to heat with a good pinch of salt. Bring to a boil. Add 4 ounces fava beans (fresh or frozen) and simmer for 5 to 6 minutes until tender (test one). Drain into a colander. Cool under running water. Remove and discard their outer skins. Toss into a bowl. Add scant ¼ cup roughly crumbled Cheddar cheese, 3 teaspoons olive oil, and 2 teaspoons lemon juice. Mash the mix with a fork, leaving some chunks. Taste and season lightly, adjusting the oil and lemon if needed.

2 TOMATO AND BLACK OLIVE

Slice 8–12 good-quality cherry or baby plum tomatoes in half lengthwise, slice in half again, and tip into a bowl. Chop 6 black olives (if the pits are still in, remove them first by cutting around using a small, sharp knife) and add to the bowl with half a diced shallot. Add 1 tablespoon oil, a pinch each of salt and sugar, black pepper, and a few arugula or basil leaves, if you like, and mix well.

3 HOT MIXED MUSHROOMS

Clean 12 ounces mixed mushrooms (e.g. portobello, cremini, or oyster) with paper towels, trim, and slice into ½-inch thick pieces. Put a heavy-bottomed medium skillet over medium heat with 4 tablespoons butter and a drop or two of oil. Add a finely diced shallot and 1 crushed garlic clove and cook, stirring for a minute or two. Add a small glass of white wine and bring to a boil. Lower to a simmer and add the mushrooms and a small pinch of dried thyme. Cook, stirring, for 2 to 3 minutes, until the mushrooms are soft but still holding their shape. Season. Remove from the heat, stir through 1½ tablespoons heavy cream and squeeze over a little lemon juice.

PUNCHY CHICORY WATERCRESS, BACON, AVOCADO
IN A HONEY MUSTARD DRESSING

HEALTHY

FEEDS 2

A good dressing pulls ingredients together. Add the oil slowly so it emulsifies. Here's a great little salad that's open to a range of other ingredient options. So go ahead and build it up. Follow the salad rules (p18) and you'll be laughing.

INGREDIENTS

2 big handfuls of watercress
a head of chicory (endive)
2 American bacon slices
1 avocado
juice of ¼ a small lemon
HONEY MUSTARD DRESSING
½ teaspoon thin honey
1 teaspoon Dijon mustard
1 tablespoon white wine vinegar
3 tablespoons extra virgin olive oil
½ small shallot, peeled
salt and pepper

—— CHANGE IT UP ——

1. Add baby spinach to the salad for extra nutrients. **2.** Switch the avocado for regular pear, sliced and tossed in lemon juice, and use walnut dressing (p33). **3.** Switch the bacon for crumbled goat cheese, Stilton, or Roquefort and add caramelized walnuts (p194). **4.** For a simple green salad, leave out the bacon and avocado.

PREP Wash and dry the watercress. Discard any woody stems. Sit the chicory on a board, trim the end or just strip the leaves off. Wash and dry them well. Leave whole, tear into bits or mix it up—your choice.

Make the dressing: put the honey and mustard into a small bowl. Using a spoon or mini-balloon whisk, beat the vinegar in gradually until creamy. Add the oil drop by drop, then in a trickle, beating as you go, so it emulsifies. Slice the shallot thinly and stir it in. Dip a leaf in to taste so you can adjust the seasoning and balance of acidity if you need to. Set aside.

Preheat the broiler to high. Lay the bacon on the rack in the pan. Cook for 2 minutes. Turn with tongs or a fork. Repeat until cooked (don't burn it). Transfer to paper towels. Sit your avocado on a board. Cut it in half by slicing horizontally through the skin and flesh until you hit the pit. Rotate the fruit as you hold the knife in place. Hold both halves of the fruit and twist in opposite directions to separate. Leave the pit in the half you're not using, rub the flesh with lemon and wrap in plastic wrap: save this for guacamole (p75). Scoop the flesh from the other half with a spoon, slice it, and toss in lemon juice.

Toss the leaves and dressing together with your fingers, judging it so you don't use too much, yet every leaf is coated.

PLATE Bang the dressed leaves onto plates or into a bowl. Add the avocado and crumble over the crisp bacon.

MILD LETTUCE SALAD WITH RADISH, CUCUMBER, CRESS, CHEESE, AND CLASSIC FRENCH DRESSING

HEALTHY   FEEDS 2

Salad is all about textures, contrasts, and excellent dressing: toss this one or any basic green leaf side salad in a classic French vinaigrette to transform it.

INGREDIENTS

½ a soft lettuce (like butterhead)
6 radishes
1 x 4-inch length of cucumber
3–4 snips of cress from a box
2–3 ounces manchego/Gruyère/
    Cheddar cheese (optional)
FRENCH DRESSING
1 tablespoon white wine vinegar
salt and black pepper
3 tablespoons extra virgin olive oil

PREP Pull as many leaves as you need off the lettuce (don't cut it as it bruises and the rest won't last as long). Wash and dry it well. Wash, dry, trim, and slice the radishes, mixing your slicing style (circles and lengths) if you like. Run a fork down the length of your piece of cucumber to score the edges for looks, then slice thinly. Snip the cress with scissors. Wash and let drain in a strainer. Slice the cheese into thin sticks, if using.

For the dressing: spoon the vinegar into a small bowl with a good pinch of salt and a few grindings of pepper. Whisk/beat the oil in drop by drop for an emulsion. Toss everything except the cress in the dressing using your fingers.

PLATE Heap into a bowl or onto plates. Scatter the cress on top.

—— CHANGE IT UP ——

Try teaming this salad with cherry tomatoes, sliced hard-boiled eggs, and ham, or a very good pork pie with cold roasted meats and hard cheeses.

A CLASSIC PEPPERY ARUGULA SIDE SALAD WITH BALSAMIC DRESSING

HEALTHY   FEEDS 2

Your classic arugula side salad in a sharp, dark dressing. Mix it up by shaving over Parmesan or adding croutons (opposite), toasted pine nuts, or cherry tomatoes. If making this—or any—salad to go, pack the dressing in a pot and dress just before eating.

INGREDIENTS

2 big handfuls of arugula
BALSAMIC DRESSING
a pinch of salt
a pinch of sugar
1 teaspoon balsamic vinegar
1 tablespoon extra virgin olive oil
1 tablespoon light olive/peanut/
    sunflower oil

PREP Wash the arugula leaves in a strainer or colander under cold running water. Handle them lightly as they easily spoil and bruise. Get them really dry by patting on a dish towel or paper towels or use a spinner. They'll hold their dressing better, it's not diluted and you'll use less.

Make the dressing: beat the salt, sugar, and balsamic together in a bowl. Add the oils in drop by drop, beating as you go so the dressing emulsifies naturally. Taste and adjust the seasoning and balance of acidity to suit your palate.

Toss the arugula and dressing together with your fingers, judging it so you don't use too much, yet every leaf is coated.

PLATE Lift and arrange the dressed leaves on plates/bowls.

CRISP CAESAR SALAD

`HEALTHY`   FEEDS 2

Here's a lighter alternative to a standard Caesar. Have it plain or throw in your choice of crunchy additions (vegetarians—use nonrennet cheese). Make your own croutons: they're way tastier than bought-ins.

INGREDIENTS

*a head of Cos/1 large Romaine heart/
    2 Boston lettuces*

CAESAR DRESSING

*2 tablespoons plain yogurt
2 tablespoons mayonnaise (p153)
¼ ounce Parmesan, plus extra to finish
1 teaspoon lemon juice
3 drops of Worcestershire sauce
a little black pepper*

ADDITIONS

*4 American bacon slices
a handful of pine nuts
a handful of croutons of your choice*

PREP Strip all or a good number of whole leaves from your chosen lettuce variety. Wash and dry them carefully and put in the refrigerator to crisp for 30 minutes.

Make the dressing: mix the yogurt and mayo in a bowl. Finely grate the cheese and stir in. Add the lemon juice, Worcestershire sauce, and pepper to season (the cheese provides salt). Taste and adjust to suit your palate.

BACON: Preheat the broiler. Lay the bacon on the pan and broil for 2 minutes. Turn with tongs. Broil until cooked. Don't burn. Cool on paper towels to crisp up. **PINE NUTS:** Put a dry skillet on to heat. Add the nuts. Shuffle or toss them so they toast evenly for 2 to 3 minutes, or until pale gold. **CROUTONS:** prep as per your chosen recipe.

Tear and toss the leaves into a bowl with some of the dressing. Turn to coat.

PLATE Pile into bowls. Top with the croutons, pine nuts, and crumbled bacon. Shave or grate over some extra Parmesan to finish.

—— CHANGE IT UP ——

For a chicken Caesar salad, top with two sliced griddled chicken breasts (p51). For a walnut Caesar, sprinkle with caramelized walnuts (p194) and chopped dates.

TIPS

1. Stale bread or baguette makes ideal croutons (it may well cook a bit faster, so keep checking it). **2.** Stale bagels make the crunchiest croutons.

TO GO WITH

CROUTONS

Preheat an oven to 350°F. Using a serrated knife, cut 3 thick slices from a loaf of bread. Slice off the crusts. Cut the remaining bread into even fingers then cubes. Toss in a thin coating of olive oil and a bit of sea salt. Bake on a baking sheet for 10 minutes or until crisp.

PEPPER CROUTONS

Bash ¼ teaspoon peppercorns in a mortar and pestle or with the end of a rolling pin. Toss in a bowl with the oil and bread. Bake as above.

GARLIC AND CHEESE CROUTONS

Mix a crushed garlic clove with a bit of olive oil and a little bit of freshly grated Parmesan or other cheese. Coat the bread cubes and bake as above.

LENTIL SALAD
THREE WAYS

HEALTHY

FEEDS 2

I love these little salads. Team your lentils with smoked fish and bacon, sausage, and caramelized onion or a good sharp cheese. Toss them in a tasty dressing: make it look extraordinary.

INGREDIENTS

½ cup Puy lentils
generous 1 cup vegetable stock (p15)
scant ⅓ cup white wine
salt and pepper

TOPPINGS

1 2 ounces smoked salmon
1 small avocado
juice of ¼ a small lemon
2 bacon slices
a small handful of fresh dill
1 x honey mustard dressing (p26)

2 1 brown onion
2 tablespoons olive/peanut oil
1 teaspoon butter
1–2 good-quality chipolatas
1 x honey mustard dressing (p26)

3 3 ounces Cheddar/feta/goat cheese
1 shallot
a handful of pea shoots/soft lettuce leaves
1 x walnut dressing (p33)

PREP Wash the lentils in a strainer under running water. Pour the stock and wine into a pan. Bring to a boil. Add the lentils and a touch of salt. Reduce the heat and simmer for 15 to 20 minutes until the lentils are tender, but still holding their shape. Be vigilant, as they can turn to mush in an instant. Meantime, make the dressing to match your topping and set it aside.

Test the lentils for doneness. Drain them into a strainer and let cool for a minute, then tip into a bowl and toss with a tablespoon or two of dressing, tasting to judge the amount.

1 Chop the salmon into thin strips. Cut the avocado in half. Remove the pit and peel. Chop and toss in lemon juice. Broil the bacon until crispy. Sit it on paper towels. Chop the dill.

2 Peel and thinly slice the onion. Heat half the oil and butter in a pan. Cook the onion over very low heat for 20 to 30 minutes, until soft and caramelized. Add the chipolatas to a separate small pan with the remaining oil and fry over low heat for 10 minutes, turning, until done.

3 Crumble the cheese and peel and slice the shallot.

PLATE Stir the lentils and taste to see if they need more dressing or seasoning.

1 Mix the dill into the lentils. Pile on the salmon, avocado, and bacon. Grind a bit of black pepper over the lot and serve with a handful of green leaves and a dollop of sour cream on the side.

2 Mix some of the onion into the lentils. Arrange slices of sausage and the rest of the onion on top. Stir a little mustard through a few dollops of sour cream and serve on the side with a few dill pickles.

3 Scatter the cheese, shallot, and leaves over the lentil base. Drizzle over the walnut dressing and serve with some good crusty bread.

CREAMY THREE BEAN AND ALMOND SALAD

  FEEDS 3 TO 4

Beans can be so boring, but I'd never do that to you. Every mouthful here is a contrast of texture and flavor. The dressing is delicious.

INGREDIENTS

1 x 16-ounce can of cannellini beans
salt and pepper
scant 1 cup frozen fava beans
7 ounces green beans
a handful of slivered almonds
DRESSING
1 teaspoon Dijon mustard
a big squeeze of lime juice
3 tablespoons chopped cilantro
4–6 tablespoons crème fraîche
a pinch of superfine sugar

PREP Tip the can of beans into a strainer or colander. Let drain and dry a bit.

COOK Boil up a pan of water. Add a pinch of salt. Tip in the fava beans and cook for 4 minutes or until tender. Drain into a colander. Refresh under cold running water. Set aside for a bit to cool and dry. Now, remove and discard the tough outer skins. Find the bit of spare skin on the edge of the bean and squeeze it—the innards should pop out easily. Put them into a bowl and set aside.

Boil a second pan of lightly salted water. Wash and trim the fine beans. Boil for 5 minutes or a little longer until tender but not overcooked (you want some bite).

Drain and hold under cold water to crisp them up again and hold their color.

Mix all the elements for the dressing in a bowl. Taste it and adjust the seasoning to suit your palate. Tip all the beans into a bowl. Add the slivered almonds and stir in your dressing.

PLATE Shift the beans to a clean bowl or plate. Enjoy with other salads and bread, or team with my leek tart (p170), egg and bacon tart (p169), or griddled lamb/chicken.

PLOUGHMAN'S STYLE BEAN AND CELERY SALAD

 HEALTHY   FAST

FEEDS 2 (on the side)

INGREDIENTS

scant ½ cup canned red kidney beans
3 celery stalks
a handful of golden raisins
2 crisp apples
a squeeze of lemon juice
4 ounces sharp Cheddar
a handful of pea shoots/corn salad/
*   other soft salad leaves*

WALNUT DRESSING

2 teaspoons Dijon mustard
a pinch of superfine sugar
a pinch of salt
2 tablespoons white wine vinegar
6 tablespoons walnut oil

—— CHANGE IT UP ——

1. Switch the walnut dressing for honey mustard dressing (p26). **2.** Use Gruyère in place of Cheddar. **3.** Tear in a few pieces of salami. **4.** Replace the cheese with bite-size chunks of freshly cooked pork sausage. **5.** Make it fruity by adding some chopped dates, dried figs, chopped pear, whole grapes. or chopped orange.

✷✷✷✷ CASH SAVER ✷✷✷✷

Replace 2 tablespoons of the walnut oil with the same quantity of peanut oil instead.

Very little effort for a great tasting plate: use good sharp apples for a taste contrast. Who doesn't love a ploughman's?

PREP Make the dressing: put the mustard, sugar, and salt into a small bowl. Beat the vinegar in gradually until creamy. Add the oil drop by drop, then in a trickle, beating as you go, so it emulsifies.

Drain the beans into a strainer or colander. Set aside.

Wash, string, and slice the celery.

Remove the cores of the apples with a corer or cut them into quarters and scoop the seeds out with a sharp knife. Chop them into large bite-size pieces. Toss them in lemon juice to stop discoloration.

Cut the cheese into bite-size cubes. Toss the beans, celery, golden raisins, and apple in a bowl with 2–3 tablespoons of your dressing. Taste and adjust the seasoning.

PLATE Pile it onto your plates. Top with the leaves and cheese. Serve alongside a plate of cold ham or roast pork or team with a big, buttered baked potato.

CRISP POLENTA
AND TOMATO
CAPONATA SALAD

FEEDS 4

Crisp, soft, hot, and cold: this one's so good. The salad's cooked ahead of time, which gives the flavors time to develop. Fry the polenta disks at the last minute for a real contrast in temperatures and textures.

INGREDIENTS

2 glossy eggplants
sea salt and black pepper
1 pound fresh tomatoes
3 celery stalks
1 onion
2 garlic cloves
generous ¼ cup dried apricots
4 tablespoons olive oil
1½ teaspoons red harissa paste
⅓ cup black olives
1½ teaspoons capers
1 tablespoon superfine sugar
4 tablespoons white wine vinegar
a handful of chopped Italian parsley
POLENTA
2½ cups water
¾ cup fast-cook cornmeal
a few pinches of dried oregano
2 tablespoons butter
a handful of freshly grated Parmesan
olive oil, for shallow-frying

TIP
When sprinkling salt on a dish, do so from a height so it covers the food lightly and evenly

---

—— CHANGE IT UP ——
1. Switch the Parmesan for Cheddar. **2.** Serve the polenta disks with bolognaise (p85) or an easy tomato sauce (p176).

PREP Trim the eggplant stalks and slice into thick rounds with a serrated/bread knife. Sprinkle both sides lightly with fine sea salt and leave for 30 minutes to draw out any juices. Wipe the slices on paper towels and chop into bite-size pieces.

Skin the tomatoes (p17) and cut into thick slices vertically. Wash, dry, then strip any stringy bits away from the celery. Slice it thinly. Peel, halve, and slice the onion. Peel and crush the garlic. Finely chop the apricots.

COOK Heat the oil in a large frying pan/shallow casserole dish. Fry the vegetables in turn so their flavors stay separate. Start with the eggplants (fry and stir for 10 minutes or until soft, brown, and cooked through). Transfer to a plate with a slotted spoon. Lower the heat and fry the celery for a few minutes. Spoon it out and set aside on the plate.

Fry the onions very gently for 5 to 10 minutes until soft, not colored. Then add the garlic, harissa paste, apricots, tomatoes, olives, and capers. Let the mix boil then reduce and simmer on very low heat for 15 minutes.

Stir in the sugar and vinegar. Simmer until sticky for 10 minutes, then bang the eggplants and celery back in the pan, add the parsley, and stir well. Adjust the balance of sweet and sour to taste (adding a little more sugar or vinegar as necessary). Tip into a dish to cool as you make the polenta.

Polenta: Measure the water into a pan. Cover and bring to a boil. In a bowl, mix the cornmeal and oregano. Season with salt and pepper. Shove the mix into the boiling water in one go, beating furiously with a wooden spoon for 5 minutes as it splutters and spits. Beat in the butter and cheese. Pour into a 8 by 8 by ¾-inch oiled pan and let cool. (If you find yourself with extra polenta, pour it into another pan, cool it, cut it out, and freeze it for later.)

Cut circles of cooled, set polenta with a 3½-inch cookie cutter or wine glass. Shallow-fry in olive oil for 3 minutes a side or until cooked through and beautifully crispy.

PLATE Sit the polenta on plates, pile on your salad, and serve (this is a good-to-go-by-itself dish, so doesn't really need accompanying with anything).

TOMATOES MARINATED IN LIME JUICE
AND HONEY WITH SALTED MOZZARELLA

HEALTHY

FEEDS 2

INGREDIENTS

3 good-sized best ripe vine tomatoes
2 tablespoons fruity extra-virgin olive
  oil, plus extra for serving
1–2 teaspoons thin honey
sea salt and black pepper
juice of ½–1 lime (to taste)
a small handful of cilantro leaves
1 x 4½-ounce ball of good mozzarella

TIP
When using tomatoes raw in a dish like this, make sure they are at room temperature to enjoy their flavor and texture at their best.

The tomato is a wonderful beast when it's at its best (in season). When it's not it can do with help and that's when interesting seasonings, herbs, and ingredient combinations really make the most of it.

PREP Wash and dry the tomatoes. Remove the stem. Working on a board, use a sharp vegetable knife or a serrated blade to slice them thinly horizontally. Shift the tomato slices over to a shallow dish or plate to marinate and pour over any juices that may have escaped while slicing.

Mix the oil, honey, a little pepper, and lime juice together and drizzle over the tomatoes. Wash, blot, and tear the cilantro. Scatter over the lot and leave for 20 minutes to an hour to marinate. Baste the tomatoes (spooning the marinade juices over them) just before serving.

Slice the mozzarella just before plating.

PLATE Spoon the tomatoes onto a fresh dish/plates or leave as they are. Arrange the cheese on top and treat it to a few drops of oil and a couple of pinches of sea salt flakes to taste. Have some warm bread in the oven ready to mop up the juices.

ROASTED TOMATO SALAD IN A PAN

HEALTHY

FEEDS 2

INGREDIENTS

4 large vine tomatoes
1 garlic clove
salt (or celery salt) and black pepper
a few pinches of dried oregano
olive oil

—— **BONUS BITE** ——
OVEN-DRIED TOMATOES
Set the oven at 250°F. Halve the tomatoes. Leave in their skins and roll in oil, seasoning, dried or fresh herbs. Bake on sheets for 6 hours until reduced and shriveled. Remove. Bang into clean jars. Add olive oil to cover and keep in the refrigerator for up to 6 months. Eat with salads.

Slow roasting transforms average tomatoes into sweet beauties. Dip your bread in the pan to soak up the juices.

PREP Preheat the oven to 425°F. Boil a kettle.

Skin the tomatoes (p17). Sit them on a board. Slice each one across into halves horizontally. Fit them cut-side up into an oiled shallow enamel pan/dish in a single layer. Cut the garlic clove in half widthways and use to rub over the tomato tops. Sprinkle with oregano and salt or celery salt and drizzle with oil.

COOK Roast for 10 minutes. Reduce the temperature to 350°F and cook for another 40 minutes, or until soft and almost caramelized. Let cool.

PLATE Share from the pan and enjoy with warm bread and cheese.

RETRO BEEFSTEAK TOMATOES FILLED WITH A CHOICE OF SALADS

HEALTHY

FEEDS 2

Don't take this dish too seriously: food needs its comedy moments. Stuff your beefsteak tomatoes with micro-salads. Prepping them this way heightens the flavors.

INGREDIENTS

2 large beefsteak or very large vine
   tomatoes
a pinch of salt
GREEK SALAD FILLING
2–2¼ ounces feta cheese
a pinch of dried oregano
a pinch of red pepper flakes
2 teaspoons olive oil
2 teaspoons lemon juice
10 black olives
1 x 2-inch piece cucumber
1 shallot
2 crisp chilled iceberg lettuce leaves
1–2 teaspoons red wine vinegar
SHRIMP COCKTAIL FILLING
4 tablespoons mayonnaise or yogurt/
   mayo mix
1 tablespoon tomato ketchup
1 teaspoon lemon juice
1 garlic clove, peeled and crushed
salt and pepper
4 cherry tomatoes
8 small cooked shrimp, shelled (p134)
12 large, whole cooked shrimp
a large iceberg lettuce, torn into pieces
a sprinkle of paprika

PREP Use a sharp chef's knife to slice the tops off the tomatoes to create lids. Hollow out the tomatoes with a teaspoon, scraping down to the shell. Rub salt around the insides. Invert on a rack to drain their moisture.

GREEK SALAD FILLING: Drain the feta if it comes in liquid. Pat dry on paper towels and dice into tiny cubes. Mix the oregano, red pepper flakes, oil, and lemon juice in a bowl to make a marinade and sit the feta in it to flavor up. Dice the olives (pit them first if they have pits). Peel, halve, seed, and finely dice the cucumber. Peel and slice the shallot. Shake moisture out of the tomatoes. Sit them up. Line each one with a torn iceberg leaf, letting it come over the top (a rough finish is good). Use a teaspoon to layer it with a bit of marinated feta, diced olive, and cucumber. Repeat, finishing with a pile of feta. Add a few drops of red wine vinegar and scatter over the shallot slices to finish.

SHRIMP COCKTAIL FILLING: Mix the mayo, ketchup, lemon juice, garlic, salt, and pepper together in a bowl to make a Marie Rose sauce. Dice the cherry tomatoes and small shrimp. Spoon a bit of sauce into the base of each tomato, then alternate layers of diced shrimp, diced tomato, and sauce, finishing with sauce. Wedge pieces of lettuce creatively down the sides of the tomatoes, alternating with whole shrimp which you can hook over the tops so they're looking out. Add more sauce and a sprinkling of paprika over the top to finish.

PLATE Prop the tomato lids back on if they go. Eat the Greek salad tomatoes with warm, soft pitas and the shrimp cocktail tomatoes with brown bread and butter.

—— CHANGE IT UP ——

1. For a caprese salad, cover a plate with overlapping layers of sliced vine/beefsteak tomato, mozzarella, and whole basil leaves. Drizzle with good olive oil. Sprinkle with sea salt. **2.** For a simple tomato salad, mix together a little superfine sugar, black pepper, crushed sea salt, olive oil, lemon juice, and torn basil. Drizzle over sliced tomatoes. **3.** For an everyday tomato and shallot salad, chop or slice a handful of vine/beefsteak tomatoes and toss in French dressing (p28) with diced/sliced shallot or red onion.

ZUCCHINI AND
FETA FRITTERS WITH HUMMUS AND MEZZE BITS

FEEDS 3 TO 4

INGREDIENTS

1 pound zucchini
salt and black pepper
1 large egg
4 ounces feta cheese
3 scallions (white and green)
4 tablespoons all-purpose flour
2 tablespoons chopped fresh dill
a pinch of dried mint
a small pinch of smoked paprika
peanut oil with a dash of olive oil, for
  shallow-frying

—— CHANGE IT UP ——

1. For yogurt hummus, stir in 1–2 tablespoons of plain or Greek yogurt to regular hummus to taste. **2.** For cilantro and lemon hummus, blitz in a little fresh cilantro and 1 teaspoons lemon zest with the chickpeas. **3.** For parsley and sundried tomato hummus, add a little Italian parsley and a few sundried tomatoes before blitzing.

TURN OVER
FOR MEZZE BITS

Make these delicious fritters the star attraction of a mezze plate. Mix it up with home-marinated olives (cheaper and better than store-bought), easy tzatziki, good punchy hummus, spectacular smoky eggplant dip, and wrap it up with steaming hot flatbreads.

PREP Wash, dry then grate the zucchini coarsely onto a board. Tip them into a bowl with a few pinches of fine salt. Mix and let sweat for 15 minutes.

Meantime, beat the egg with a fork. Crumble the feta cheese roughly. Bunch the scallions together on a board, trim the roots then slice across thinly.

Tip the zucchini into a colander/strainer to drain. Squeeze them with your hands to remove moisture, then put half into the center of a dish towel. Pull it around them then twist and squeeze. (You need to remove as much moisture as possible so the fritters aren't wet). Repeat with the rest.

Tip the dried zucchini into a large dry bowl. Mix in the flour, scallion, dill, mint, paprika, and feta cheese and season with salt and pepper. Add the egg gradually, stirring, until evenly distributed.

COOK Put a medium skillet on to heat and add enough oil to cover the bottom of the pan. Test the heat of the oil—it's hot enough when it can brown a bread crumb in 10 seconds. Carefully add the fritter mix a tablespoon at a time. Cook for 2 to 3 minutes per side or until golden (check with a spatula). Turn very gently as these guys aren't robust. Set aside on paper towels.

PLATE Sprinkle with salt. Serve hot with mezze bits: lemon and garlic marinated olives, eggplant dip, cucumber tzatziki, hummus, and cilantro flatbreads.

TO GO WITH

HUMMUS

Tip a 14-ounce can of chickpeas into a strainer over a bowl, saving the water. By machine: Pulse the chickpeas until fine as wet sand in a processor. Add water from the can (2 tablespoons), 2 tablespoons tahini paste, 3 tablespoons lemon juice, 4 garlic cloves, and salt. Blitz to a smooth paste then start to trickle scant ½ cup olive oil in through the funnel. Stop before it's all in. Sample for taste and texture, adjusting lemon/salt as necessary. Add a little more oil or add water for a lighter mix. Taste and adjust again. By hand: Use a stick blender or mash the same ingredients together. Spoon the hummus into a bowl and drizzle olive oil over the surface. Sprinkle over a little paprika and a few pine nuts/chopped cilantro leaves to finish.

LEMON AND GARLIC MARINATED OLIVES

Slice the top and base off a medium lemon and sit on a board. Using a sharp or serrated knife, cut down the curve of the fruit to remove the peel and pith. Lay the bare fruit on its side. Hold it firmly with one hand as you cut down along the inside of each of the segment lines to the center of the fruit until neat wedges of membrane-free lemon can be removed easily. Cut each one into three. Tip 3 thinly sliced garlic cloves and a pot each of black and green olives into a bowl that can take them snugly in a layer. Add the lemon. Sprinkle with 1 teaspoon dried oregano and cover with fruity extra virgin olive oil. Let marinate in the refrigerator, covered, for a few hours at least (preferably 24 hours). Return to room temperature before serving.

EGGPLANT DIP

Preheat the oven to 400°F. Wash and dry 2 medium eggplants. Roast on a baking sheet for 30 minutes until blackened, soft, and collapsing. Or hold them over a gas flame on a fork to blacken and smoke for a few minutes before finishing in the oven. Cool for 5 minutes. Slit them open. Spoon and scrape the flesh free and discard the skins. Squeeze the flesh gently to remove some of the juices. Drop it into a processor (or use a stick blender). Add half a chopped shallot, a garlic clove, the juice of 1 lemon, 2 tablespoons extra virgin olive oil, and 1 tablespoon chopped Italian parsley. Blitz until smooth. Season lightly. Cool and cover. Serve in a bowl for spreading/dipping.

CUCUMBER TZATZIKI

Wash and dry ½ a cucumber. Grate it thickly and put in a colander. Let it drain a little and squeeze out a bit of the water with paper towels. Bang 1¼ cups thick Greek yogurt, 1 tablespoon minced mint (or a pinch of dried mint/dill), 2 teaspoons olive oil, 1 teaspoon lemon juice, a crushed clove of garlic, and a pinch of superfine sugar into a large bowl. Season to taste. Stir in the cucumber. Eat now or chill.

CILANTRO FLATBREADS

Combine scant ¼ cup boiling water/1 scant ½ cup cold water in a pitcher. Sift generous 1¾ cups white bread flour into a bowl, adding 1½ teaspoons cumin seeds and a few fresh cilantro leaves. Mix the water in gradually, using a fork or your hand until it integrates into a smooth (not sticky) ball. Divide equally into 4 on a lightly floured board. Roll one piece out into a very thin circle. Fold it in half and then half again before rolling it out very thinly again. Cover with a dish towel and repeat with the other pieces. Put a crepe pan or large flat skillet onto very high heat for 3 minutes. Add the first flatbread. Cook for 1 to 2 minutes per side or until puffed and charred. Remove. Brush with a bit of oil and sprinkle with a little coarse salt. Eat immediately. Repeat with the remaining flatbreads.

BUTTERNUT SQUASH FALAFEL-STYLE FRITTERS

HEALTHY

FEEDS 3

Butternut squash takes on a more exotic identity in this one, teaming up with cheap and nutritious chickpeas and spices for an extravagant tasting, festival-style fritter.

INGREDIENTS

14 ounces butternut squash
2 tablespoons olive oil
a pinch of dried cumin
salt and black pepper
a pinch of red pepper flakes
1 x 16-ounce can of chickpeas
3 scallions
2¼ ounces Cheddar
a small handful of fresh cilantro
a pinch of ground ginger
a pinch of dried oregano
scant ½ cup white bread crumbs made from stale bread (p201)
a pinch of dried mint
a squeeze of lime juice
4–5 tablespoons all-purpose or gram flour, for coating
peanut oil with a dash of olive oil, for shallow-frying

PREP Preheat the oven to 400°F. Using a sawing action, cut into your squash with a bread knife. Scoop out any seeds with a spoon and chop into large, fairly equal pieces, keeping the skins on. Sit on a baking sheet and roll in olive oil to coat. Sprinkle with cumin, salt, and red pepper flakes and roast for 20 minutes, or until the flesh is tender. Remove and let cool, then scoop the flesh from the skins (these can be discarded). Blitz into a puree in a blender, put in a large bowl, and set aside.

Drain the chickpeas into a strainer. Dry them with a dish towel or on paper towels, then tip into a bowl and mash roughly, leaving some almost whole for texture. Finely chop the scallions. Finely grate the Cheddar and tear the cilantro roughly.

Mix a good big pinch of ginger (as much as you can get between thumb and index finger) and one of oregano into the squash puree. Throw in the chickpeas, bread crumbs, cheese, scallion, mint, lime juice, and cilantro. Mix well with a fork. Taste to check it's well seasoned. The mix should be firm, not sloppy.

Coat the fritters: scatter a bit of flour over a large plate. Dampen your hands. Scoop up tablespoons of the mix and shape into fritters then roll them in the flour to coat. Chill for 30 minutes at least. Preheat the oven to 350°F.

COOK Pour enough peanut oil into a wok to about ½-inch depth, adding a dash of olive oil. When it's hot enough to crisp a bread crumb to a count of 10, add the fritters. Cook for 2 minutes per side (without overbrowning) then transfer to a baking sheet and finish in the oven for 10 minutes.

PLATE Serve these up on a pile of couscous or tabbouleh (p128) with a plate of lightly griddled vegetables, or bang them into pitas with leaves and hummus (p38). Save any extra for a lunch box.

SWEET POTATO AND BLACK-EYE PEA BURGER

FEEDS 4

INGREDIENTS

14 ounces sweet potato
2 teaspoons dried oregano
1 teaspoon ground cumin
salt and black pepper
1–2 tablespoons olive oil, for coating
1 x 14-ounce can of black-eye peas
2 ounces crustless fresh white bread
a good handful of torn cilantro
juice of ½ a lime
¼ teaspoon smoked paprika
4 homemade (p82) or store-bought
    burger buns
EXTRAS
lime mayo (p45)
corn salsa (opposite)
guacamole (p75)
grated Cheddar
shredded iceberg lettuce leaves

TIP
Why ruin a burger with bad bread? Try making your own buns (p82).

This Mexican-inspired gourmet vegetable burger is full of spicy flavors which ping off all over the place. It's delicious.

PREP Preheat the oven to 350°F. Peel the sweet potatoes and cut into ½-inch slices. Chuck them onto a baking sheet and sprinkle with oregano, cumin, salt, and pepper. Toss them in olive oil and roast for 30 minutes, or until soft and golden (test with a knife at 20 minutes). Remove. Tip them into a bowl and mash to a smooth paste. Let cool.

Meantime, drain the beans into a strainer. Shake them dry. Tip them into a bowl. Mash roughly with a fork. Blitz the bread to crumbs (p201). Mix the mashed beans, bread crumbs, cilantro, lime juice smoked paprika, and some salt and pepper into the sweet potato mash. Divide and shape into 4 flat burgers with your hands. Chill for 10 minutes. Make your mayo, salsa, and guacamole. Slice the burger buns across and broil or toast lightly. Set aside.

COOK Put a skillet on medium-high heat. Fry the burgers for 5 minutes per side or until golden, crispy, and hot all though, regulating the heat so they don't burn. (Alternatively, fry for a minute each side to seal the burger before finishing in a hot oven for 10 minutes).

PLATE Stack the warm buns with lime mayo, corn salsa, the burgers, and guacamole before finishing with the Cheddar and lettuce. Serve with tortilla crisps, spiced sweet potato wedges (p82), or a healthy salad.

TO GO WITH

CORN SALSA

Drain a 9-ounce can of corn into a bowl. Squeeze over the juice of 1 fat lime, add 1–2 tablespoons thin honey and stir together. Throw in 2 tablespoons chopped cilantro, ½ a seeded, finely diced chile (p16), and 1 small finely diced red onion. Stir together and season to taste. Set aside for the flavors to develop until needed and stir before using.

EGGPLANT AND GOAT CHEESE BURGER WITH OLIVE MAYO AND TOMATO

FEEDS 2

There's a Mediterranean vibe going on here: this burger's fresh, zingy, and totally satisfying. Don't be tempted to buy standard bread crumbs —they're no good here. Get a pack of light tasty panko bread crumbs from your Asian supermarket or make your own (p201) instead— they're easy.

INGREDIENTS

2 x ½-inch firm goat cheese rounds
1 egg
4–5 tablespoons all-purpose flour
a handful of panko/panko-style bread crumbs (p201)
salt and black pepper
1 small eggplant
2–3 tablespoons olive oil
a pinch of dried thyme
2 homemade (p82) or store-bought burger buns
2–4 sunblush/sundried tomatoes
a handful of soft green leaves
peanut oil, for shallow-frying

OLIVE MAYO
1 tablespoon mayonnaise (p153)
a few chopped black olives or 1 teaspoon olive tapenade

PREP Coat the cheese: Beat the egg and tip it into a bowl. Put your flour and bread crumbs onto separate plates. Season the flour lightly with salt and pepper. Toss the cheese disks one at a time into the flour, turning to coat well. Dip the floured disks into the beaten egg (making sure to cover) then toss and turn in the bread crumbs. Dunk them back into the egg and finally into the crumbs. Refrigerate on a plate for at least 30 minutes.

Meantime, slice the eggplant into ½-inch disks using a sharp knife/bread knife. Sit the pieces in a colander and sprinkle with a little salt to draw out any bitterness. After 20 minutes, wipe off any moisture then brush sparingly with olive oil and a sprinkle of thyme. Heat the remaining olive oil in a large pan. Add the slices and fry for 1 to 2 minutes per side, until well browned and soft. Drain on paper towels and set aside in a warm place.

Prep your mayo by mixing it with the chopped olives/tapenade in a bowl. Set aside.

Slice the burger buns across and broil or toast lightly. Spread with mayo. Add a couple of slices of eggplant, a sunblush or sundried tomato, then top with a few of the green leaves and the remaining eggplant.

COOK Pour peanut oil into a small shallow skillet so it's around ½-inch deep. If you have a cooking thermometer, heat the oil to around 350°F. Otherwise, drop a bread crumb in and count to 10. If it's crisp and lightly golden after this time, the oil is ready.

Gently place the crumbed cheese disks in the oil. Cook for 1 to 2 minutes per side, turning carefully using a spatula, until they're hot and soft inside, crisp,and golden outside. Sit them briefly on paper towels.

PLATE Bang the hot cheese disks on top of the eggplant. Top with leaves. Leave open with the lids leaning jauntily against the stack. Eat with fries and some dressed leaves.

SMOTHERED GARLIC AND TARRAGON PORTOBELLO MUSHROOM BURGER WITH LIME MAYO

FAST

FEEDS 2

You definitely don't miss the meat with this gorgeous combination of flavors. So good that I've had them for breakfast. Not baking your own buns? Ciabatta rolls are excellent for soaking up the juices.

INGREDIENTS

1 garlic clove
a few fresh tarragon leaves
  (or a pinch of dried)
2 teaspoons softened butter
2 fat portobello mushrooms
a glug of olive oil
salt and black pepper
a handful of fresh green leaves
  (arugula/spinach)
2 homemade (p82) or store-bought
  burger buns
LIME MAYO
3 tablespoons mayonnaise (p153)
juice of ½–1 lime

PREP Peel and crush the garlic and finely chop the tarragon. Add to the butter in a bowl and cream together with the back of a spoon. Brush the heads of the mushrooms with paper towels if they need cleaning. Don't wash them. Cut off the stalks. Smear the whole of each mushroom with a generous coating of olive oil.

Make up the lime mayo by mixing up regular mayonnaise with a good squeeze of fresh lime juice to taste. Get it nice and sharp to contrast with the burger.

COOK Heat a griddle pan. Once hot, put the mushrooms bottom-side down to cook for 5 minutes. Turn them over. Smear a teaspoon of the butter mix over each and cook for another 5 minutes, or until soft. (Thin mushrooms may take less time so keep your eye on them). Season. Meantime, lightly toast or broil your burger buns separately.

PLATE Stack both bottom halves of the toasted rolls with lime mayo and green leaves and top with the mushrooms.

TIP
If you have a roomy pan, try griddling the buns in it with the mushrooms rather than toasting them separately. This way they'll absorb some of the lovely mushroom juices.

——— BONUS BITE ———

BACON AND CHEESE MUSHROOM BURGER
Brush the mushrooms with oil and griddle as above. Broil 2 bacon slices and chop roughly. Grate some Cheddar cheese. Top the mushrooms with both the bacon and cheese and place under a preheated broiler until the cheese is melting and bubbling hot. Bang into toasted rolls and serve with ketchup and iceberg lettuce.

Chicken

Chicken has done me a great service over the years. A proper roast dinner was the first meal I ever cooked and since then Mrs Chicken and I haven't looked back; I've eaten and cooked loads of it. And for good reason; a good chicken is irresistible. As with other meats (perhaps even more so with chicken) it's all about bagging the best bird you can get. The arguments are well rehearsed: using free-range organic and other well looked after chicken is the key to fuller flavor, and it's humane. The birds get to lead happier lives and you get a meat that's lower in fat, nutritionally superior, and way tastier. From the cook's point of view a chicken's a gracious bird—the meat is beautiful when simply cooked but it permits the addition of a huge number of flavors that can take your skills and your palate traveling anywhere. Enjoy…

TALKING CHICKEN BITS

BREAST (OFF THE BONE) Makes for a great simple fast cook (thin it out) and has very low fat content without skin. Cook with care to avoid chewiness or cook with skin for the flavor and then remove if it's an issue. Perfect for stir-fry, skewers, scallop, griddling, schnitzel, pan-fries, casseroles.

WING A tender, juicy, flavorsome, and very cheap cut, perfect for sharing and parties (or just pigging out on)—my favorite bit.

THIGH Carries more fat so has deeper flavor and is less likely to dry out than breast meat. It's also cheaper which makes it a top buy. Cook it bone-in (best) or off. Sauté or bake it then get in there with your fingers or whack it into stews and casseroles. Tender and juicy.

BREAST ON THE BONE Cooking on the bone imparts a beautiful juicy sweetness—sear off then slow roast or casserole.

LEG Made up of the thigh and the drumstick, this part of the chicken is great for a really tasty budget feed. Treat it like a small roast or use in casseroles.

DRUMSTICK Ideal for mucky eating. Slather in your choice of marinade, bake, broil, or start in the oven then bang on the BBQ for summer eating. Good in stews.

OYSTER A right little gem, tucked under the bird at the end of the leg. It's the tenderest part of the chicken—chef's treat.

CHICKEN LIVERS Trim, season, and fry in a little butter and oil. Bang them on salads or griddled bread and use them for pâté.

WHOLE BIRD Roast in the oven or shoot in to a pot-roast with stock, vegetables, and seasoning.

GIBLETS Inner bits stored in a plastic bag in some whole birds. Use for stock.

POUSSIN A mini-chicken great for one person. It's low on taste but takes flavors well. Roast, spatchcock, griddle, or broil it.

BUY IT—STASH IT

Flight time from **STORE TO REFRIGERATOR** shouldn't be more than **3 HOURS MAX**. Bang it into the refrigerator in the original packaging unless it has giblets inside (it'll say on the label). Remove these at once and keep separately. Store naked chicken, loosely covered, on a plate. **PLACE IT WELL AWAY FROM OTHER FOODS—** especially cooked food. Fresh meat lasts up to **2 DAYS**. Top organic birds from the butcher can last **4 DAYS**. Follow sell-by labels.

CHICKEN COSMETICS

Appearance counts. If buying a whole bird, look for one that's fat, well-rounded, and neatly shaped. Its skin wants to be creamy and pretty uniformly smooth. Avoid anything with tears, marks, stubble, or marks from freezer burn. Check the packaging too. It should be unscathed. Press before you buy: a properly stored bird should feel cold. Take it home in separate wrap.

WHAT'S THE BEST BIRD?
Cutting through the jargon

Be canny and work out where the chicken's from and what sort of quality you're getting. It's all about reading the labels and interpreting them (or asking your butcher).

STANDARD These guys have very little room to move. They grow unnaturally fast, and are often loaded with hormones and antibiotics. Stress affects the quality and flavor of the meat. It's cheaper, but cruel? There's no distinctive labeling.

HIGHER WELFARE INDOOR-REARED Means less-intensive rearing with a better environment leading to better life and better flavor.

FREE-RANGE The birds are allowed to roam outdoors and have a longer, more natural life. The label may specify the farm and farmer. It's more expensive.

ORGANIC Same as free-range but fed organic feed so fewer chemicals involved—never a bad thing. If money's tight, consider getting a cheaper cut of this more expensive bird or only eating organic free-range but less often.

CORN-FED Fed on corn, these guys should be clearly labeled and slightly juicer with a more intense flavor, but check where they've come from.

∿∿∿∿∿ *Scare Tactics* ∿∿∿∿∿

Keep it clean and you won't wind up in the emergency room. Wash your hands after handling raw chicken and scrub your utensils to avoid contamination. Chicken should be freshly fragrant, by the way. If the inevitable smell from the wrapping doesn't disappear in seconds, ditch the bird.

FRIENDS
AVOCADO, BACON, BLUE CHEESE, CAESAR DRESSING, CHILE, CILANTRO, CRANBERRY JELLY, CREAM, CRÈME FRAÎCHE, CHICORY, COCONUT MILK, FETA, FISH SAUCE, GARLIC, GINGER, ICEBERG LETTUCE, LEMON, LEMONGRASS, LIME, MARJORAM, MAYO, MUSTARD, OREGANO, OYSTER SAUCE, PAPRIKA, PARMESAN, PEANUT, POTATOES, RED CURRANT JELLY, ROSEMARY, SAGE, SEA SALT, SOY SAUCE, TARRAGON, THYME, TOMATO KETCHUP, WALNUT, WATERCRESS, WINE

CHICKEN NUTRITION

BRILLIANT FOR:

PROTEIN
Builds muscles and cells and helps with repair and general body maintenance.

Tryptophan
An essential amino acid which allows the release of the cheer-you-up happy hormone S E R O T O N I N

IRON
FOUND IN THE DARK MEAT AND LIVER HELPS CARRY OXYGEN THROUGH the bloodstream, fights anemia and helps you think straight.

VITAMIN B6
Produces insulin for stability, helps with PMT (*I'm told*), AND PROTECTS AGAINST CARDIOVASCULAR DISEASE.

ZINC
STRENGTHENS THE IMMUNE SYSTEM, helping fight off colds, infections, etc.

CALCIUM
WORKS TO STRENGTHEN TEETH AND BONES.

FATTY ACIDS
in the bird help to LOWER CHOLESTEROL, helping your heart out, while the

LACK OF FAT
(in the white meat in particular) makes chicken the popular choice for anyone with health concerns or weight watching.

———— BIRD ACTION ————

TRUSSING
Binding a whole chicken's bits together with string means it doesn't flap about during cooking. It holds any stuffing in and neatens it. I don't bother to do it with a smaller bird and many come pre-tied anyway. However, if you're going for a bigger chicken and where presentation matters, it's worth a go.

Spatchcocking
Opening the bird up by cutting out the backbone then griddling or broiling it whole means faster even cooking—it's really easy, try it (p63)

JOINTING
Take a whole chicken and divide it up into its component parts. Ideal for economical eating as it's much cheaper than buying everything separately. Cut into 8 using a sharpened filleting or other good knife with a bit of a flex to it.

1. Place the bird flat on board with the breast facing up and legs toward you.

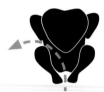

2. Cut through skin between leg and breast following the line of the carcass to keep maximum meat.

5. Sit the chicken back up. Find the backbone with your finger and cut along the edge of the left side all along it.

6. Use long, clean slices to follow the shape of the ribcage round and cut the breast meat off neatly including the wing.

3. Push and twist to break leg out of socket.
4. Turn bird on side and cut around the oyster so it stays attached to the leg, taking it all off in one piece.

7. Remove the wings from the breasts. Snip the tips and discard. Repeat on the other side.

CHICKEN TRICK

Velveting chicken stir-fry Chinese-style like this keeps it tender.
1. Slice skinless breast into strips across the grain.
2. Bang in a bowl with a smooth mix of egg white and cornstarch.

3. Add sesame and vegetable oil to a hot wok to heat. Add meat.
4. Toss and turn on medium/hot heat for 4 to 5 minutes or until cooked.
5. Use as is or add sauce. Bang on noodles or use with whatever.

APPROXIMATE COOKING TIMES

Here's a very rough idea for chicken cooking times but you'll need to test your meat for doneness—chicken has to be cooked right through (overcooking ruins it).

WHOLE ROAST CHICKEN: 20 minutes per 1 pound + an extra 20 minutes at 350°F.

ROAST CHICKEN LEG: 35 to 40 minutes at 350°F.

CHICKEN BREAST (BONELESS): pan-fry for 2 minutes each side or until golden then bang in the oven at 350°F for 8 to 10 minutes depending on the size of the breast.

DRUMSTICKS: slash, marinate then roast in the oven for 40 minutes at 400°F.

A CHICKEN STOCK (*or three*)

Stock's your best friend. Use it as the base for soups, risottos, sauces, casseroles. Here are a few different ways of making it.

LAST-MINUTE FIX VERSION Mix a good chicken stock cube with boiling water. It won't taste nearly as good as proper homemade stuff and may be salty, so remember that as you're seasoning your dish.

EMERGENCY VERSION Bang a few slashed chicken wings or small joints into a pan with an onion, carrot, a bit of celery, a few peppercorns, and some salt. Cover with lots of water then boil for 30 minutes and strain. Discard the bits. Makes a light but very useful stock.

POST-ROAST CHICKEN VERSION Tip the chicken carcass with any spare meat and gravy, an onion, carrot, whatever herbs you have to hand, and some seasoning into a large pan with lots of water. Boil then simmer it for an hour. Strain and discard the bits. Chill to use the next day (it lasts 4 days in the refrigerator) or freeze in small containers for stock shots when cold or in pour-in storage bags. This makes a top stock and a great soup base.

IS IT DONE YET?

Sometimes, timings don't do it. To know for sure whether your chicken's cooked use these methods.

SIGHT TEST

Cut into the meat to check it's white all through (no pink). See if the juices run clear. Put a skewer into the bird at the thickest part and catch any juice that comes out with a teaspoon. Good to go if not pink.

Touch test

Push a metal skewer into the thickest part. Count to 5 and remove. If it's burning to the touch, it's done.

MEAT THERMOMETER NEEDS TO READ...

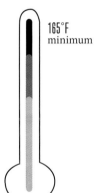

165°F minimum

A COUPLE OF CLASSIC MARINADES

PIRI-PIRI

Make this classic chicken sauce as hot as you like by playing with the chiles. For a good base, seed and chop 4 hot red chiles (or keep seeds for heat). Bang in a pan with 4 fat garlic cloves, 1½ tablespoons paprika, 1 teaspoon salt, 1 teaspoon dried oregano, lemon juice to taste, and 6 tablespoons oil. Heat gently for 5 minutes without browning the garlic. Remove. Blitz. Cool. Slap over your chicken.

YOGURT RUB

Mix a bit of plain yogurt with harissa paste, garlic, lemon juice, oil, cumin, fresh cilantro, cinnamon, salt, and pepper. Rub into skinless breasts or chunks for skewers.

BUTTERFLIED GRIDDLED
HERB CHICKEN
WITH ZINGY TOMATO GREEN BEANS

HEALTHY **FAST** FEEDS 2

Fresh, tasty, and quicker than any ready-meal: butterfly your bird for even cooking and griddle it for a BBQ effect all-year round.

INGREDIENTS

*2 plump boneless, skinless chicken
    breasts*
1 tablespoon olive oil
*a handful of torn fresh herbs
    (cilantro/oregano/rosemary/thyme/
    marjoram)*
2 garlic cloves, peeled and crushed
salt and pepper
grated zest and juice of 1 lemon
*a few slices of coarse bread, for
    griddling*
*a dollop of hummus
    (store-bought or homemade, p38)*
ZINGY TOMATO GREEN BEANS
7 ounces fine green beans, trimmed
1 tablespoon olive oil
1 garlic clove, peeled and diced
6 cherry tomatoes, halved

✳✳✳✳ CASH SAVER ✳✳✳✳
Buy and use skinless chicken thigh fillets.
Open them up then roll them out with a
rolling pin. Griddle for a bit longer.

—— CHANGE IT UP ——
For mustard and honey butterflies, marinate
the chicken in a mix of 2 tablespoons
white wine vinegar, 1 crushed garlic
clove, 2 teaspoons dried herbs (oregano/
thyme/rosemary) 1 teaspoon honey, and 3
teaspoons each of Dijon mustard and olive
oil. Cook as above, adding lemon juice and
sea salt.

PREP Butterfly the chicken: first, take a look at the bottom of the chicken breasts. If they have tenders attached (mini-fillets) slice them off to cook separately. Sit the breasts on a board, smooth sides up. Using a sharp chef's knife held parallel to the board, slice cleanly sideways through the centers of each one but NOT all the way through. Leave a hinge. Open each breast out into one thinner piece like a book. Lay the first butterfly between two pieces of plastic wrap. Flatten it some more by hitting it with the flat of your hand or by rolling and bashing it with a rolling pin. Take care not to rip it. Transfer to a plate. Repeat with the second piece. Add any tenders.

Make the marinade: Mix the oil, herbs, garlic, pepper, lemon zest, and half of the juice in a bowl. Tip it over the chicken and rub in. Set aside.

Blanch the beans in a pan of boiling water for 2 minutes or until *al dente* (bite one to test). Tip them into a colander held under running cold water for 30 seconds to fix the color and texture. Set aside to drain.

COOK Heat a griddle or stovetop grill pan until almost smoking hot. Slap the butterflies down. Let them cook for 2 minutes, pressing down a bit with your spatula, until golden brown. Flip. Repeat for 2 minutes or until cooked (test with a knife: the flesh should be white, not pink). Remove to a plate. Sprinkle with salt and remaining lemon juice. Griddle the bread on the pan until crisp and marked each side.

Finish the beans: heat the olive oil in a skillet. Add the diced garlic and cook for a few seconds but don't brown it up. Add the beans, turning, and cook for a minute or two. Add the tomatoes, turning, and cook for another minute until warmed through.

PLATE Pile the beans and tomato artistically onto your plates. Sit the butterfly at a jaunty angle. Add a dollop of hummus and hot bread. Sit on the couch and enjoy.

BONUS BITES

HERBED CHICKEN SKEWERS
Chop the nonbutterflied meat into bite-size chunks. Add your marinade. Thread onto metal or presoaked wooden skewers. Cook under a hot broiler, turning, until white all through and still juicy. Eat on rice or in warmed pitas with salad.
CHICKEN FAJITAS
Thin meat as above before cutting into long thin strips. Add 2 teaspoons paprika, 1 crushed garlic clove, and a squeeze of lemon. Pan-fry quickly before banging into warmed tortillas with guacamole (p75), grated Cheddar, sliced red onion, and shredded iceberg lettuce.

SCHNITZEL WITH A TWIST

FAST

FEEDS 1

These gorgeous hot chicken sandwiches are crisp on the outside and ooze with a tasty herb and blue cheese center. If that topping's not to your taste, head for the garlic cream cheese or prosciutto and banana options. Plain schnitzel, meanwhile, is a classic fast-food favorite: if that's what you're after, thin the chicken, skip the topping, coat, and fry.

INGREDIENTS

1 large boneless, skinless chicken breast
¾ tablespoon olive oil
a little piece of butter
TOPPING
1 plump shallot, peeled and diced
2 teaspoons olive oil
1 teaspoon chopped sage
scant ¼ cup crumbled blue cheese
COATING
generous ⅓ cup all-purpose flour,
    seasoned
1 small egg
2 slices of white bread, crusts removed

PREP Thin the chicken breast: Place it between sheets of plastic wrap or wax paper on a board and roll or bash it with a rolling pin until it's about 1¼ inches thick. Set aside.

Make the topping: fry the shallot very gently in the oil in a small pan over low heat for a few minutes until soft. Tip it into a bowl. Add the sage and blue cheese and mix until smooth. Cool for 2 minutes. Spread the mix over the top of the chicken breast, using your hands to encourage it to stick. Set aside.

Organize the coating: spread the flour over a plate. Crack the egg onto a second plate and beat with a fork. Roughly tear the bread and blitz it to rough crumbs in a processor/blender or with a stick blender. Sprinkle onto a third plate.

Very carefully, place the topped chicken in the flour (bottom first). To coat the top, flick flour over the meat and pat it on to cover the cheese mix. Or turn the whole thing very carefully. Then, with care, dip it into the egg, flicking again for a good sticky covering. Finally, sit it in the bread crumbs, flicking or turning to coat it completely. Cook it now or chill until you need it.

COOK Preheat the oven to 350°F. Put an ovenproof pan onto medium/high heat. Add the oil and butter. When it's frothing, carefully add the schnitzel. Fry for 3 minutes, or until golden. Use a wide spatula and in one smooth movement turn it carefully. Fry for another 3 minutes (check and adjust the heat to ensure it doesn't burn at any point). Shove the pan into the oven for 5 minutes to finish off. Remove. Check it's cooked through (test with a knife). Sprinkle with sea salt.

PLATE Serve with chunks of lemon. Team with a crisp salad and shallow-fry fries (p78) or spaghetti with easy tomato sauce (p176).

TIP
Make loads if you've crowds heading around. Mix and match the topping options.

·········· **TIME SAVER** ··········
Use a jar of panko bread crumbs instead of making your own.

—— **CHANGE IT UP** ——
1. For garlic, cream cheese, and prosciutto schnitzel, soften 1–2 tablespoons cream cheese in a bowl. Smear a little over the top of the thinned meat. Lay on a slice of prosciutto, smear over the remaining cheese, and coat and cook as before.
2. For banana and ham schnitzel, butterfly the breast (p51) and lay in a slice of ham and half a mashed banana. Close it up. Coat and cook in the pan or fry and bake in the oven at 400°F.

BONUS BITES

CHICKEN FINGERS
Cut the thinned breast into long slices with a sharp chef's knife. Coat in flour, egg, and crumbs as above. Fry in oil and butter until cooked through or for a minute per side before finishing in the oven at 400°F until white all through.
CHICKEN KIEV
Slice into the side of the breast to create a pocket. Stuff it with well-chilled garlic butter. Seal with a couple of toothpicks before coating as above, frying then finishing in the oven for 15 minutes or until cooked through.

CRISPY CHICKEN WINGS AND DIPS

FAST

FEEDS 6 TO 8

INGREDIENTS

2 pounds chicken wings
 (whole or prebutchered)
2–3 tablespoons olive oil
a light sprinkling of paprika/smoked
 paprika (optional)
salt and pepper

✵✵✵✵ CASH SAVER ✵✵✵✵

For a cheap solo or shared meal, pile chicken wings onto bowls of basmati or sticky rice, drizzle with one of the dips below, and serve with stir-fried greens.

········· TIME SAVER ·········

Prep the wings and the dipping sauces a few hours ahead.

—— CHANGE IT UP ——

Marinate the wings in olive oil, lemon juice and rind, crushed garlic, and cayenne pepper. Oven-bake as before then toss in chopped parsley/cilantro.

These little beauties are perfect for sharing and dipping. Wings are the sweetest bits of the bird. If you're treating yourself, just reduce the quantities. Choose a cooking style to suit your event: oven-bake, griddle, broil, or BBQ.

PREP If you've bought whole wings (still wing-shaped), trim them. Cut off the tips at the end joint with kitchen scissors or a sharp knife at an angle. Discard or use for stock. Find the remaining joint by flexing the wing. Cut cleanly through it at an angle into two. Dry these pieces on paper towels, then tip into a large bowl. Coat with the olive oil, sprinkle over the paprika (use it if you're making plain wings), and grind over a little pepper. Chill in the refrigerator while you make your chosen dip or cook now and enjoy plain.

COOK OVEN: Preheat the oven to 425°F. Bang the wings onto a rack over a baking sheet/roasting pan. Cook for 20 to 30 minutes until golden and crispy. GRIDDLE: Put the griddle or stovetop grill pan onto medium/high heat. Put the wings (and extractor fan) on. Cook for 10 to 15 minutes, turning and pressing with a spatula. Finish under a very hot broiler for a few seconds if you like. BROIL: Turn regularly for 10 to 15 minutes. BBQ: Place the wings directly over medium coals, turning frequently until golden (10 to 15 minutes). To check for doneness, cut to the bone to make sure there's no redness.

PLATE Lightly salt the wings and pile onto a big plate; serve with dips in bowls and let everyone help themselves.

━━━━━━ DIPS ━━━━━━

1 THAI BOUNTY
Mix a 1½-ounce piece of grated, creamed coconut with 4 tablespoons boiling water until it looks like toothpaste. Mix together with 2 tablespoons fish sauce, 2 tablespoons soy sauce, 1 tablespoon tamarind paste, 3 teaspoons superfine sugar, 1 chopped small red chile, a ¾-inch piece of bruised, minced lemongrass and a little cilantro.

2 SICHUAN
Seed and slice 1 large red chile and thinly slice 2 scallions. Mix together with 2 crushed garlic cloves, 1 tablespoon sesame oil, 3 tablespoons low-salt soy sauce, 2 teaspoons mirin/rice vinegar, ¾ teaspoon brown sugar, and lots of torn cilantro. Tip into a food processor or use a stick blender and blitz to a thick liquid.

3 TERIYAKI
Mix together 2 teaspoons grated fresh ginger, 8 tablespoons soy sauce, 3 tablespoons Chinese rice wine, 4 tablespoons rice vinegar, ½ tablespoon superfine sugar, and a good squeeze of lemon juice.

4 SCORCHING DIJON
Mix together 4 tablespoons white balsamic vinegar, 2 tablespoons dried oregano, 6 teaspoons Dijon mustard, 1 chopped red chile, and a pinch each of salt and sugar. Squeeze a little lime juice onto the chicken wings before adding to this dip.

A SIMPLE ROAST
CHICKEN (AND BITS)

HEALTHY

FEEDS 6

INGREDIENTS
THE BIRD

1 x 4½–5 pounds good-quality chicken, giblets removed
salt and black pepper
1 small eating apple/1 lemon
a small handful of fresh herbs (sage/tarragon/rosemary/thyme)
a little piece of butter
a squeeze or two of lemon juice
2 tablespoons olive oil
a good sprinkling of dried herbs (oregano/tarragon/marjoram/rosemary/thyme)
5–8 unsmoked American bacon slices (or sufficient to cover breast)
generous 1 cup chicken stock/water/white wine/cider

TIP

Rub the naked bird all over with softened butter instead of using bacon. If it browns early, slip a bit of foil or wax paper over it.

✳✳✳✳ CASH SAVER ✳✳✳✳

For a cheaper roast for two, bang 2 large chicken legs or a poussin (small bird) into an ovenproof skillet/dish/pan. Add chopped root vegetables. Sprinkle with a few dried herbs, scatter over some sliced garlic, and season. Squeeze over a bit of lemon juice and drizzle with olive oil before roasting as above for 40 minutes to 1 hour.

You can't beat a roast bird; it's one of the all time greats. But don't restrict it to weekends—any night can be a roast night. Stuff it the no-fuss way with fruit and herbs, or flavor it up with my sweet sage and onion stuffing. This one multitasks: cook it in the bird or in a separate dish so it crisps up (it makes a great meal in its own right).

PREP Remove the chicken from the refrigerator an hour before cooking so it returns to room temperature. Check the weight to calculate cooking time (p49). Preheat the oven to 350°F.

Sprinkle a little salt and pepper into the cavity, then push the fruit, fresh herbs, and butter inside. Larger birds may be sold trussed (legs tied) in which case you'll need to undo it, add the bits and retruss it. If going for the weekend option, push a few tablespoons of cooled sage and onion stuffing (p56) into the cavity. But don't pack it in as it slows the cooking process. Cook any extra separately in a dish alongside the chicken.

Sit the bird, breast up, in a large roasting pan. Squeeze a little lemon juice over it then brush or drizzle with olive oil. Sprinkle over the dried herbs and a little salt and pepper.

COOK Put the pan into the oven. Watch the top of your bird as it doesn't want to get too brown. A third of the way into the cooking time, remove from the oven. Spoon the juices over the breast. Lay the bacon slices over the breast in a single layer to cover and protect it. Return to the oven.

Once your calculated cooking time has elapsed, remove the chicken from the oven. Test for doneness (p49). Transfer to a plate and let rest in a warm place for 10 to 15 minutes. To make the gravy: place the pan directly onto the stove. Add stock or your liquid of choice to the juices along with those from the chicken plate. Stir and scrape the mix with a wooden spoon. Let it boil to reduce a bit. When you're happy with the consistency, add lemon juice and taste for seasoning.

PLATE Cut any trussing string, sharpen your steel, and carve the chicken at the table, sharing out the white and dark meat, crisp bacon, and stuffing, if using. Bang your chosen veg into bowls and gravy into a pitcher. Fight over the wishbone and enjoy...

SWEET SAGE AND ONION
STUFFING

Blitz 3 ounces crustless white bread in a processor for 2 seconds to make crumbs. Tip them into a bowl with the grated zest of ½ lemon and 4 chopped sage leaves. Slit 3 pork and apple sausages along their sides. Cut the meat into rough chunks (discarding the skins). Add to the bowl. Fry a finely diced medium onion in 1 tablespoon butter on medium heat until soft. Mix evenly into the stuffing with 1 tablespoon brandy/cider. Spoon into an 7 by 5-inch greased ovenproof dish. Bake for 30 to 40 minutes (put it in the oven 20 minutes before the bird is due to come out) or until crisping up and browning on top. Let it rest for 5 minutes. Spoon or carve it out.

A GREEN VEGETABLE PLATE

Put a steamer of water onto boil or set a colander or strainer into the top of a pan of boiling water. Break a head or two of broccoli into florets, trim the ends off a handful of green beans, and wash both vegetables well. Put the broccoli in the steamer and cook for 5 minutes, then add the beans and cook for another 5 minutes. Drain, then chuck into a dish—adding salt, butter, and lemon juice if you like.

BITS

ROAST POTATOES

Parboil 3¼ pounds peeled mealy white potatoes for 10 minutes. Drain. Bang them back into the pan. Shuffle over the heat for a few seconds to dry and ruffle their edges for a crisper finish. Add to the pan with the bird along with a pinch of salt and ½ lemon, cut into chunks. You may need a drop more oil. While the chicken is resting, turn the oven up to 425°F and bang the potatoes back in to cook for an additional 10 to 15 minutes, until golden and crispy.

A ROAST ROOT VEGETABLE PLATE

Peel and chop a mix of carrots/parsnips/sweet potato/butternut squash/beet into chunks. Cut 2 red/white onions into quarters and slice the tops off 2 heads of garlic. Drizzle the lot in olive oil, salt, lemon juice, and sprinkle over a pinch dried oregano. Bang onto a baking sheet to roast 20 minutes before the bird comes out. Cook for another 10 to 15 minutes or until soft and starting to caramelize.

FAST TANDOORI-STYLE ROAST WITH ONIONS

FEEDS 4

INGREDIENTS

1 x 3 pounds chicken
3 large onions, peeled and thinly sliced
1¼ cups chicken stock (p49)
sea salt
a handful of cilantro leaves, torn
MARINADE
¾ cup plain yogurt
5 garlic cloves, crushed
2 ounces ginger, peeled and grated
2 tablespoons paprika
2 tablespoons lemon juice
2 tablespoons peanut/vegetable oil
1 teaspoon garam masala
1 teaspoon chili powder/cayenne
*   pepper*
1 teaspoon ground turmeric
1 teaspoon ground cumin
½ teaspoon cinnamon
1 tablespoon tomato paste/ketchup
scant ½ cup grated Cheddar
½ teaspoon black pepper
1 teaspoon salt

TIP

Chicken wings, skinless breasts, chopped breast meat (for skewers), drumsticks, poussins, and lamb chops taste amazing in this marinade: just adjust your cooking method and timings to suit the ingredient.

········· **TIME SAVER** ·········

In place of the spices listed, blend 4 tablespoons good tandoori/tikka paste with the yogurt, lemon juice, Cheddar, garlic, and let marinate as above.

Roast chicken goes to Bollywood—and why not? Eat as it is or make this one the star of a curry banquet.

PREP Mix the marinade ingredients together in a bowl. Spoon and rub over the chicken so it's completely coated. Chill on a plate for a few hours, or overnight. Return to room temperature before cooking.

COOK Preheat the oven to 425°F. Put the chicken in a roasting pan. Surround with the onions and add half of the stock. Cook for 20 minutes. Add remaining stock and baste the chicken. Cook for another 20 minutes before checking for doneness (p49). Give it longer if you need to.

PLATE Let rest on a plate for 10 minutes. Sprinke with sea salt. Carve or tear the bird onto plates, pile on the onions and cilantro. Enjoy with honey mint raita (p130), lemon chunks, mango chutney, naan bread (p130), rice, and crisp shredded lettuce.

BONUS BITES

SUMMER ROAST CHICKEN ON COUSCOUS WITH ROASTED VEGETABLES AND FETA CHEESE
Mix 4 tablespoons soft butter with minced mint, crushed garlic, and lemon rind. Taking a whole chicken, gently release the skin over the breast, working your fingers in from the edge of the cavity to create space. Spread the butter over the top of the chicken then pull the skin back into place over it. Drizzle with oil. Roast in an oven preheated to 350°F for 20 minutes per 1 pound plus an extra 20 minutes until cooked. Leave until warm. Carve or chop into pieces. Throw onto a plate of cooled couscous with crumbled feta, roasted root vegetables, and a dressing of yogurt and crushed garlic.

ROAST POUSSIN IN WINE, CREAM AND TARRAGON
Preheat the oven to 375°F. Mix 4 tablespoons soft butter with a few handfuls of minced tarragon and use to stuff and coat the outsides of 2 poussins. Roast in a pan with 1 large glass of white wine for 30 to 40 minutes until tender. Remove. Stir a bit more tarragon, 4 tablespoons crème fraîche or sour cream, and 1 teaspoon mustard into the gravy and bring to a boil and stir. Pour over the birds.

ROAST CHICKEN LEFTOVERS

Remember, there's more to life than a plain cold chicken sandwich (although it is good). Check out these other tasty ways with leftover roast chicken.

1 ROAST CHICKEN AND STUFFING SANDWICH

Spread slices of good bread with mayo/butter, cranberry sauce, sliced chicken, and cold cooked stuffing. Classic.

2 TANDOORI WRAP

Fry off cooked potato chunks in diced shallot, butter, a pinch or two of curry powder, lemon juice, and a bit of torn cilantro. Cool. Pile into warmed wraps with cold tandoori chicken, yogurt mixed with crushed garlic, thin cucumber sticks, thinly sliced red onion and tomato, mango chutney, and more fresh cilantro.

3 CHICKEN AND VEGETABLE SOUP

Make a homemade stock (p49). Boil then reduce to a simmer. Add finely diced carrot, sliced green or fava beans, and chopped asparagus. Simmer until tender. Add a little finely shredded cold chicken. Season to taste with salt, pepper, lemon juice, and scatter over minced parsley or tarragon to finish.

4 CHICKEN RISOTTO

Check out page 197 for one of the best leftover meals ever.

5 SHREDDED CHICKEN AND SPICY SAUCE

Shred 1 pound 4 ounces cold chicken or as much as you have with two forks. Peel, halve, seed, and cut ¼ of a cucumber into thin sticks. Slice 4 scallions thinly lengthwise. Finely dice a chile. Cook, drain, and cool 2 nests of thin egg noodles (following the package directions). Toss in a few drops of oil. SAUCE: mix 2 tablespoons tahini (sesame seed paste) and 2 tablespoons water until smooth. Stir in 2 teaspoons sesame oil, 2 teaspoons chili oil, 1 teaspoon red wine vinegar, 2 crushed garlic cloves, ¾-inch piece finely grated ginger, 2 teaspoons superfine sugar, and a pinch of salt. Pile the chicken, onions, cucumber, and chile over the noodles and drizzle over the sauce. A great lunch box.

SAUTÉED CHICKEN THIGHS

FEEDS 2

INGREDIENTS

4 chicken thighs, bone in, skin on
5–6 medium new potatoes, washed
2 shallots
2 tablespoons olive oil
a bit of butter
a small handful of fresh tarragon
    leaves
scant ¼ cup white wine or Noilly Prat
generous ¾ cup heavy cream/crème
    fraîche
1 teaspoon Dijon/English mustard
salt and pepper
a good squeeze of lemon juice

—— BONUS BITES ——

ROSEMARY BAKED GARLIC THIGHS
Sit the thighs in a roasting pan. Slip half
a garlic clove under each one with a bit of
fresh rosemary if available. Sprinkle with
dried oregano/thyme/rosemary. Squeeze
juice of ½ a lemon over the top. Sprinkle
with sea salt. Chuck chunks of lemon into
the pan. Bake at 425°F for 20 to 30 minutes
until crisp and golden.

STICKY CHINESE STYLE THIGHS
Slash boneless thighs in a few places with
a sharp knife. Marinate for a few hours or
overnight in a mix of 2 tablespoons hoisin
sauce, 1 tablespoon soy, 1 tablespoon sugar/
honey, 2 scallions, 1 crushed garlic clove,
and a chunk of ginger, finely grated. Bake as
above but for less time as boneless or broil
for 4 to 5 minutes per side until cooked.

········ TIME SAVER ········

No time for a marinade or sauce? Toss
chicken thighs in oil, salt, and paprika and
cook as per rosemary baked garlic thighs for
20 to 30 minutes. Sprinkle with a handful
of chopped Italian parsley mixed with 1
teaspoon grated lemon rind, 1 diced garlic
clove, and sea salt.

Take a classic French dish, whack in some potatoes, and you've got yourself a cracking meal-in-one. The chicken/tarragon partnership is a winner and this one is just beautiful…

PREP Blot the chicken thighs on paper towels. Let them return to room temperature. Using a sharp vegetable knife, cut the potatoes into ¾-inch chunks. Peel and dice the shallots.

COOK Heat a heavy-bottom skillet or sauté pan. Add the oil and butter. When it's hot and bubbling, place the thighs in the pan, skin-side down to brown and crisp. They should sizzle as they hit the oil. Give them 5 minutes or until good and golden.

Turn the chicken over using tongs. Add the potato chunks and half of the tarragon, tearing the leaves. Put a lid on the pan and let cook through on medium/low heat for 15 minutes.

Just before the 15 minutes are up, preheat the broiler. Check the chicken is white all through (give it another minute or two if needed). Remove from the pan and slap under the broiler to crisp the skin for a minute or two. Remove.

Meantime, drain the majority of the fat from the pan, leaving the potatoes in there. Add the shallot and the wine and turn the heat up slightly. Cook for 2 minutes. Add the cream/crème fraîche, mustard, and the rest of the torn tarragon. Let it bubble until it reduces by a third and thickens slightly. Taste it and season with salt, pepper, and lemon juice. Return the chicken to the pan for a minute so it starts to soak up the gorgeous sauce.

PLATE Arrange the chicken bits on the plates with the potatoes neatly on either side. Spoon the sauce over the top. Eat with a sharply dressed green salad.

COQ AU VIN

FEEDS 4

INGREDIENTS

1 medium/large chicken
5 ounces thick American bacon/
 pancetta
1 large onion
12 baby/2 large carrots
12 small mushrooms
1–2 tablespoons oil
3 tablespoons butter
8–12 shallots, peeled
salt and black pepper
1 petal from a star anise
3 fat garlic cloves, peeled and crushed
1 bay leaf
a small handful of fresh tarragon leaves
1 tablespoon flour
1¼ cups good red wine
2 tablespoons brandy or a glug of
 balsamic vinegar
generous 3 cups chicken stock (p49)
2–3 tablespoons water
a small pinch of sugar
a handful of Italian parsley, minced

TIP
If you prefer oven cooking to cooking on the stove, bang this in the oven at 350°F for 45 minutes after adding the chicken stock.

—— CHANGE IT UP ——
For a thicker sauce, spoon the veg and bits out of the cooked coq and into a dish. Boil the sauce, stirring until it thickens to your taste and reduces a bit. Taste and season before returning the bits to the pan.

········ TIME SAVER ········
If you don't fancy having a go at jointing your own chicken or just want to save a little time, buy a mix of breasts, thighs, and drumsticks instead.

Raise your game and joint a whole bird. It's satisfying to do and saves cash. Make sure to use a nice wine for the best result in this meltingly lovely classic French chicken dish.

PREP Remove the chicken from the refrigerator. Cut it into joints (p48) and return to room temperature. Cut the bacon into thick strips. Peel and thickly slice the onion. Peel and chop large carrots if using (leave small ones whole). Brush the mushrooms.

COOK Heat the oil and two-thirds of the butter in a large, shallow casserole dish. Chuck in the bacon and cook for 5 minutes or so, turning, so it releases fat and browns. Remove with a slotted spoon and set aside. Add half the shallots. Fry for 5 minutes, turning or until just coloring all over. Remove and set aside. The fat in the pan will be brown and sticky.

Season the bits of chicken well. Bang them skin-side down into the hot fat in a single layer. Fry until just starting to brown (and flavor) well. Turn. Reduce the heat slightly. Cook for another 4 to 5 minutes. Remove.

Add the carrot, onion, and star anise to the pan. Fry on low heat, stirring, until the onion is soft, about 5 to 10 minutes. Discard the star anise. Add the garlic, browned shallots, chicken, bacon, bay, and tarragon. Sprinkle with flour and cook for 2 minutes before adding the wine and brandy/balsamic. Increase the heat and let it bubble for a minute then add enough chicken stock to cover the chicken but not drown it. Boil for a second then reduce to a simmer and cook very slowly for 30 to 40 minutes, or until the meat is tender.

Meantime, melt the remaining butter with a little water and sugar on low heat. Add the remaining shallots. Simmer until soft and glazed (check they don't dry out), add the mushrooms, and cook for another minute. Add the mix to the casserole for the final 10 minutes of cooking.

PLATE Sprinkle with parsley, bang the pan on the table, and serve with parsley and lemon potatoes. Or spoon into big shallow pasta dishes with freshly cooked pasta (like tagliatelle) tossed in butter and seasoned.

······· TO GO WITH ·······

PARSLEY AND LEMON POTATOES
Peel and halve 3 pounds mealy potatoes and chuck into cold water. Add a pinch of salt, bring to a boil, and cook until tender (check after 10 minutes). Drain and tip them back into the pan. Add 2 teaspoons butter, a squeeze of lemon juice, and a handful of chopped parsley and season with salt and pepper.

CHICKEN POT PIE

FEEDS 4

INGREDIENTS

PIE BASE

2 pounds skinless, boneless chicken
   (a mix of thighs and breasts)
a pinch of dried tarragon
2½ tablespoons flour
salt and pepper
2 tablespoons butter
1–2 tablespoons olive oil
3 bacon slices, cut into strips
3 good pork and apple sausages,
   roughly chopped
7 ounces white mushrooms
4 garlic cloves, peeled and crushed
2 onions, peeled and sliced
scant 2 cups white wine
scant 2 cups chicken stock (p49)
a small handful of fresh tarragon leaves
½–1 teaspoon Dijon mustard
a squeeze of lemon juice
1 teaspoon honey (optional)
1 x quick flaky pastry (p199) or 1 x 1
   pound 2 ounces package puff pastry
1 egg beaten with a little water,
   for glazing
1 tablespoon poppy/black onion seeds
   (optional)

****** CASH SAVER ******

Use sliced carrots or a few butter
beans in place of some of the chicken.

—— CHANGE IT UP ——

1. Substitute red wine for white and use
thyme or rosemary instead of tarragon.
2. Use mini-meatballs instead of sausages.
Fry 1 diced shallot in butter until soft. Mix
into 6 ounces sausagemeat with grated

Part of the point of a pie is that it tastes different every time you make it. Try this one from scratch topped with your own flaky pastry; or use what's left over from your coq au vin and slap a crisp, buttery lid on top.

PREP Dice the chicken into large bite-size bits. Slap into a bowl with the dried tarragon, 1½ tablespoons of the flour, and a bit of salt and pepper. Stir to coat.

COOK Heat the butter and olive oil in a wide pan or casserole. Add the bacon. Cook until crisp. Remove and set aside. Add the chicken without crowding. Fry and turn for 5 minutes or so until browned. Remove and set aside. Repeat in batches. Quickly fry the bits of sausage to brown them up. Set aside.

Add more butter if needed. Add the mushrooms and a crushed garlic clove and fry for 3 to 4 minutes. Set aside. Add the onions and the remaining garlic. Fry gently until soft. Add the remaining flour, stirring well for a minute. Don't let it burn. Pour in the wine and increase the heat. Stir as it bubbles and thickens.

Add half the stock, the tarragon, chicken, bacon, and mushrooms. Simmer for 3 minutes. Add more stock. You want enough liquid to cover the chicken plus a bit (so your pie will have a gravy) but without drowning it. Cover and simmer on low heat for 15 minutes. Taste the sauce. Add Dijon mustard and lemon juice to sharpen, plus a dab of honey if you like. Set aside to cool. Preheat the oven to 425°F. Transfer the cooled chicken mix to a 11 by 8½ by 2¾-inch ovenproof dish. Include enough of the gravy to cover the chicken well. Save any extra for pouring gravy.

Roll your chosen pastry out on a lightly floured board to a size that's larger than the top of your dish. Slip a rolling pin underneath and lift it over the pie. Sit it down. Crimp the edges to make it seal and fit. Reroll any extra, and cut out leaves or shapes if you like. Cut a slit in the center of the pie to release steam. Brush with egg wash. Stick on your leaves and scatter over seeds if using. Sit on a baking sheet and cook for 20 minutes. Reduce the heat to 350°F and cook for another 20 to 30 minutes, until golden brown and bubbling.

PLATE Serve with gravy and creamy mash with shredded blanched green cabbage tossed in butter, crushed garlic, and lemon juice.

SPATCHCOCK
AND SIDES

FEEDS 2 TO 3

A posh way with a squashed chicken; it tastes bloody good though. Try this with piri-piri sauce (p49) if you like it spicier…

INGREDIENTS

1 x 2¾ pounds small chicken
  (or 1 poussin per person)
2 tablespoons olive oil
juice of 1 lemon, plus extra for serving
2 teaspoons paprika
a good sprinkling of dried oregano
sea salt and pepper

TIP

Put your prepped spatchcocked bird on a baking sheet. Oven-cook for 30 to 40 minutes or broil/BBQ for 15 minutes per side.

PREP
Sit the bird on a board, breast up. Cut any string away. Turn it upside down with the legs facing you. Have a pair of kitchen scissors or poultry shears ready.

Run your fingers along the backbone of your chicken/poussin. Place the open scissors, one blade into the cavity, the other on top of the bird, and cut slowly down the right of the spine—alongside it, not through it—and then down the left. Remove the spine.

Turn your bird breast up. Hold onto the legs and pull it open. Now place the heels of each hand on the top and push down slowly but forcibly. You should hear a crack as the whole thing flattens. Repeat with any remaining birds.

Brush the bird/birds with a mix of olive oil and lemon juice. Sprinkle with the paprika and dried oregano and season. Leave for 30 minutes or chill for a few hours until needed (remembering to return your bird/birds to room temperature before cooking).

COOK
Heat a griddle or stovetop grill pan. Preheat the oven to 400°F.

Bang the bird/birds breast-side down in the pan. For chicken, cook for 10 minutes. Press down lightly with a spatula occasionally. Turn and repeat for 5 minutes. For poussin, cook for 5 minutes per side.

Transfer to a baking sheet and finish in the oven for 10 minutes or until cooked through. Check and test (p49)—it's size-dependent. Don't overcook. Let rest for 5 minutes.

PLATE
Sit the bird/birds on a plate and pull apart with your fingers or cut with clean scissors or shears. Sprinkle with salt and squeeze over a bit more lemon juice. Enjoy with French fries, mayo, ketchup, and a green salad or treat yourself to spatchcock sides: sweet and sour slaw, spiced potato wedges, baked potatoes with bacon and sour cream, and mango salsa.

TURN OVER
FOR SIDES

SWEET AND SOUR SLAW

Place half a head of crisp white cabbage on a board. Cut into long, thin shreds with a sharp chef's knife then tip into a bowl. Roughly grate 2 carrots and mix into the cabbage with a fork. Put ¾ cup good mayonnaise (p153), 2½ tablespoons white wine vinegar, 1 tablespoon superfine sugar in a small bowl, season, and stir to combine. Tip into the slaw and mix well.

SPICED POTATO WEDGES

Preheat the oven to 425°F. Using a sharp knife, cut 2 pounds mealy potatoes into quarters or sixths lengthwise (size-dependent). Dry them off on paper towels and throw them into a freezer bag or bowl. Add 2 tablespoons olive oil, 2 teaspoons ground paprika, and a little salt and pepper and shake or turn. Arrange the wedges in a single layer on a baking sheet and bake for 30 to 40 minutes, until crisp and cooked through.

BAKED POTATOES WITH BACON AND SOUR CREAM

Preheat the oven to 400°F. Scrub and dry 4 baking potatoes, then prick them with a fork or stick metal skewers through to speed up the cooking time. For crisp skins, rub them with oil and roll in salt. For soft skins, wrap naked in foil. Bake for 1 hour or until tender. Meantime, fry or broil 4 American bacon slices for 5 minutes or until crisp. Drain on paper towels and cut into small pieces. Punch, squeeze, or cut the cooked potatoes across to open. Add a little butter and seasoning and top with ⅔ cup sour cream, the bacon pieces, and a few bits of fresh dill/snipped chives/scallion tops.

MANGO SALSA

Take a large mango: upend it on a board and, holding firmly, slice down each side of the large central flat seed, getting as close to it as you can. Sit each halved section flesh up on the board and score horizontally and vertically without cutting the bottom skin (it should look a bit like graph paper). Now turn each half inside out, cut the dice from the skin, and tip into a bowl. Add 1–2 red chiles, 1 diced red onion, 1–2 tablespoons lime juice, and a handful of chopped cilantro leaves. Mix well and season to taste.

SLOW-ROAST
CHICKEN BREAST
WITH MUSHROOM CAPPUCCINO SAUCE

FEEDS 2

Time to get sophisticated: dress to impress. A slow roast makes for the most tender bird and the sauce is silky rich. You'll be winning hearts with this one. Make the sauce a day ahead and reheat if it suits you.

INGREDIENTS

a drizzle of olive oil

a little bit of butter

2 good skin-on chicken breasts
   (preferably on the bone),
   at room temperature

sea salt and pepper

a squeeze of lemon juice

MUSHROOM STOCK

1 ounce dried mushrooms
   (mixed/porcini/shiitake)

a handful of fresh white mushrooms,
   sliced

4 garlic cloves, peeled and bashed/
   crushed

1 onion, peeled and halved

2 carrots, halved

½ tseaspoon peppercorns

a few sprigs of fresh herbs
   (rosemary/tarragon/sage)

2 tablespoons black coffee

4 cups water

SAUCE

4 cups good chicken stock (p49)

1 tablespoon sherry (optional)

4 cups heavy cream

a few tarragon/thyme leaves

a squeeze of lemon juice

PREP MUSHROOM STOCK: Tip all the ingredients into a medium pan. Bring to a boil then simmer for 20 to 30 minutes. Sit a strainer over a large bowl. Tip the mix in, pressing with a wooden spoon to get the liquid (not solids) through. Discard the bits.

Pour the mushroom stock into a pan. Add the chicken stock and optional sherry/Madeira. Bring it to a good boil. Keep it rolling on high heat until the liquid has hugely reduced. You want about scant ½ cup of black sticky liquid (this can take 20 minutes plus, but watch it). Transfer to a large pan. Add the cream. Put it on the heat and bring to a boil (it will bubble up). Let it bubble for 5 minutes or until it thickens a bit to look like thin custard. Add the chopped tarragon/thyme leaves, a squeeze of lemon juice, and season with salt and pepper. Set aside or chill until needed.

COOK Preheat the oven to 275°F. Put an ovenproof pan on medium/high heat. Add the oil and butter. Put both chicken bits in, skin-side down, for 2 to 3 minutes to get a good color. Turn the breasts skin over and spoon the oil and butter over the top to coat. Slap the pan in the oven to slow cook until done, basting the juices over with a spoon a few times to keep it all juicy. Test for doneness (p49) after 20 minutes (though bear in mind it can take up to 30 and meat on the bone takes longer). Let it rest for 4 minutes. Season with sea salt and squeeze over lemon to taste. Warm the sauce.

PLATE Place the breasts on the plate then spoon the warmed sauce over. Serve with bread to soak up the sauce and a sharply dressed green salad, or go for shallow-fry fries (p78) and crunchy green beans (p87).

TIP

This sauce is also great with griddled steak.

········· TIME SAVER ·········

For a faster but still tender pan-fried breast, bash boneless breasts until half their thickness. Pan-fry skin-side down for 2 minutes. Turn and sear for another minute. Bang into a preheated oven in the pan or on a baking sheet at 350°F and test after 10 minutes. Serve with the mushroom sauce made up in advance or with hot mixed mushrooms (p25).

BEEF.

Beef and me go way back: steaks, roasts, cottage pies, marrow roasted up and straight from the bone, beef raw and naked as carpaccio—you name it, I've cooked and eaten it. I guess it's in the blood, coming as I do from a farming family. The cow is a magnificent beast and beef's a quintessentially British meat. Treat it with respect and nothing beats it. This big, bold ingredient is a pleasure to cook. From that moment when you catch your butcher's eye across the counter and you both know it's a case of beef love (and maybe the start of a very special retail relationship), to serving up the finished dish to family and friends. Get your skills right and it's all good.

WHICH COW FOR NOW?

For fast suppers go for steaks...

TENDERLOIN Extra tender, delicate flavor, no fat and expensive. Pan-fry/fast roast.

PORTERHOUSE STEAK Tender, tasty, and fringed with fat—a great regular choice. Pan-fry/griddle/BBQ/skewer.

SIRLOIN/TOP ROUND Intense flavor, great texture, and cheaper. Loves rubs and marinades. Broil/griddle/stir-fry/skewer/grind.

SKIRT Cheap. Needs marinades and careful cooking but very tasty.

For Sunday roasts (or midweek treats) go for joints...

PORTERHOUSE STEAK A top choice. Expensive but delicious. On the bone is sweeter.

PRIME RIB A great choice roast with a good price and a rich taste. On the bone is sweeter and cheaper.

ROUND Needs cooking at a low temperature and with a good fat layer, but much cheaper.

For anyday budget pot roasts go for cheaper joints...

TOP ROUND Tenderize lean cuts with long slow roasting in stock with vegetables.

For casseroles, braises, pies, stews, and ground meat go for cheaper cuts...

CHUCK/BLADE/SHIN Sear then cook slowly at low temperatures with vegetables and stock.

FLANK/SKIRT/BRISKET Grind up for burgers, bolognaise, meatloaf, meatballs, kofta.

For stock, go for bones...

BOUGHT IT

TAKE OFF ANY OUTER WRAPPING AND STORE ON A PLATE, COVERED LOOSELY,
AWAY FROM COOKED STUFF.

MEAT LASTS 3 TO 5 DAYS IN THE REFRIGERATOR.

COOK GROUND MEAT WITHIN 24 HOURS.

FREEZE FRESH MEAT IMMEDIATELY.

BEEF STOCK
Preheat the oven to 425°F. Put 3¼ pounds marrow/shin bones in the sink and cover with cold water. Add 4 teaspoons salt and soak for 10 minutes. Drain well, blot dry, and shove in a roasting tray. Drizzle with 1 tablespoon oil. Bang into the oven and cook for 30 minutes. Add 1 chopped carrot, 1 quartered onion, 1 chopped celery stalk, and 1 halved garlic bulb to the tray and cook for another 20 minutes. Tip into a stock pan, add 5 peppercorns, 2 cloves, ½ teaspoon tomato paste, and a bouquet garni (p19) and cover with water. Simmer very gently for 5 hours, checking and skimming off the fat as you go. Strain through a strainer or cheesecloth-lined colander, cool, and chill overnight. Remove the solidified fat on top to finish. Keep chilled in the refrigerator for up to 3 days or freeze in ice-cube trays or freezer bags.

WHAT TO LOOK FOR

Butchers love a bit of chat and will tell you what they know, so never be intimidated—get in there. If you're not sure what you want or can't see what you need, just ask. Those big refrigerators at the back of the store will be full of meat, often the more unusual cuts. Go with a plan and see what's looking good or buy to budget and ask them to recommend. When I'm buying beef here's what I'm looking for...

BREED AND SOURCE OF BEEF

Butchers (and best supermarkets) often stock locally reared beef and will label or advertise the breed. I love the rich flavor of Aberdeen Angus and Hereford but these meats are much more expensive. So treat yourself when you can or get a cheaper cut of that meat. Otherwise, use the rules and use your judgment. A meat that's local will usually have come from a happier cow, by the way. I don't fuss too much about organic but I'd rather not eat meat that's clocked up air miles.

BONES

Are essential for stocks and the butcher will often hand them out for free. It's likely he or she will only have them in on butchering/delivery days so check when that is or go in and order some specially.

GROUND MEAT

If buying ground meat from a butcher check that it's freshly made as it spoils quickly. Better to buy the right cut (see opposite), grind your own and even mix them up for great flavor.

COLOR OF MEAT

Don't just point at a joint or gaze at the top. Ask to look at the side of the meat so you can judge the color. You want a deep red with a network or marbling of creamy white fat throughout. It's an indicator of quality, a tender juiciness and flavor to come. If it looks gray, slimy, or a uniform bright red color then get out of there. The fat should be creamy white.

SUPERMARKETS

Choose one with a butchery counter if you can so you can get into conversation and see the meat properly. If you're just grabbing a steak or joint off the shelf, no problem, just use the rules, take a bit of time to weigh up the options and use your skill-set to cook it right.

AGE OF MEAT

Hanging meat over time matures the flavor. The majority is wet-hung (vac packed) to speed the process so it's cheaper. Dry-aged meat is hung naturally for a fuller flavor and tenderness but as it takes longer it's a more expensive meat. Well-hung is darker, often purple, and will taste amazing—your choice.

How much?

If you don't know how much of a meat to buy, tell your butcher "I'm cooking for so many..." and he'll tell you what you need. If the steaks on display are too big, ask for a smaller one and they'll cut it for you and you can specify size. Small roasting joints shrink, so get a bigger one and be creative with your leftovers.

BEEF ACTION—HOW TO DEAL WITH IT

BARDING tying a bit of pork fat to the top of a lean beef joint so it doesn't dry out—use string
BASTING spooning the hot oils, juices, sauces back over the meat during cooking
CUTTING ACROSS THE GRAIN slicing beef the right way to keep it tender
POUNDING using a meat hammer or improvising with a rolling pin/clean bottle to thin and tenderize
RESTING after cooking means beef relaxes and tenderizes—even steaks need it
SALTING adding salt at the last minute to steaks to draw out juices and flavor
TEMPERING getting beef to room temperature before cooking so it cooks evenly
TRIMMING using a tenderloining, a chef's or your sharpest knife to trim exterior fat and membrane

COOKING TIMES FOR YOUR STEAK
A ROUGH GUIDE

It's dependent on type of cut, thickness and heat so this is approximate.
For a steak that's 1 inch thick and at room temperature:

 RARE 1 to 2 minutes

 MEDIUM 3 minutes

 **MEDIUM-RARE** 2 to 2½ minutes

 WELL-DONE 4 minutes

COW TRICK

Press your steak to judge how well cooked it is. Here's how to judge.

Hold out a relaxed hand. Press the fleshy bump under your thumb. **RARE** steak feels like this.

 Bring the tips of the thumb and first finger together. Now press the fleshy bump under your thumb again. **MEDIUM-RARE** feels like this.

Touch the thumb and middle finger for **MEDIUM**.

 Thumb and little finger is **WELL-DONE**.

MOO-TRITION

BRILLIANT FOR:

P R O T E I N
BUILDS MUSCLE & BODY STRENGTH

ZINC
BOOSTS IMMUNE SYSTEM, HEALS WOUNDS, BOOSTS SKIN & HAIR

IRON
helps carry oxygen to all body cells & muscles to fight fatigue; keeps you sharp & focused; eat with vitamin C rich foods to beat anemia

Phosphorus
STRONGER TEETH & BONES

VITAMIN B12
attacks anemia
and helps central nervous system.

OMEGA 3S
FOUND IN GRASS-FED BEEF
AIDS BRAIN FUNCTION

FAT EQUALS FLAVOR
BUT TRIM IF IT MATTERS;
USE ROUND, TENDERLOIN, AND TOP ROUND, GRIND-YOUR-OWN. BROIL, OR ROAST ON A RACK FOR LOWER FAT.

COOKING TIMES FOR YOUR ROAST

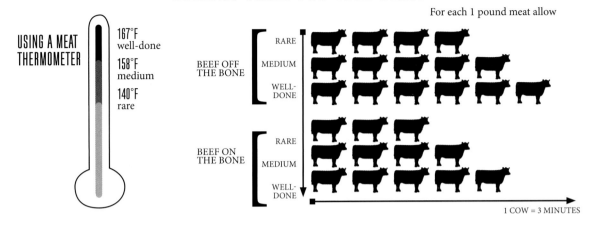

USING A MEAT THERMOMETER

167°F well-done
158°F medium
140°F rare

For each 1 pound meat allow

BEEF OFF THE BONE
- RARE
- MEDIUM
- WELL-DONE

BEEF ON THE BONE
- RARE
- MEDIUM
- WELL-DONE

1 COW = 3 MINUTES

WAYS WITH STEAK

QUICK PASTES

Blast a mix of fresh and dried herbs with spices and just enough liquid (maybe oil, lemon/orange juice, wine or vinegar, ketchup, mustard, soy, or Worcestershire sauce) for a thick paste. A bit of crushed garlic and fresh ginger's also good. Crush with mortar and pestle or mix by hand. Spread onto your steak.

fast rubs

Bang a mix of dried herbs and spices together. Coat steaks or roasts (rub in or sprinkle). Leave for 20 minutes as the beef draws the essential oils and flavors into itself. Experiment with your choice of black pepper, chili powder, mustard powder, ground ginger, garlic powder or crushed fresh cumin, cinnamon, smoked or hot paprika, cayenne, coriander, dried thyme, rosemary, oregano, marjoram, tarragon, a little sugar (too much burns).

SIMPLE MARINADES

Slap an easy mix of beef-loving herbs, spices, and liquids together. Sit smaller steaks on a nonmetallic dish, roll them in the mix. Leave for 30 minutes. To cook: blot/dry the marinade off or the beef won't sear/flavor well. Save surplus marinade to boil up fiercely for a sauce if you want to. Marinades are brilliant for griddling/BBQs.

FRIENDS

ANCHOVY ESSENCE, ARUGULA, BALSAMIC VINEGAR, BEER, BEET, CAPERS, CABBAGE, CAYENNE, CHEESE, CHILE, CINNAMON, COFFEE, COCONUT MILK, EGGS, FISH SAUCE, GARLIC, GINGER, GOAT CHEESE, GUINNESS, HORSERADISH, KETCHUP, LEMON JUICE, MADERIA, MUSHROOM, MUSTARD, ONION, ONION RINGS, ORANGE ZEST, OYSTER SAUCE, PAPRIKA, PEANUTS, PORK, POTATOES, RED WINE, RED WINE VINEGAR, ROSEMARY, STAR ANISE, TABASCO SAUCE, TARRAGON, TERIYAKI SAUCE, THYME, TOMATO, SOY SAUCE, WALNUTS, WATERCRESS, WORCESTERSHIRE SAUCE

BEEF FAJITAS
HARISSA-STYLE

  FEEDS 2

Perfect for when you're just back from work or the gym, these fajitas are packed full of lean protein, are fast to make and don't skimp on flavor. Cut the steak across the grain for a tender eat and don't hold back on the extras. Bang up the quantities if you've got loads of people coming around.

INGREDIENTS

2 x 43¾ ounces top round steaks
salt
4–6 tortilla wraps, store-bought or
    homemade (see overleaf)

MARINADE

1½ teaspoons red harissa paste
½ teaspoons hot smoked paprika
1 teaspoon dried oregano
2 tablespoons olive oil
½ lemon

EXTRAS

sour cream
guacamole (see overleaf)
tomato salsa (see overleaf)
grated Cheddar
shredded iceberg lettuce

TIP

If you can't get hold of sour cream, add 1 tablespoon lemon juice to a 11-ounce tub of heavy cream, leave for 1 hour, and use in its place (or substitute with yogurt).

**** **CASH SAVER** ****

Use skirt steak from a good butcher. It's cheap and tasty—just marinade for longer.

--- **BONUS BITE** ---

MARGARITA FAJITAS

Mix a marinade from the juice of 1 lemon or lime, a good splash of gin/rum/tequila, 2 tablespoons torn cilantro leaves, ½ tablespoon brown sugar, 2 crushed garlic cloves, 4 pinches of red pepper flakes, and a splash of olive oil. Add to beef strips and proceed as above.

PREP 30 minutes before cooking, remove your steak from the refrigerator and slap it onto a board. Trim off any exterior fat using a very sharp chef's or tenderloining knife. Check which way the protein and fat lines run through the steak (the grain of the meat). Take your knife and make swift, clean cuts across the grain, dividing the steak into ½–¾-inch wide strips.

Combine the marinade ingredients in a nonmetallic bowl and mix well. Place your meat in a bowl and cover with the marinade. Organize your extras.

COOK 5 minutes before eating, put a griddle or stovetop grill pan onto high heat until almost smoking. To check if it's hot enough, drop a bit of cold water on the griddle or pan—if it spits and evaporates, it's ready. Use a pair of tongs to drop strips of steak, well apart, down onto it.

Cook for 10 seconds then turn quickly. Cook for another 10 seconds. Shift the meat to a plate and sprinkle with a little salt. Rest for 2 minutes.

Meantime, warm the tortillas either foil-wrapped in a preheated oven, or one at a time, a few seconds a side, in a dry hot pan or a microwave, until soft and pliable.

PLATE Spoon a bit of sour cream, guacamole, and tomato salsa into the center of your tortilla. Layer in strips of beef and add the grated cheese and lettuce. Now roll up like a cigar using a bit of guacamole to hold it together. If you're making more of these to feed loads of people, bang your extras into bowls on the table and let everyone help themselves instead.

TORTILLAS Sift scant 1½ cups all-purpose flour, ½ teaspoon salt, and ½ teaspoon baking powder into a large bowl. Rub 1 ounce lard/white vegetable fat into the flour, then add a pinch of cumin seeds, a pinch of red pepper flakes, and 1 tablespoon chopped cilantro leaves. Pour in ½ cup hot water gradually, mixing with a fork. Pull the dough into a ball, then knead it in the bowl for 3 minutes until smooth and elastic. Cover with a dish towel and leave for 15 minutes. Divide it into 6. Take 1 piece (covering the rest to stop them drying out) and knead it in the palm of your hand, pressing with your knuckles and pinching for 1 to 2 minutes until soft. Roll into a ball. Cover and repeat with the rest. Place a ball on a lightly floured counter and roll into an oval. Quarter turn and roll again. Keep going until you get a large, thin tortilla. Heat a large, dry skillet, add the tortilla, and cook for a minute until the underside starts to color. Turn and repeat. Place in a dish towel to keep soft and warm while you roll and cook the rest.

SIMPLY SMOOTH GUACAMOLE Cut around 1 ripe avocado, twist, and pull to separate the two halves. Remove the pit with a large metal spoon, then scoop the flesh out. By machine: Tip into a processor with 1 garlic clove, 1 shallot, the juice of ½ a lemon, a good pinch of cayenne pepper or a finely diced fresh chile, 2 teaspoons chopped cilantro leaves, salt, and pepper. Blitz a few seconds until smooth. Taste, and adjust the seasoning. By hand: Finely dice the shallot and mash all the ingredients together with a fork. Chill until needed, but don't make more than 4 hours ahead. Sit the pit in the bowl to stop oxidation or smear lemon juice onto plastic wrap and lay over the mix.

FRESH AND SPICY TOMATO SALSA
Slice, seed, and chop 2 ripe vine tomatoes into rough cubes or dice. Finely dice 1 small red onion. Seed and finely dice ½ a red chile. Crush 1 garlic clove. Slap it all into a bowl and stir well. Add 1 tablespoon chopped cilantro leaves, lemon juice to taste, and a good glug of olive oil. Just before eating, season with salt, pepper, and a pinch of sugar. Taste. If your tomatoes aren't so good, add a pinch more sugar to balance the acidity. Spoon into a good-looking bowl if serving at the table.

ULTIMATE STEAK
AND THE WORKS

HEALTHY FAST FEEDS 2

INGREDIENTS

2 great sirloin/top round/rib-eye/
  tenderloin steaks (approx. 9 ounces
  depending on appetite/budget)
1 garlic clove, peeled and cut across
a splash of good olive/peanut oil
salt and black pepper
2 teaspoons Dijon mustard (to taste)
2 teaspoons soft butter

THE WORKS (SEE OVERLEAF)

**** CASH SAVER ****
Make your steak go further by bashing and
rolling cheaper top round and skirt steaks
between layers of plastic wrap with a rolling
pin to get them thinner. Pan-fry or griddle
for 1 minute per side. Season, rest, and serve
as before but with more veg, or in a warm
panini with mustard/horseradish/ketchup/
salad or a fried egg.

—— CHANGE IT UP ——
Customize steaks with flavored butters.
Beat ½ cup (1 stick) soft butter, 1 crushed
garlic clove, and 1 tablespoon lemon juice
with herbs (2 tablespoons minced tarragon/
Italian parsley/cilantro/rosemary) or 2
tablespoons horseradish cream/¼ cup
crumbled blue cheese, and a finely diced
shallot. Roll into sausage shapes in wax
paper to chill. Slice off what you need.

TIP
If you want to broil your steak, cut all but
½ inch of fat from the edge, snipping the
remaining fat with scissors so it stays flat
when cooking. Brush with oil, garlic, and
herbs. Cook and turn under high heat to
suit your taste. To BBQ: sit the steak over
medium/ash white coals. Sit on an oiled
rack for 4 minutes before sliding a spatula
under to shift and turn it. Cook for another
4 minutes.

*You're only allowed to cook this if you satisfy two conditions. One: get
the best meat cash allows (preferably from a butcher so you can chat
over options). Two: dress it properly in the instant butter and mustard
sauce as it's resting, or serve with luxurious Béarnaise sauce.*

PREP Get the steaks from the refrigerator. Leave on any of the fatty edge
to maximize flavor and texture or remove after cooking. Rub the
meat gently all over with the cut garlic and oil to tenderize it and prepare it
for the dry pan. Add a few grinds of black pepper and leave to get to room
temperature while you prep your chosen accompaniments.

Just before cooking, get a large dinner plate. On one side, put half the mustard
and butter. Add a generous pinch of salt and pepper. Do the same on the other
side of the plate. You'll be using this for fast saucing/seasoning once your
steaks are cooked and resting. (You won't need to do this if you're making
Béarnaise sauce to accompany your steak.)

COOK Put a heavy-bottom skillet, griddle, or stovetop grill pan big enough
to take the steaks onto high. Once it's almost smoking, slap the
steaks down. If you're not sure if the heat's right, just touch the side of one
steak to the pan—it should sizzle.

Cook for the required time to suit your tastes, the cut of meat, its thickness,
and temperature. For medium-rare, I give a 1-inch thick steak 2 minutes on
one side (don't shift it—you want that crust and color) then turn with tongs or
a spatula and cook again for 2 minutes. For a thicker steak, turn for another
minute, then repeat. Really thick steaks may need finishing off in a hot oven
for a minute or two, so make sure yours is preheated if you've got a big piece
of cow there. Check the introduction (p70) for notes on steak doneness.

Steaks continue to cook a bit as they rest, so take them out of the pan just
before they get to the perfect stage for your taste. Place each on its pile of
seasonings on the dinner plate, turning once. Rest somewhere warm for 4
minutes to ensure your steak will be tender.

PLATE Transfer the steaks to clean plates with all their lovely, flavorsome
juices. Serve with dauphinoise potatoes (p126) and a simple
green or tomato salad. Or eat with the works—shallow-fry fries, roasted vine
tomatoes, stir-fry spinach, and béarnaise sauce (see overleaf) instead of the
mustard/butter.

CRISP SHALLOW-FRY FRIES

Put a pan of cold water onto high heat, adding a pinch of salt. Peel 2–3 medium mealy potatoes and cut into even-sized wedges. Add to the water, bring to a boil, and parboil for 8 minutes. Drain. Quickly blot them on paper towels so they'll crisp up. Cool. Heat a skillet and add enough peanut oil to cover the bottom. Add the fries in a single layer. Fry for a couple of minutes then turn with a spatula. Repeat, cooking for 8 to 10 minutes or until golden on the outside, fluffy in the center. Sit on paper towels to drain. Salt immediately.

ROASTED VINE TOMATOES

Preheat the oven to 400°F. Sit 2 medium/4 small vine tomatoes per person in a small roasting pn or on a baking sheet. Leave them attached to the vine if they came with it. Scatter them with 2 finely diced cloves of garlic, a little fresh thyme/rosemary/basil, and drizzle with olive oil. Season well and add a pinch of sugar. Roast larger tomatoes for 25 minutes, smaller ones for 15 minutes. Sit them next to your steak and use bread to mop up the juices.

STIR-FRY SPINACH

Heat a wok or large pan as your steak rests. Add a little bit of butter and a 9-ounce bag of washed spinach (it reduces—don't worry). Stir-fry for a minute or so to wilt. Gently press out any excess water. Season it with salt and pepper.

EASY LUXURY BÉARNAISE SAUCE

Melt ½ cup (1 stick) butter in a pan without stirring. Remove from the heat and skim off the solids floating on top. Put 5 tablespoons white wine vinegar, a few chopped tarragon leaves, and a chopped shallot into a small pan. Boil to reduce by a third. Strain it into an ovenproof bowl. Set the bowl over a pan half-full of simmering water. Whisk in two medium egg yolks and 2 teaspoons cold water until the mix thickens —about 5 minutes. Remove and trickle in the butter, whisking as you go. Season to taste and keep warm until needed. Don't reheat.

CRUNCHY THAI-STYLE BEEF SALAD

HEALTHY

FEEDS 2

There's a lovely fresh, zingy character to this beautiful little salad. Fresh herbs take it somewhere else and the chili/lime/fish sauce combination is classic.

INGREDIENTS

2 steaks (sirloin/top round)
1 tablespoon olive oil
2 teaspoons sesame oil
salt and black pepper
a small handful of dry roasted peanuts, roughly chopped

DRESSING
2½ teaspoons palm/superfine sugar
⅓ cup fish sauce
1 small red chile
juice of 2 small limes

SALAD
4 ripe vine tomatoes
3 small shallots
4 scallions
½ cucumber
a handful of mint leaves
a handful of cilantro leaves
½ iceberg lettuce, washed and dried

TIP

If you're not into peanuts, top with crunchy onion rings (p82) or try a crispy shallot topping instead. Peel and thinly slice 1 large banana shallot or 4 small ones. Heat ½-inch depth of peanut oil in a skillet. Once really hot, add the shallot for a few seconds. Turn with a slotted spoon until golden. Scoop onto paper towels, sprinkle with salt, and toss onto salad.

—— CHANGE IT UP ——

1. Drizzle your beef with spicy sauce (p58) for a satay-style beef salad. **2.** Stuff the dressed meat salad into warmed pitas or yogurt flatbreads (p128). **3.** For a Thai beef salad wrap, peel off and chill the iceberg leaves separately. Prep remaining salad, dressing, and cook and slice meat as above. Serve in separate piles on one big plate. Spoon into the lettuce leaves, wrap, and eat.

PREP Dressing: finely grate the palm sugar, if using. Mix the palm/superfine sugar in a bowl with the fish sauce. Finely slice the chile and add to the bowl with the lime juice. Set aside.

Salad: slice the tomatoes into quarters. Peel and slice the shallot. Trim the scallions and slice lengthwise with a sharp chef's knife. Peel and halve the cucumber lengthwise. Seed it with a teaspoon. Slice the flesh into half-moons. Tear the herbs. Throw the lot into a bowl. Tear or shred the lettuce with a carving knife and set aside.

Put the steaks onto a plate. Mix the oils together and pour over the steaks, turning to coat. Season with black pepper.

COOK Heat a griddle or stovetop grill pan until almost smoking. Cook your steaks to medium-rare—I give a 1-inch thick steak 2 minutes on one side (don't shift it—you want that crust and color) then turn with tongs or a spatula and cook again for 2 minutes. For a thicker steak, turn for another minute, then repeat. Check the introduction (p70) for notes on steak doneness.

Remove your steaks from the pan, season lightly with salt, and rest for 3 minutes. Add the lettuce to the salad bowl and toss in the dressing. Sit the steaks on a board. Slice them across the grain in ½–¾-inch strips using a sharp chef's knife.

PLATE Pile the salad onto a plate or into bowls and arrange the steak slices neatly on top. Sprinkle over the crushed peanuts to finish.

THE ULTIMATE NEW YORK CHEESEBURGER

FEEDS 4

INGREDIENTS

4 homemade or best store-bought
 burger buns (see overleaf)
10½ ounces chuck steak
4¾ ounces skirt
4¾ ounces brisket
2 smoked bacon slices
salt and pepper
olive oil, for frying
CARAMELIZED ONION
1 large onion, peeled and thinly sliced
1 tablespoon olive oil
a pinch of sugar
EXTRAS
1 cup grated Cheddar
1 cup grated mozzarella
2 smoked American bacon slices
2 hamisha/large dill pickles, sliced

TIP
Chop into ground meat by hand. The
strands aren't distinct but it means you can
still use cheap cuts. Cut chilled meat into
small cubes on a board. Chop into coarse
ground meat with a sharpened chef's knife.
If you've got two, hold one in each hand and
chop rhythmically as if using drumsticks.

········ **TIME SAVER** ········
Prep the caramelized onion up to a day
ahead, just reheat gently when needed. The
burger buns can be made days ahead and
frozen until needed.

────── **BONUS BITES** ──────
EVERYDAY FAST SMOKY BURGER
Mix 1 minced and gently fried medium
onion with 2 pounds ground beef, ⅓ cup
grated Cheddar, 1 teaspoon smoked paprika,
½ teaspoon mustard, a shake of Tabasco/hot
sauce, 1 pinch each of dried oregano/thyme/
mint, 2 teaspoons apple chutney or ketchup,
1 handful of chopped fresh parsley, salt, and
pepper. Test for seasoning. Shape. Chill. Fry.

*Get your meat right and the technique down (grinding it yourself so
the strands are separate for least resistance) and you've got yourself
the ultimate burger. Don't kill it with a cheap bun—make mine or buy
something nice. Skip the cheese if you don't do dairy and dice the meat
up with a chef's knife if you don't have a grinder.*

PREP Timings: start the burgers 40 minutes before you want to cook. They
take 30 minutes to chill. If making your own buns (they transform
a burger) start at least 3 hours before you need them. They're fast to prep and
easy to make but need time to rise, cook, and cool.

Set up your grinder. If you don't have a processor/mixer with attachment, use
a hand-operated one—they're cheap, good, and easy to get hold of. Fit it with
a medium grinder plate. Slap your beef and bacon onto a board. Use a sharp
chef's knife to cut it into chunks small enough to fit through the feeding tube.
Season it lightly with salt and pepper.

Turn the grinder to top speed or get ready to turn. Cover a large baking sheet
with plastic wrap and hold it underneath the grinder to catch the ground meat.
Push the meat through the machine in a constant flow so the strands come out
unbroken. Simultaneously, move the baking sheet away and then back toward
you a few times until the meat is used up. This makes a heaped sausage shape
of ground beef with all the proteins running in the same direction; which
means your burger will be beautifully tender. (N.B. This is doable by yourself
but an extra pair of hands at this stage is useful).

Without disturbing the strands, bring the sides of the plastic wrap up to wrap
the meat like a thick cracker, twisting the ends tightly to seal. Roll it in another
layer of plastic wrap and chill in the refrigerator for at least 30 minutes.

Meantime, caramelize the onion. Whack it in a pan with the oil and the sugar
and cook very gently for about 20 minutes, or until it's soft. Set aside. Prep
the rolls by slicing in two cleanly. Mix together the cheeses and spread evenly
across the bottom halves of the bread. Cook the bacon on a broiler preheated
to high. Place on a rack for 2 minutes per side or until crisp, turning.

COOK Slice the chilled meat, through the wrap, into 2½-inch thick
burgers. Put a heavy-bottom pan onto high heat. Add a glug of oil.
Peel the fwrap from the burgers. Lift them carefully into the pan. Fry for
30 seconds per side, flipping with a spatula. Repeat so they cook over
2 minutes (or another minute or two for well-done). Sit on a warm plate.
Season well. Let rest.

Broil the cheese-topped roll bottoms for 3 to 4 seconds until melting/gooey. Sit
the tops, cut-side down, in the hot burger pan to absorb the juices.

PLATE Place each burger on a gooey, cheesy bread base. Add a bit of
onion, pickle, half a strip of crispy bacon, and the lids. Eat with a
simple green/tomato salad, shallow-fry fries (p78), or sweet potato wedges.

HOMEMADE BURGER BUNS

Sift generous 4 cups white bread flour, ½ teaspoon salt, and ½ teaspoon sugar into a bowl. Add 2 tablespoons butter, 2 x ¼-ounce sachets of active dry yeast, and rub everything together with your fingers. Add 1 teaspoon black onion seeds and scant ½ cup grated Cheddar and pour over scant 1⅔ cups of warm water. Mix well with your hands. Pull it into a ball. Knead by hand (p200) on a floured board or in a processor for 8 minutes. Bang it into a covered bowl and let rise for 1 hour or until doubled in size. Knead again for 2 minutes. Divide into 8 even pieces and shape each into a roll. Grease two baking sheets, space the rolls evenly between each, and let rise, covered with dampened dish towels, for a second time for 30 minutes. Preheat the oven to 425°F. Brush the buns with a mix of 1 beaten egg/2 tablespoons milk and sprinkle over a few extra onion seeds. Cook for 25 minutes or until the domes are golden brown. Tap the base of a bun from each sheet—they should sound hollow. Give them a bit of extra time if needed. Cool on a rack.

----- CHANGE IT UP -----

1. BOOST EVERYDAY BURGER FLAVORS by adding:
LEMON ZEST/GRATED GINGER/SCALLION/ ROASTED GARLIC/GRATED APPLE OR CARROT/FRESH HERBS/CUMIN/FENNEL SEEDS/HORSERADISH SAUCE/ONION CHUTNEY

2. PLAY WITH THE BREAD using:
BAGUETTE/GRIDDLED BUNS/TOASTED BRIOCHE/FLATBREADS /CHILLED LETTUCE LEAVES

3. STACK with:
OTHER GOOD MELTING CHEESES/ONION RINGS/PICKLED GINGER/GRIDDLED BUTTERNUT SQUASH SLICES/SLICED MANGO OR APPLE/GRIDDLED MUSHROOMS/ ARUGULA/WATERCRESS/YOGURT DRESSING/ CAESAR DRESSING/SALSAS/TAPENADE OR COLESLAWS/FLAVORED MAYOS

SPICED SWEET POTATO WEDGES

Preheat the oven to 425°F. Peel 2 pounds sweet potatoes. Pat them dry. Slice each one into very large fries/ wedges. Dry again. Drop them into a freezer bag. Add 2 tablespoons olive/sunflower/peanut oil, 1–2 teaspoons ground cumin or paprika, 1–2 teaspoon red pepper flakes, a squeeze of lime if you have any, and season with salt and pepper. Shake well. Tip onto a baking sheet. Bake in a layer for 20 to 30 minutes (size-dependent) until tender and golden. Serve with sour cream or mayo, and a chunk of lime for squeezing, if you like.

CRUNCHY ONION RINGS

Slice 1 medium onion into ¼-inch rings. Separate the rings and cover with milk in a bowl. Scatter 3 tablespoons white flour on a plate with salt, pepper, and a pinch of paprika. Drop the rings in to coat. Heat peanut oil to a depth of 3¼ inches in a deep pan or wok until 350°F (an onion ring should sizzle at once when added). Add a few rings at a time and cook for a few seconds, turning once with a slotted spoon. Drain on paper towels and salt before eating.

CARPACCIO

FEEDS 4

Here's a personal favorite. It's raw meat (or just seared) but don't let that put you off. It's bloody gorgeous. This makes a great light lunch or dinner party appetizer. Tenderloin is the finest piece of meat and this makes the most of it. Mix and match the toppings or go for a favorite.

INGREDIENTS

*1 pound 2 ounces beef tenderloin
(in one piece and not the tail end)
a few drops of extra virgin olive oil
a good squeeze of lemon juice, to taste
sea salt and pepper*

✳✳✳✳ CASH SAVER ✳✳✳✳
Use good sirloin steak or even very cheap skirt from a good butcher.

TIP
For an even easier slice, wrap the trimmed tenderloin tightly in foil or wrap and freeze for 2 to 4 hours. Peel the foil/wrap back gradually as you slice very thinly using a sawing action. Return to room temperature before serving.

—— BONUS BITE ——
FAST TOAST CHIPS
Preheat the oven to 300°F. Meantime, toast 6 slices of white bread lightly in a toaster. Remove the crusts with a serrated knife and slide a knife through the center of each slice. Peel the two sides apart gently. Sit the slices, cut sides up, on a baking sheet and bake for 10 minutes or until crisp and golden. Cool on a rack.

—— CHANGE IT UP ——
If you're not keen on the raw concept then sear your meat. Heat a wide skillet/roasting pan that can fit the tenderloin. Add a glug of olive oil. Rub ground black pepper into the meat to sweeten it or roll in a handful of minced rosemary and thyme leaves. When the skillet/pan's good and hot, add the meat and sear for 30 seconds to 1 minute each side. Remove. Wrap in foil/plastic wrap and cool in the refrigerator for at least 30 minutes before slicing.

PREP
Buy a trimmed tenderloin or do it yourself. Sharpen a tenderloining or chef's knife. With the beef on a board, take hold of any white sinewy membrane or fat on the surface with one hand. Pull it away from you while sliding the knife underneath it to cut it cleanly away. Cover and chill the tenderloin for a few hours or overnight in the refrigerator (cold meat slices more easily).

Just before eating, remove the meat and sit it on a board. Using the sharpened knife, slice the tenderloin vertically very thinly. Spread a large sheet of plastic wrap over a cutting board or clean surface. Distribute the slices neatly over the top in one layer, about ½ inch apart. Cover with another piece of plastic wrap. Very gently, run a rolling pin over the lot—don't be too vigorous or you'll break up the fibers. Hold up the plastic wrap, it should look like a thin sheet of meaty wallpaper.

Remove the top bit of wrap and carefully peel the slices off the bottom layer. Divide between individual plates as elegantly as you can, overlapping slightly.

PLATE
Drizzle with olive oil, squeeze over lemon juice, and season with salt and pepper. Serve with breadsticks or fast toast crisps (see left) or a simple tomato and shallot salad (p37). Alternatively, add any of the following toppings.

TOPPINGS

1 MOZZARELLA, TOMATO, ARUGULA & LEMON JUICE
Seed and dice 4 good ripe tomatoes. Roughly tear a 4½-ounce ball of mozzarella. Distribute between plates of sliced naked carpaccio with a good handful of arugula leaves. Drizzle with a good glug of olive oil, a good squeeze of lemon juice, pepper, and sea salt.

2 ROAST BEET & GOAT CHEESE
Roast 1 pound 2 ounce beet wrapped in foil at 450°F. Cool. Peel. Square off the edges, cut into dice, and toss in lemon juice. Leave for 20 minutes. Chop 4 ounces hard goat's cheese or tear a soft one. Scatter the beet and cheese over naked carpaccio with arugula leaves, olive oil, a good squeeze of lemon juice, and sea salt.

3 WARM BEANS, ROSEMARY & GARLIC
Drain a 14-ounce can/jar of large lima beans. Tip into a pan with a glug of olive oil, 1–2 minced garlic cloves, a sprig of fresh rosemary, and a squeeze of lemon juice. Warm very gently on low heat for a few minutes (add a bit of water if you want). Let the flavors infuse or use immediately. Divide the beans between 4 small dishes. Place centrally on plates and arrange the beef slices around them.

SPAGHETTI BOLOGNAISE

FEEDS 6

INGREDIENTS

1½ pounds best ground steak
  (or own ground chuck steak)
3 ounces smoked American bacon/
  pancetta
2 ounces chicken livers
  (optional, but add depth)
2 tablespoons olive oil
3 teaspoons butter
1 large onion, peeled and minced
½ a star anise
salt and pepper
3 garlic cloves, peeled and crushed
1 carrot, peeled and finely diced
1 small celery stalk, finely chopped
1¼ cups red/white wine
4 tablespoons milk
1 bay leaf
a pinch of all-purpose flour
a good pinch of nutmeg
1 x 14-ounce carton strained tomatoes
2–3 tablespoons tomato paste
a pinch of oregano
a pinch of sugar
a dash of fish sauce/lemon juice
  (optional)
14 ounces dried spaghetti/tagliatelle
a hunk of Parmesan, for serving

This is a traditional Italian sauce (ragu) and it's delicious. The long slow cook means all the great ingredients have time to integrate. Make it ahead and let the flavors develop further: a great dish if you've got mates heading around; just get out the wine and garlic bread.

PREP

Return your ground meat to room temperature. Dice the bacon/pancetta. Wash and dry the chicken livers if using. Remove any fat or gristle and chop into tiny pieces.

COOK

Heat the oil and a teaspoon of butter in a wide skillet/pan on medium heat. Add the bacon/pancetta. Fry for 2 minutes, stirring, until brown. Reduce the heat. Add the onion, star anise, and a pinch of salt. Cook for 5 minutes or until soft and translucent. Discard the star anise. Add the garlic, carrot, and celery. Fry and stir on low for 5 minutes until softening. Increase the heat a bit.

Crumble the ground meat in with your hands, stirring as the meat caramelizes. Once it's browned, add the chopped liver. Cook for 2 minutes. Increase the heat. Add the wine. Let it bubble up for 2 minutes to burn off the alcohol. Reduce the heat. Add the milk, bay leaf, flour, nutmeg, tomatoes, tomato paste, oregano, sugar, optional lemon juice/fish sauce, and lots of black pepper. Stir to mix well and let it simmer gently for 5 minutes.

To oven cook: Preheat the oven to 275°F. Tip the sauce into a lidded dish. Cook for 2 to 3 hours. Check occasionally, adding more milk if it's too thick or a bit more paste if it needs more substance. To cook on the stove: Reduce the heat to minimum and cover. Cook for 1 to 2 hours, checking and stirring regularly, adding more liquid if needed. Taste and adjust the seasoning with salt, pepper, and lemon juice as needed.

Add the spaghetti/tagliatelle to a pan of boiling water and cook until *al dente* or as you like it (see p173 or check your package for timings). Drain well. Return to the pan. Add the remaining butter and season. Mix the sauce and spaghetti together (or serve separately).

PLATE

Tip into warmed bowls and grate over Parmesan at the table. Eat with a sharply dressed green salad and crunchy garlic bread (p178)

BONUS BITE

CLASSIC LASAGNA

Make the ragu as above, but omit the chicken livers. Make a cheese béchamel (p185). Get a 9-ounce pack of fresh lasagna or soak dried, no-cook lasagna sheets in water for 10 mins and drain well. Grate 5 ounces Parmesan. Butter a lasagna or large ovenproof dish that's at least 2 inches deep. Layer it up with béchamel, meat sauce, grated cheese, more béchamel, and lasagna sheets. Repeat the layering until the meat sauce is finished. Top with lasagna sheets and cover with béchamel. Scatter over extra Parmesan and dabs of garlic butter (p138). Bake at 425°F for about 40 minutes. Remove from the oven and let settle for 10 minutes before spooning out.

SMOKING CHILI CON CARNE

FEEDS 3 TO 4

INGREDIENTS

3 strong red chiles, trimmed
2 x 14-ounce cans of chopped tomatoes
3 fat garlic cloves, peeled
1 teaspoon ground cumin
2–3 tablespoons olive oil
1 large onion, peeled and minced
1 star anise
1½ pounds best ground steak (or grind
*   your own chuck/skirt steak)*
a small bunch of fresh cilantro leaves,
*   chopped*
2 tablespoons tomato paste
a pinch of sugar
a good pinch of dried oregano
1 cinnamon stick
¾ cup beef/chicken stock (p68/p49)
1 x 14-ounce can of kidney/black
*   beans, drained*
salt and pepper

✳✳✳✳ CASH SAVER ✳✳✳✳

Make your chili go further by turning it into burritos. Pile the mix into wheat tortillas with a bit of sour cream, Cheddar, and scallion. Fold into parcels and sit them in a buttered dish. Bake, foil covered at 425°F for 20 minutes. Eat as is or add tomato sauce and grated cheese and broil until bubbling.

TIP
Take chili into work to microwave with a baked potato.

This is a particularly zingy chili. Supercharge the beef by adding chiles you've toasted on the griddle to release their oils and heat. Shower with sour cream and extras for fresh taste and contrast.

PREP Heat a griddle pan to smoking. Slice the chiles in half lengthwise and add to the pan cut-side down, to toast. Press them down with a spatula for 15 seconds. Turn and repeat. Lift into a dish and cover with hot water. Set aside for 10 minutes.

Drain the chiles. Tip the tomatoes, garlic, cumin, and drained chiles into a food processor or use a stick blender and blitz well. Sieve the mix into a bowl. Set aside.

COOK Heat a wide pan or a large, deep skillet to medium-low. Add the oil, onion, and star anise. Cook until soft, not colored. Increase the heat. Crumble the ground meat in gradually, stirring. Cook for 5 minutes, or until colored. Remove the star anise.

Stir in your strained tomato sauce. Cook for 5 minutes. Add everything else, except the beans and half the cilantro. Stir and boil for 2 minutes. Reduce to the lowest heat and cook for another 30 to 40 minutes, stirring sometimes. Taste and adjust the seasoning, adding water if it looks too dry. Stir in the beans and the remaining cilantro 5 minutes before serving.

PLATE Heap onto bowls of cooked rice and serve with soft tortillas (p74), sour cream, yogurt, tortilla crisps, guacamole (p75), diced red bell pepper, chopped scallion/red onion, grated Cheddar, diced red chile, and lime wedges. It's also good in warmed tortillas with fried eggs.

BONUS BITE

FAVORITE COTTAGE PIE

Heat 1 tablespoon olive oil in a large casserole or pan. Cook 1 pound best ground steak, turning, for 3 to 4 minutes until browned. Add 1 very finely minced large onion, 1 large grated/finely diced carrot, 1 finely diced celery stalk, and 3 crushed garlic cloves and cook for 3 minutes. Add 2 tablespoons Worcestershire sauce/mushroom ketchup, 2 tablespoons tomato paste, and a pinch of dried thyme. Cook for 2 minutes. Increase the heat. Add 1 small glass of red wine and scant 1¼ cups chicken/beef stock. Boil for 2 minutes. Reduce the heat. Simmer for 15 minutes on low heat. Meanwhile, boil 2 pounds mealyy potatoes until soft. Drain and mash with 4 tablespoons butter, ½ cup grated Cheddar, 2 egg yolks, salt, and pepper. Tip the cooled meat mix into a dish and top with mashed potato. Dab with garlic butter (p138) and bake at 400°F for 30 to 40 minutes, until browned and bubbling.

ROUGH BEEF AND VEGETABLE STEW WITH HERB DUMPLINGS

FEEDS 4

INGREDIENTS

2 large onions
4 carrots
2 parsnips
9 ounces butternut squash
1 leek, washed
2 garlic cloves, peeled
2 pounds good stewing/chuck steak
2 tablespoons all-purpose flour
salt and pepper
1 tablespoon oil
2 tablespoons butter
generous 2 cups chicken stock (p49)
1–2 tablespoons Worcestershire sauce
1 tablespoon tomato paste
1 teaspoon sugar
1 bay leaf
a few pinches of dried/fresh thyme
a splash of balsamic vinegar/lemon juice
6 small white/cremini mushrooms,
    chopped (optional)
1 x 2-inch strip of orange zest (optional)
a small handful of parsley, chopped
HERB DUMPLINGS
generous ¾ cup self-rising flour
4 tablespoons butter
2 teaspoons dried marjoram
1 small egg

✴✴✴✴ CASH SAVER ✴✴✴✴
Substitute a drained 14-ounce can of lima
beans for half the meat.

—— CHANGE IT UP ——

1. Enhance the flavor with a sprinkle of gremolata (p88). **2.** Add dried prunes or apricots for a fruity comfort food. **3.** For goulash, stir 14 ounces chopped tomatoes, 4 teaspoons paprika, and a few caraway seeds into the stew. Omit the stock—use ale instead. Stir in a dollop of sour cream. **4.** For hotchpotch, cook the stew, then cover with thin slices of overlapping potatoes. Dot with butter, cover in foil, and bake for 2 to 3 hours. Uncover for the last 30 minutes.

Here's a really good basic stew with loads of vegetables to balance out the meat and get your cash going further. I'd make this for a weekend and then enjoy it through the week or freeze some for later.

PREP Preheat the oven to 350°F. Peel and chop the onions, carrots, parsnips, and butternut squash. Slice the leek. Crush the garlic. Cut the meat into 2-inch cubes. Shake it in a bag with the flour, salt, and pepper.

COOK Heat a large casserole dish or pan. Add the oil, butter, and a pinch of salt. Fry the vegetables and garlic in batches gently until slightly softened, not colored. Remove from the pan and set aside.

If the pan is dry, add a bit more oil. In small batches, add the meat and sear quickly on all sides, turning with tongs, until nice and brown. Remove to the plate as it's done. Repeat until all the meat is seared.

Tip the meat and vegetables back into the pan. Add the stock, Worcestershire sauce, paste, sugar, herbs, vinegar/lemon juice, mushrooms, and orange rind. Boil for a minute. Reduce the heat. Oven-cook for 2 to 3 hours or simmer on the stove on very low heat for ½ to 2 hours. Check that it doesn't dry out.

Make the herb dumplings. Sift the flour into a bowl. Rub in the butter, add the dried marjoram and the egg, and mix together with a fork to form a sticky dough. Shape into dumplings, add to the casserole, cover, and cook for another 20 to 30 minutes. Taste and adjust the seasoning.

PLATE Spoon into big bowls, sprinkle with parsley, and eat with crunchy green beans and mashed potatoes (see below); crushed lemon and parsley potatoes (p60), or just scooped up with slices of thick bread and butter.

· · · · · · · · · · · · TO GO WITH · · · · · · · · · · · ·

CRUNCHY GREEN BEANS

Wash 2¼ ounces of fine green beans per person. Cut the tops off with a paring knife and add to a pan of boiling salted water. Boil for 4 to 5 minutes or until softening but with a bit of bite. Drain and season.

CREAMY FRENCH MASHED POTATO

Put 2 pounds mealy potatoes (unpeeled) and 2 garlic cloves into a pan of cold salted water. Boil for 20 minutes or until tender. Drain. Put them through a ricer or strip the skins off as soon as you can handle them. Put the potato back into the warm pan. Mash with 4 tablespoons butter and 4 tablespoons milk. Beat in 4 ounces gruyére cheese and add 2 finely chopped scallions. Taste and season.

BOEUF BOURGUIGNON WITH GARLIC CROUTONS

FEEDS 4

INGREDIENTS

4 ounces American bacon
2½ pounds chuck steak, in a piece or
    cubed
1 tablespoon olive oil
2 tablespoons butter, plus extra for frying
1 large onion, peeled and sliced across
1 medium carrot, sliced across
4 garlic cloves, peeled and crushed
1 star anise
2 tablespoons all-purpose flour
salt and pepper
2½ cups red wine
1¾ cups beef/chicken stock (p68/p49)
1 tablespoon tomato paste
1 bay leaf
a pinch of dried thyme
12 shallots, peeled
a pinch of sugar
12 baby mushrooms
GARLIC CROUTONS
3 tablespoons oil
1 garlic clove, peeled and crushed
6 slices of coarse bread

——— CHANGE IT UP ———

1. For a taste blast, spread the garlic croutons
with strong mustard (serving mustard-side
down). **2.** Replace the garlic croutons with
gremolata. Sprinkle with a mix of 1 minced
garlic clove, 3 tablespoons chopped parsley,
grated zest of ½ a lemon, and scatter over the
bourguignon before serving.

········ TIME SAVER ········

1. Make the day before to let the flavors
develop and take the pressure off. **2.** To skin
shallots or baby onions easily, cover with
boiling water for 60 seconds. Drain. Run
under cold water. Slice the tips and stems.
Peel the skins off.

A brilliant traditional French dish packing layers of flavor. Unlike most casseroles where the textures melt together, these stay distinct. Add the mushrooms and onions toward the end of cooking. Top the finished dish with crunchy croutons and other bits and pieces for even more contrast. Enjoy with French mashed potato and crunchy green beans (p87) for a perfect marriage.

PREP Blanch your bacon to desalt it: put a pan of water onto boil. Cut the bacon into ¾-inch strips. Add to the pan. Simmer for 5 minutes. Drain and let cool. Trim any excess fat from your beef. Cut it into regular 2-inch cubes so that it cooks evenly. Dry them really well on paper towels.

COOK Put a large, wide casserole dish onto medium heat. Add the oil and a little bit of butter. Preheat the oven to 425°F. Sit a plate near the stove. Add the bacon to the hot fat and cook for 5 minutes until crispy, turning using a wooden or slotted spoon. Spoon onto a plate. Increase the heat. Add a few cubes of meat to the bacon fat to brown. Don't overcrowd the pan or it'll stew (you want a good dry brown crust without overcooking). As each edge browns, turn it quickly with tongs. Once browned, remove from the pan and place on the plate. Repeat until all the meat is seared.

Decrease the heat. Add the onion, carrot, 3 of the crushed garlic cloves, and star anise. Cook gently for 5 to 10 minutes until softening, not colored. Remove the star anise.

Sprinkle the beef and bacon with the flour and some pepper. Stir to coat it well. Tip it all back in with the vegetables. Stick it in the oven for 5 minutes or until the flour browns up. Reduce the temperature to 300°F.

Remove the casserole dish from the oven and place it on medium heat. Add the wine and just enough stock to cover the ingredients—don't swamp them. Add the paste and herbs. Boil for 1 minute, then cover. Return to the oven and cook for 3 hours (check after 2 to see it's not drying out) until deliciously tender.

Meantime, put the shallots in a pan with just enough water to cover. Add the sugar and butter. Simmer on very low heat for 10 to 15 minutes until tender but still holding their shape. Fry the whole mushrooms in a little butter with the remaining garlic, shaking to turn brown. Season lightly. Add to the bourguignon with the onions to heat through. Taste and adjust the seasoning.

Make the garlic croutons. Mix the oil with the garlic and rub over the bread slices. Place on a baking sheet, add to the oven, and bake for 10 minutes or until very crisp.

PLATE Spoon the bourguignon into bowls. Top with garlic croutons. Serve with green beans and creamy French mashed potato or slices of good thick bread and butter for mopping up the gravy.

ROAST BEEF WITH ALL THE TRIMMINGS

FEEDS 4 TO 6

INGREDIENTS

4 pounds well-hung beef rib on the
    bone
sea salt and pepper
a little minced rosemary/dry mustard
2 tablespoons olive oil/beef dripping
TRIMMINGS (see overleaf)

········· TIME SAVERS ·········

1. Prep the potatoes the night before and
chill in the refrigerator in cold water.
2. Make the Yorkshire batter the night
before. Get to room temperature and whisk
again before using.

TIP
Make the most of your leftovers. For a hot
roast beef sandwich, carve cold meat thinly.
Add to 2 thick slices of white bread with a
slathering of hot mustard or horseradish
sauce. Heat any leftover gravy. Pour it over.
Sandwich it (it's messy—enjoy it!). If you've
got Yorkshire puddings left over, reheat in a
warm oven or microwave and fill with thinly
sliced meat and piping hot gravy.

────── CHANGE IT UP──────

1. To give your beef a crisp crust, rub
1 tablespoon flour and 1 tablespoon mustard
powder into the fat.
2. For fat-free joints ask a butcher for a bit
of pork fat (it's free). Sit it on top of the meat
and tie with bits of string. The fat will melt,
protecting the meat while cooking.

Recipes for roast beef are one of those things that get passed down through the generations and I'm not about to change that, so this is my mom's version. Once again, the key is buying a great piece of meat as no amount of skill can transform a scraggy piece of beast. Get a joint with a decent covering of fat which will baste the meat naturally as it cooks, and go for a joint with bones. It makes any Sunday.

PREP Start early—maybe the night before so the beef can take up flavors. Check its weight and calculate and record cooking times (p71). Using a sharp knife, slash the top of the fat lightly across into a crisscross pattern. This will release fat as the meat cooks to keep it tender. Mix salt, pepper, and a little chopped rosemary/mustard powder together and rub into the fat only. Bang the meat in the refrigerator. Remove 2 hours ahead to get it to room temperature.

COOK Preheat the oven to 450°F. Sit the beef, fat-side up, in a roasting pan (preferably one big enough to take some potatoes). Rub half the oil/dripping into the meat and season lightly all over. Add the remaining oil/dripping to the pan. Put it into the oven. After 15 minutes, reduce the temperature to 350°F. Spoon juices over the meat a few times. Prep your trimmings, adding your roasties to the pan when the time is right.

10 minutes before the cooking time is up, stick a metal skewer into the joint for 30 seconds. Remove then lay it on your wrist. If the beef is rare, it'll feel cool. For medium-rare it's just warm (my choice). For medium, it's warm. For well-done, it's hot. Juices run red for rare, pink for medium, clear for well-done. Put it back to cook for longer if you need (though it cooks on a bit as it rests, so don't overdo it). Move to a warm plate. Cover loosely with foil. Rest for 20 to 30 minutes in a warm place—don't worry, it'll stay hot.

PLATE Sit the meat on a board, fat-side up. Using a freshly sharpened carving knife, cut through the string and follow the contour of the meat down between the bones (hold onto the bones to steady the operation with your free hand). The bones will come away as one. Hold the deboned meat with a fork and, using an easy sawing action, slice the joint vertically across the grain in slices as thick or thin as you like. Serve with loads of gravy and your trimmings of choice.

BONUS BITE

ROAST ROUND (FOR 2 TO 3)
Preheat the oven to 350°F. Heat a skillet large enough to take a 2-pound beef round joint. Rub the joint all over with 1 tablespoon olive/peanut oil. Add the meat, fat-side down first to sizzle and brown. Turn and sear for another 2 minutes, until all the sides are sealed. Transfer to a roasting pan, adding some parboiled potatoes if you like or throw in a mix of halved red onions, beet, carrots, and potatoes with a bit of oil or a splash of wine. Season the beef with salt and pepper. Reduce the heat to 325°F. Roast for 40 to 50 minutes for rare/medium. Test with a skewer or meat thermometer. Let rest for 15 minutes before carving.

ROASTIES

Peel, cut, and boil 12 medium mealy potatoes for 10 minutes. Drain well. Shuffle them in the colander to roughen their edges. Bang them in with the beef, 45 minutes before it's cooked, adding a bit more oil or fat to the pan if you think it's needed. As you take the meat out to rest, increase the temperature to 425°F and crisp the potatoes. Sprinkle with sea salt.

YORKIES

Make up a Yorkshire batter:
By machine: mix 4 large eggs, 1¼ cups milk, and a pinch of salt in a processor or with a stick blender. 10 minutes before the meat is done, blitz in generous 1¾ cups all-purpose flour until smooth. By hand: beat the eggs, milk, and salt with a whisk. Sift the flour into a bowl. Whisk the liquid bit by bit into a hollow in the center.

Before cooking, put 2 x 4-hole Yorkshire pudding trays or muffin pans into the very hot oven while the meat is resting to preheat for 5 minutes. Add a dash of dripping or oil to each hole and heat for another 5 minutes (the hotter they are, the higher the puddings rise). Pour the batter into the smoking pans until two-thirds full and cook for 20 minutes.

GRAVY

Once the meat and potatoes have been removed from the pan, spoon out any excess oil, leaving 1–2 tablespoons. Sit the pan on the stove over medium heat and add 1¼ cups water/stock. Using a wooden spoon, scrape the tasty bits off the bottom to incorporate. Simmer gently to reduce for a thin, tasty jus. Add any juices that seep from the meat as it rests. Season. Pour into a pitcher, skimming off any fat.

CARROTS IN FOIL

Cut 4 large peeled carrots into sticks with a paring knife. Cut out a large piece of foil. Turn the edges up slightly. Distribute the carrots. Add a squeeze of lemon/orange juice, the grated rind of ½ a lemon/orange, and a star anise. Season. Add a little bit of butter and a sprinkle of dried thyme. Bake with the beef for 30 minutes.

NO-FUSS TASTY BAKED ONIONS

Cut 6 medium red onions (skin on) in half lengthwise. Drizzle a glug of olive oil on a plate sprinkled with sea salt and dried thyme. Rub the onions into it cut-side down. Sit on a baking sheet and rub the tops with a cut garlic clove. Add black pepper. Roast for 20 to 30 minutes as the potatoes are crisping up.

PORK

Oh isn't the pig a beautiful beast? Not only lovely in life, it serves up a rich bounty of amazing meat in its passing. From nose to tail there's barely a bit I wouldn't consider cooking and eating. Ok we'll quickly pass over the deep-fried tail and slow braised pig's foot just for now anyway (they're both delicious by the way) but who'd not go for a classic bacon sandwich or a great hunk of deliciously roasted meat with a cheeky bit of crackling. Pork's the only meat that features large in the UK's national breakfast—and that has to mean something. But it doesn't stop there. This meat's a globetrotter. Try gorgeous melt-in-the mouth Chinese style belly pork or a finger-licking scorching southern rack of ribs. It's an international star in my book. Now when it comes to buying it—get yourself to a proper butcher or the meat counter in your local supermarket. See what they've got. If in doubt ask for a rare breed pork, which will have been properly cared for, have a much richer flavor, and is far less likely to dry out in the cooking. Get piggy…

STASH IT

BANG pork into the refrigerator as soon as you get it back.

KEEP it in its original plastic wrapped trays.

REMOVE butcher's paper. Plate it and cover with foil/wax paper.

WRAP bacon once the pack has been opened or store in a container.

KEEP pork, bacon, and sausages away from cooked and fresh foods.

Use **ground meat** within a day.

Smoked bacon lasts for 10 days. Unsmoked bacon keeps for 7.

Pork will keep in the freezer for up to 6 months.

Fresh **pork** lasts for 2 to 3 days chilled.

Cooked pork lasts for 4 days.

Bacon freezes for a short time in vacuum packs.

PORK
Buyer's Guide

LOOK FOR:

SKIN THAT'S DRY AND SMOOTH

MEAT THAT'S PINK AND FIRM WITHOUT A DAMP OR OILY SHEEN

FAT THAT'S WHITE AND THICK

JOINTS WITH A GOOD LAYERING OF FAT (IT CONDUCTS HEAT TO THE SKIN WHICH HELPS MAKE GREAT CRACKLING)

AVOID:

MEAT THAT LOOKS SLIPPERY

YELLOW FAT

THIS LITTLE PIGGY WENT TO MARKET .... TO BUY

1 SHOULDER

A versatile cut and not too expensive. A shoulder joint makes a great cheaper **slow roast** *for loads of people. Get* **SHOULDER CHOPS** *for* **slow braising**. **DICE IT** *up for* **stews and casseroles** *made with cider and apples and friends.* **GRIND IT** *up for* **burgers** *and create your own* **sausages and sausage rolls**. *Shoulder is* **CURED** *to make* **bacon joints**.

2 LOIN

Your everyday pork purchase could well come from this cut and be a loin chop or loin steak. Easy to cook (but don't dry them out). Healthy (cut any fat off after cooking if you want but remember fat is flavor). Loin is cured for making back and short back bacon.

TENDERLOIN Very lean and versatile, it absorbs flavors. Thin it for saltimbocca. Roast with care (it can dry out fast). Stuff it. Wrap it. Slice into medallions. It's great for stir-fry.

LOIN EYE STEAK Equivalent to beef top round. A premium cut.

RIB CHOP Fry, griddle, or roast it fast. This is a lovely, tender bit of pork.

RACK A proper joint on the bone, this looks great on the table.

LOIN JOINT A very nice roasting joint.

3 PORK BELLY

One of the cheaper sweeter cuts and packed with juicy flavor. Belly is cured for making American bacon and pancetta.

SPARE RIBS Get them in a rack or ask the butcher to separate. Marinate then roast, deep-fry, or BBQ to keep everyone happy.

FLAT BELLY A really beautiful cheaper joint that's perfect for long, slow cooking so the fat disappears as the skin crisps and crackles.

BELLY JOINT Rolled flat belly is ideal for stuffing and long slow cooking.

BELLY SLICES Try marinating then braising until tender.

4 PORK LEG

Home of the classic roast and leg steaks but less fat so cook carefully. Gammon joints are cured from pork leg.

LEG STEAK A cheap lean cut which you can griddle, fry, broil, stew, or braise.

LEG JOINT Ask your butcher to score it for crisp crackling or buy a Stanley knife. Roast, braise, or pot-roast.

SCALLOP Thin it out and fry for an easy fast meal.

PIG NUTRITION

PORK IS A RICH SOURCE OF

VITAMIN B1 (THIAMIN)

METABOLIZES CARBS essential for growth and repair of nerve and muscle tissue.

RIBOFLAVIN

facilitates the release of energy from food and promotes HEALTHY SKIN AND EYES.

NIACIN

SUPPORTS THE NERVOUS SYSTEM and digestion and energy release from carbs, proteins, and fats.

Phosphorus

BUILDS BONES AND TEETH

PORK CONTAINS **B6 + B12** WHICH WORK ALONGSIDE ➤ **IRON** AND **PANTOTHENATE** to promote blood health and keep you mentally alert.

PORK'S RICH IN

ZINC

a deficit of which undermines THE NERVOUS SYSTEM. LEAN PORK CONTAINS **29G** OF **PROTEIN** PER **100G** MAKING IT GREAT FOR BODY BUILDING AND MAINTENANCE. OK IT CONTAINS **FAT** but it's generally a lean meat and we need some fat to stay healthy.

TEMPERATURES AND ROUGH TIMINGS FOR YOUR PORK JOINT

Start your joint at **450°F** for 10 minutes.

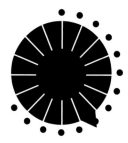

Reduce to **350°F** for the rest of your cooking time.

JOINTS ON THE BONE

30 MINUTES PER 1 POUND

plus an extra 30

JOINTS OFF THE BONE

35 MINUTES PER 1 POUND

plus an extra 30

COOK IT

Pork should be cooked through until the juice runs clear and it's no longer pink. But don't overcompensate or you'll create leather … Test and use your judgment.

IS IT DONE YET?

SKEWER IT

Thrust into the joint of meat at the thickest point, avoiding the bone. Count to 10. Place it on your wrist. If it's very hot (and the juices are clear) it's done.

Science

Insert a meat thermometer, avoiding the bone. It should read 176°F.

VISION

Cut into it with your knife. The meat should be moist and just white.

Pork Secrets
A CRACKLING LOVER'S GUIDE

Buy pork with the rind still intact. Ask the butcher to score it. To do it yourself, get your sharpest knife or a Stanley knife. Sit the meat on a board. Cut in the direction of carving to make life easier. Stab down into the rind and the top of the skin then bring your knife down a bit and score your line. Do this at ¼-inch intervals. Pat the meat dry with paper towels (purists use a hairdryer). Leave uncovered in the refrigerator for up to 24 hours if possible. Heat your oven to its highest temperature. Once it's there, rub the rind generously with sea salt (too soon and it draws out the moisture). Don't put any fats/oils on it. Blast with heat for 15 minutes before dropping the temperature to 350°F (or much lower for belly pork/long slow cooks). Don't baste it. If it doesn't crackle to your taste, cut it away from the cooked joint and while that rests, crank up the oven and blast it with extra heat.

WET CURE Often oozes water as it cooks, so not so good.

DRY CURE Cooks up nicely and good value, also lower in nitrates so healthier.

SINGLE PIECE Chop or slice as an ingredient.

SLICES Neat and convenient for instant cooking.

SMOKED Distinctive flavor (bear this in mind if including in a recipe).

UNSMOKED A blander taste.

CANADIAN BACON Leaner but more expensive.

AMERICAN Very tasty because it's fattier.

MIDDLE BACK Contains a bit of Canadian and American.

BACON/HAM JOINTS

COLLAR Good for boiling as a cheap, tasty joint.

HOCK Great cheap cut, really tasty.

HAM Boil or roast, or boil then roast. Lovely, lean, and versatile.

HAM & BACON

Perfect if you're working crazy hours; these guys have a long shelf life uncooked and cooked. And they're cash-stretchers, so perfect for feeding yourself for days or a load of people. Cook: remove packaging. Immerse in cold water. Chill for hours. Change the water. Chill again. This reduces the saltiness and moistens the meat.

BOIL AND GLAZE

1. Put the *joint* (string intact to keep it whole) into a pan of cold water or mix of *water and cider*. **2.** Leave plain or add an *onion/carrot/bay leaf*. **3.** Cover and boil (if scummy replace the water). **4.** Reduce to simmer for 20 minutes per 1 pound. **5.** Remove. **6.** Score diamond shapes into the fat. **7.** Stud with *cloves* and slap a glaze of *honey/mustard* on top. **8.** Finish for 10 minutes in a hot oven.

FRIENDS APPLE, APRICOT, BLUE CHEESE, CARAWAY SEEDS, CHESTNUT, CHILE, CIDER, CILANTRO, CINNAMON, COCONUT, CREAM, CUMIN, FENNEL, FIG, GARLIC, GINGER, GRUYÈRE, HONEY, LEMON, MARMALADE, MUSHROOMS, MUSTARD, ONION, ORANGE, PAPRIKA, PEAR, PEAR CIDER, PLUM, POMEGRANATE MOLASSES, POTATO, RHUBARB, ROSEMARY, SAGE, SOY, STAR ANISE, THYME, WATERCRESS

SPANISH MEATBALLS

FEEDS 4

INGREDIENTS

9 ounces good-quality ground pork
9 ounces good-quality ground beef
1 cup fresh white bread crumbs (p201)
scant ½ cup grated Parmesan
2 scallions, finely sliced
3 garlic cloves, peeled and crushed
½ teaspoon turmeric
grated zest of ½ lemon
½–1 teaspoon smoked paprika
2–3 tablespoons minced parsley,
   plus extra for serving
salt and pepper
a glug of olive oil, for frying
TOMATO SAUCE
olive oil, for frying
3 garlic cloves, peeled and sliced
a pinch of red pepper flakes
2 x 14-ounce cans good-quality
   chopped tomatoes
1 tablespoon tomato paste
a pinch of sugar

········· TIME SAVER ·········

Stir crushed garlic and a squeeze of lemon
into store-bought mayo for a quick aioli.

TIP
If you're having trouble getting the meatball mixture to hold together, add a little beaten egg to it.

One of the stars on a table of tapas, these tasty little meatballs tick all the boxes and make a cracking meal anytime. Treat them lightly as you're shaping and cooking so they stay nice and soft and sweet. Team with garlicky aioli and paprika potatoes.

PREP Make the meatballs: Tip all the ingredients except the oil into a bowl and mix together lightly with a fork. Dampen your hands. Divide the mix and roll it very lightly into large, walnut-sized balls. Place on a plate and let chill in the refrigerator until needed.

COOK Make the sauce: Heat a little oil in a pan over low heat. Add the garlic and chile and cook for 1 minute without coloring before adding the tomatoes, tomato paste, and sugar. Season lightly. Whack up the heat to high and bring to a boil, then reduce and let simmer for at least 10 minutes. Taste and season again. Set aside.

Heat the oil in your biggest skillet. Add the meatballs (in batches if necessary) and fry gently for a couple of minutes or until browned all over, rolling to turn with tongs or a spatula. Shift each one to a plate once done. Return the balls to the pan. Pour the sauce around them (you may not need it all). Simmer very gently. Turn them with care after 2 minutes for even cooking. Cook for 10 minutes or until done, but don't overdo it or they dry out. Add a splash of water to the sauce if needed. Taste and season.

PLATE Spoon the meatballs and sauce into earthenware tapas dishes (or equivalent) and sprinkle with parsley. Drizzle with aioli and serve with paprika potatoes or any of the tapas suggestions overleaf. These are also great with mussels baked in garlic butter (p138), paprika chicken wings (p53), a good red wine, and some nice bread.

BONUS BITES

ITALIAN BAKED MEATBALLS
Preheat the oven to 375°F. Cook the meatballs as above until browned all over. Spread three-quarters of the tomato sauce over the bottom of a large heatproof dish and arrange the meatballs on top. Add the remaining sauce, a handful of torn basil, and a handful of grated Parmesan or mozzarella cheese. Drizzle over a little oil and bake at 375°F for 20 to 30 minutes, or until the cheese is melted and golden.

MEATBALLS AND PASTA
Cook up a big pot of ribbon noodles or spaghetti following the package directions. Drain and toss in a little oil. Sit the meatballs and sauce on top. Sprinkle with a little Parmesan. Eat with garlic bread (p178).

TAPAS EXTRAS

PAPRIKA POTATOES

Preheat the oven to 400°F. Peel and cut 4 large mealy potatoes into 2-inch cubes with a sharp knife. Roll them in paper towels or on a dish towel to dry before throwing them onto a baking sheet. Add 1 teaspoon oregano, 1 teaspoon smoked paprika, salt, and olive oil to coat. Toss to combine. Bang into the oven and cook for 30 to 40 minutes, turning once, until crisp.

AIOLI

Measure generous ¾ cup light olive oil and scant ¼ cup peanut/vegetable oil into a pitcher. Put 2 egg yolks, 3 crushed garlic cloves, and 1½ tablespoons of lemon juice/white wine vinegar in a bowl. Beat vigorously with a wooden spoon or a balloon whisk. Whisking steadily all the time, add the oil, drop by drop at first, then in a thin, steady stream once the mayo starts to form. Taste and adjust the seasoning, Add a drop more lemon juice/vinegar if it lacks acidity, or water if too thick. Chill in the refrigerator until ready to use.

CATALAN TOASTS

Toast or griddle thick slices of French stick/coarse white loaf. Rub with a cut garlic clove and halved ripe tomatoes (discarding the squashed shells). Drizzle with olive oil and sea salt. For tapenade toasts: Rub the crisp toasted bread with tapenade (black olive paste).

CHORIZO AND SHERRY

Preheat the oven to 350°F. Slice a length of chorizo cooking sausage into ¾-inch pieces. Share between individual ovenproof dishes in a single layer. Add enough dry sherry to cover. Bake for 10 minutes or until sizzling hot. Mop up with good bread.

HOT DATES AND BACON

Run the back of a chef's knife along the back of slices of American bacon to thin them. Halve them across. Wrap each half around a whole fresh pitted date. Spear on mini-skewers. Broil 4 minutes per side or until hot and crispy.

SALTIMBOCCA

FAST

FEEDS 2

INGREDIENTS

1 x 11-ounce pork tenderloin
salt and pepper
3 slices of serrano/prosciutto,
  cut in half
6 large sage leaves
½ cup all-purpose flour
1 tablespoon olive oil
2 heaping tablespoons butter
⅔ cup pear cider (perry)
⅔ cup heavy cream
1½ teaspoons English mustard
1 lemon, cut into wedges

——— BONUS BITES ———

LEMON SALTIMBOCCA

Cook the meat as before, but skip the sauce.
Deglaze the pan with a glug of white wine
to bubble (stir to pick up the meaty bits/
flavors) then add a squeeze of lemon juice
and a little bit of butter. Season to taste.
Drizzle over the saltimbocca to finish.

MOZZARELLA SALTIMBOCCA

Place a thin slice of mozzarella in the center
of each thinned tenderloin slice before
adding the ham and sage. Cook as above
but without the sauce. Deglaze the pan with
white wine, pour over the meat, and serve
with lemon, easy tomato sauce (p176),
mashed potato, or pasta.

Saltimbocca is Italian for "jump in the mouth." Squeeze a little lemon juice over these thinned pork tenderloin and sage leaf beauties and they'll do just that. This dish delivers a complex set of flavors for very little effort and makes an impressive supper.

PREP
Pat the pork tenderloin dry with paper towels. Sit it on a board and, using a sharp tenderloining or chef's knife, cut it into 6 equal pieces with clean, smooth movements. Place the first slice, cut surface facing up, between two pieces of plastic wrap. Roll and bash it with a rolling pin (without tearing it) until it's ¼ inch thick. Repeat with the remaining slices.

Season the slices with pepper and cover each with a piece of ham. Sit a sage leaf in the center of each ham slice. Fix all three together securely with a toothpick threaded from one edge through to the other and back again. Tip the flour onto a plate. Season it with salt and pepper. Dip the *saltimbocca* pieces in to cover completely.

COOK
Heat the oil and butter in a pan. When foaming, add the pork slices, sage-side down, without crowding the pan (you may need to cook in batches). Fry for 1½ minutes, until the underside is golden and crispy. Check with a spatula. Flip and cook for 45 seconds, or until just cooked through. Lift them onto a warm plate. Sprinkle with sea salt.

Increase the heat under the pan and add the pear cider. Let it bubble to reduce by two-thirds. Add the cream and mustard, stirring. Reduce by a third again. Taste the sauce and season. Return the pork to the pan to warm for a few seconds or serve separately.

PLATE
Sit the saltimbocca on your plates with lemon wedges for squeezing to jazz it up. Drizzle the sauce artfully, if serving separately. Eat with a twist of buttered ribbon pasta and a watercress salad with chicory and caramelized walnuts (p194).

SOUTHERN
RIBS

FEEDS 6

INGREDIENTS

2 pork spare rib racks
   (approx. 2¾ pounds each)

THE RUB

3 tablespoons smoked paprika
1½ tablespoons sea salt
1½ tablespoons cracked black pepper
1½ tablespoons ground cumin
1½ tablespoons chili powder
1½ tablespoons dark brown sugar
1 tablespoons cayenne pepper
½ tablespoon ground ginger

THE BBQ SAUCE

2 tablespoons thin honey
2 tablespoons maple syrup
1 tablespoon Worcestershire sauce
3 tablespoons low-salt soy sauce
4 tablespoons tomato ketchup
4 tablespoons cider vinegar
2 garlic cloves, crushed
1 teaspoon grated fresh ginger
2 teaspoons English mustard
4 tablespoons orange juice
a pinch of paprika

—— BONUS BITE——

SWEET BBQ RIBS

Mince a small onion and fry until soft. Add
1 cup chopped tomatoes. Simmer for 5
minutes. Add to the BBQ sauce ingredients
and blitz until smooth. Pour over separated
spare ribs. Marinate for at least 30 mins.
Preheat the oven to 400°F. Cook on a rack,
turning once, or in a foil parcel in a pan for
1 hour (open and brown for 10 mins).

TIP
If you don't have cracked pepper handy, bash regular black peppercorns in a mortar and pestle.

These slow-oven-cook ribs come with a heat warning. The spice mix is scorching but deliciously addictive: tone it down (just a bit) with sweet BBQ sauce. Mightily impressive—enjoy all year round. Team with wings, burgers, sweet and sour slaw (p65), and a lager loaf (p205) for a big event.

PREP
Preheat the oven to 250°C.

Take the ribs out of any vacuum packaging. Dry them on paper towels. Sit them on a board and let return to room temperature. Meantime, mix the ingredients for the rub in a bowl. Spoon half of it over the racks to coat them well. Rub it in thoroughly. Store the excess in a jar (it keeps for months). Sit the racks on a baking sheet.

Mix all the ingredients for the BBQ sauce in a pitcher. Chill until needed.

COOK
Roast the racks for 3 hours, or until the meat is so tender they pull apart easily. Rest for 10 minutes. If you're having a BBQ, sit the roasted racks on the grill in a high position over very low coals. Let them smoke for 10 minutes to finish.

PLATE
Brush the ribs with a little of the BBQ sauce to glaze before separating (carve or pull them apart). Pile onto a big plate. Serve with the remainder of the sauce in a bowl for dipping.

CASSOULET

FEEDS 6

INGREDIENTS

2–3 duck legs
sea salt and pepper
2 large onions, peeled and sliced
5 garlic cloves, peeled and crushed
3 carrots, peeled and sliced
11 ounces butternut squash, peeled
    and cut into chunks
2 tomatoes, roughly chopped
1 bouquet garni (p19)
1 x 4 ounces belly pork
    (from a joint or slices)
7 ounces American bacon slices
2 ounces chorizo sausage
3 tablespoons olive oil
1 x 14-ounce can of lima beans,
    drained
1 x 14-ounce can of haricot beans,
    drained
1¼ cups cider
generous 2 cups chicken stock (p49)
1⅓ cups fresh bread crumbs (p201)
12 Toulouse sausages
a handful of parsley, chopped

TIP
If you feel the flavors here need lifting, add a squeeze of lemon juice with the seasoning.

Get a load of people around to share this version of a French classic. Strictly speaking you should soak dried beans overnight before cooking them for hours, but I've cheated and used canned beans. The roasted duck legs here add flavor and texture and make a great meal in their own right.

PREP A day ahead: Preheat the oven to 400°F. Put the duck legs on a baking sheet, prick all over with a fork, and sprinkle with sea salt. Roast for 30 to 40 minutes, until crisp. Remove. Cool, then cover and let chill in the refrigerator. Save the fat by tipping it into a bowl, cooling, covering, and chilling (use for this recipe or for frying crispy potatoes).

On the day: Prep the veg and bouquet garni and set aside. Sit the belly pork on a board. Slice the skin away, then cut the meat into 1½-inch pieces. Cut the bacon into 1-inch squares. Slice the chorizo.

COOK Heat the olive oil and a tablespoon of the reserved duck fat in a large, wide casserole. Fry the belly pork for 2 to 3 minutes, turning with tongs. Transfer to a plate. Add the bacon and fry, turning, until crisp and golden. Transfer to the plate. Add the onions to the pan and cook, stirring, for 8 to 10 minutes until softened. Stir in the garlic, carrot, and butternut squash. Cook for another 2 to 3 minutes. Add the chorizo and drained beans. Increase the heat. Add the cider. Boil for 2 minutes then add the chicken stock. Boil for another 2 minutes. Add the tomato, bacon, bouquet garni, and black pepper. Reduce the heat. Simmer gently for 15 minutes.

Preheat the oven to 350°F. Spread the bread crumbs on a sheet to dry out as it heats up. Remove when they're golden. Heat a little oil in a skillet. Add the sausages and fry gently, turning, for a few minutes to brown them up.

Take the casserole off the stove. Tuck the sausages and pork belly into the mix to cover well. Push the duck legs in around the edges. Add a bit more liquid if it's looking dry. Taste and adjust the seasoning. Scatter the dried bread crumbs evenly over the lot. Put it in the oven and cook for an hour. Remove and let settle for 10 minutes before serving.

PLATE Scatter over the parsley and bang on the table with a bowl of aioli (p100), mustard, apple chutney, and warm bread. Get everyone to spoon it into warm wide bowls. Enjoy with a good red wine or chilled cider.

A BOX OF HOT SAUSAGE ROLLS AND RHUBARB CHUTNEY

MAKES 6 ROLLS

INGREDIENTS

9 good-quality sausages (or 1¼ pounds sausage meat)
salt and pepper
1 x 13-ounce pack butter puff pastry
1 egg, beaten with 1 teaspoon water
poppy seeds for topping (optional)
PORK AND BLACK PUDDING
½ ounce blood sausage, roughly crumbled
2 fresh sage leaves, chopped
PORK AND LEMON
½ cup fresh white bread crumbs
grated zest of ½ lemon
a pinch of dried sage
¼ of an onion, grated
1–2 teaspoon beaten egg
PORK AND BEAN
grated zest of ¼ lemon rind
2 sage leaves
4 tablespoons baked beans
RHUBARB CHUTNEY
4 sticks of rhubarb
1 eating apple
scant ¼ cup water
1 small onion, peeled and sliced
¾-inch piece of fresh ginger, grated
scant ¼ cup cider vinegar
½ cup superfine sugar
2 teaspoons brown sugar

——— CHANGE IT UP ———

1. Make your own sausages: grind up 1 pound pork belly slices. Mix with 2 cups fresh white bread crumbs, 1 beaten egg, 1–2 teaspoons dried sage, salt and pepper, and additional flavors such as crushed garlic/paprika/lemon zest. Shape and fry a small piece to test the seasoning. Adjust if you need to. Divide the rest equally and shape into sausages. **2.** Replace puff pastry with quick flaky pastry (p199).

Who doesn't love a sausage roll? Do a huge batch for a party and watch them go missing. Get creative with your own sausage mix variations. The chutney gives these babies a different dimension.

PREP

Make the chutney: Slice the rhubarb and chop the apple. Put them into a pan with the water. Cook over low heat for a few minutes, stirring, until they start to soften. Add the onion and ginger to the pan and cook down for a minute or so. Stir in the vinegar and sugars. Boil for 1 minute then cover. Simmer on very low heat for 25 minutes, stirring occasionally.

Make the sausage roll mixes: if using sausages, split them lengthwise to release the meat and divide it equally between three bowls. If using sausage meat; split as before and season it lightly with salt and pepper.

Break the meat up with a fork. Now add each of the 3 flavorings to the bowls so you have 3 fillings (don't add the beans to number 3 yet!) Mix lightly with a fork and then your hands.

Preheat the oven to 425°F. Grease a large baking sheet.

On a large lightly floured board or clean counter, roll the pastry into a 12 by 10-inch rectangle. Neaten the sides with a sharp knife and divide into 6.

Divide each of your fillings in two and roll into thick, even sausages. Sit each sausage in the middle of a pastry rectangle. For the sausage and bean roll, spoon 1–2 teaspoons of beans on top of the meat.

Brush the surrounding pastry lightly with beaten egg. Fold the pastry over the roll and join the edges securely. Neaten the ends if you need to. Turn and sit them seam-side down on the baking sheet. Make 4 light diagonal slashes across the top of each one. Brush with beaten egg and sprinkle with poppy seeds, if using.

COOK

Bake for 20 minutes, or until cooked and golden. Place on a rack.

PLATE

Serve warm or cold with the rhubarb and ginger chutney and ketchup. They also make a great snack to go or a good lunch with cheese, fruit, bread, and pickles.

BEER BATTERED
TOAD IN THE HOLE

FEEDS 4

INGREDIENTS

2 tablespoons beef/pork dripping
   (or 2 tablespoons olive/peanut oil)
6–8 pork/pork and apple sausages
4 ounces butternut squash, cubed
   (optional)

BATTER

⅔ cup cold milk
5 tablespoons cold water
scant 1 cup all-purpose flour
a pinch of salt
½ teaspoon mustard powder
2 large free-range eggs
5 tablespoons chilled light beer/lager/
   hard cider (or more cold water)

—— **BONUS BITES** ——

BACON TOADS

Slit the sausages down one side. Peel off the skins. Twist a strip of pancetta or a slice of thinned, stretched American bacon around each one. Add to the sizzling fat 8 minutes before you add the batter. Turn once.

VEGGIE TOADS

Add good vegetarian sausages to sizzling oil 2 minutes before you add the batter. Throw in quartered onions with the oil if you like.

BAKED BANGERS

Roll sausages (skins intact) in very thin bacon. Brown and bake with chunks of potato, butternut squash, onion quarters, lemon, garlic, herbs, and oil in a roasting pan at 400°F for 30 to 40 minutes.

········ **TIME SAVER** ········

For fast gravy: mix and heat 3 tablespoons water and a squeeze of lemon juice/3 tablespoons red wine with 3 tablespoons onion marmalade (p144).

Banging beer in your batter lightens it and boosts the flavor. Dripping gives it an extra dimension. Get the pan and the fat good and hot to guarantee a good rise. Buy a quality sausage for this classic.

PREP Make the batter 30 minutes before you cook the toad (chilling improves it). By hand: Measure the milk and water into a pitcher (if using beer, add that at a later stage). Sift the flour, salt, and mustard into a bowl. Make a well in the center. Crack the eggs into it. Add 2 tablespoons of liquid. Beat with a wooden spoon or balloon whisk, gradually incorporating the flour as you pour the rest of the milk and water in very slowly for a smooth batter. By machine: Blitz everything (except beer/lager/cider if using).

Make the gravy (see below) at this stage so the onions have time to caramelize.

COOK Preheat the oven to 450°F. Put the dripping or oil into a roasting/enamel pan (I use a 12 by 5 by 2¾-inch pan as it gives the batter room to rise, but a small one works too). Heat it up for a good 10 minutes. Remove the pan. Close the oven door to retain heat. Add the sausages and return the pan to the oven immediately. Cook for 5 minutes. Remove the pan again, add the squash, and turn the sausages. Brush fat up the sides of the pan with a pastry brush. Return to the oven for 5 minutes.

If using beer/lager/cider, beat it into the batter for 1 minute. Take the pan from the oven and pour your batter straight in. Return to the oven immediately. Cook for 25 minutes without opening the oven door, until the toad is puffed and golden.

PLATE Get your toad to the table before it sinks. Spoon or cut it out (it's not elegant). Spoon over the gravy and serve up with mustard mash (opposite) and shredded savoy cabbage, blanched then tossed in a little butter and garlic.

········ **TO GO WITH** ········

ONION GRAVY

Finely slice 2 large onions. Heat a little butter and 2 tablespoons oil in a pan over medium heat. Add the onion slices, 1 crushed garlic clove, and a pinch of sugar. Cook very gently, stirring, for 10 to 15 minutes until the onions are softened and slightly browned. Stir in 1 tablespoon flour, before slowly pouring in ¾ cup chicken stock and 1 cup beer or hard cider, stirring all the time. Add 1 teaspoon each of Worcestershire sauce and balsamic vinegar. Season. Simmer for 10 to 15 minutes.

A PROPER PORK CHOP
WITH MAPLE SYRUP APPLES

 FAST

FEEDS 2

A proper chop is a great test of some key skills: track down the best meat and judge exactly how far to push it with the heat so your pork isn't overcooked. You want it to hang onto its juices and yet develop the best flavor it can from the pan before slapping on those sweet apples…

INGREDIENTS

2 x 5–7 ounces good pork chops
   (bone in or out)
2 sharp eating apples
a squeeze of lemon juice
salt and pepper
1 tablespoon olive oil
a little bit of butter
a glug of maple syrup

PREP Remove the chops from the refrigerator and let return to room temperature. 5 minutes before cooking, core your apples and slice lengthwise into ½-inch-thick half moons. Toss in lemon juice. Season the chops with salt and pepper.

COOK Add the oil and butter to a heavy-bottom pan over medium-high heat. When it's good and hot, slap the chops down. Let the undersides brown for 2 to 3 minutes as you spoon the juices over the top of the chops. Turn, spooning still, and fry until the pork is white all through but soft and juicy still (6 to 8 minutes altogether but test it). Remove to a plate to rest in a warm place. Add a sprinkle more salt.

Spoon off some of the fat from the pan if you think you need to. Return it to the heat. Add the apple pieces and fry for a minute or two, turning with a spatula, until they're just softening but holding their shape. Add a glug of maple syrup and stir to coat the apple in the hot toffee, turning the heat off under the pan so it doesn't burn.

PLATE Sit the chops on a plate. Spoon the apple pieces neatly on top with the lovely sweet sauce. Enjoy with mustard mashed potatoes and steamed broccoli or cabbage.

——— BONUS BITES ———

GRIDDLED HERB CHOPS

Bash a garlic clove and a little snipped rosemary/sage/thyme in a mortar and pestle with 2 pinches of sea salt, zest of ½ lemon, 2 tablespoons lemon juice, and olive oil. Rub into your chops. Get a griddle pan searing hot. Cook for 2 to 3 minutes per side until golden, rest, and plate up with a fresh and spicy tomato salsa (p75) and baked baby potatoes.

CRISPY BUTTERFLY CHOPS

Butterfly 2 large, thick, bone-in pork chops, open them up, and thin out. Dip in seasoned flour, then beaten egg, then a mix of panko bread crumbs (p201) and Parmesan. Fry for 3 minutes per side until white and juicy inside, crispy outside. These are brilliant hot with salad or cold to go for a lunch or picnic.

FREESTYLE BROILED/BBQ CHOPS WITH FRUIT SALSA

Trim the fat off the chops with scissors, making a few snips in the remaining fat on the edges to stop them curling in the heat. Rub them with a mix of chili, paprika, ground coriander, and oil. Cook over a high heat, broil, or BBQ until done. Eat with a mix of chopped mango/peach, lime, cilantro, diced fresh red chile, and sea salt.

TO GO WITH

MUSTARD MASHED POTATOES

Put 1¼ pounds peeled potatoes onto boil in a pan of cold water and with a pinch of salt. Cook for 15 to 20 minutes or until tender. Drain. Return to the pan, adding a splash of hot milk, 4 tablespoons butter, 1 teaspoon mustard, a squeeze of lemon juice, and seasoning. Mash and beat until creamy, adding a little bit of chopped basil/parsley if you have some handy.

SIMPLE ROAST PORK
AND BAKED APPLES

FEEDS 4

INGREDIENTS

1 x 3 pounds pork loin joint (bone in)
1–2 teaspoons fennel seeds
½ tablespoon dried thyme/sage
a few sprigs of rosemary/sage
a few garlic cloves, peeled
sea salt and pepper
4 eating apples, halved
generous ¾ cup cider
1¼ cups chicken stock/water
1 star anise
juice of ½ a lemon (optional)

TIP
If you'd rather use a boneless rolled joint just adjust the cooking times (p96).

—— CHANGE IT UP——
1. Replace the apples with plum halves drizzled with honey and cinnamon. **2.** Add potato, red onion, and beet wedges to the pan for the last hour. **3.** Fry walnut-sized balls of my sausage meat, sage, and blood sausage mix (p106) until brown before finishing in the pan for 20 minutes.

Fall on a plate and unashamedly traditional. Check out page 97 for notes on crackling and look forward to sweet meat, crunchy skin, and apple gravy. Totally delicious.

PREP Weigh the joint and calculate the cooking time (p96). Before it returns to room temperature, score the fat on the pork using a sharp paring or Stanley knife. Don't add any oil. Squeeze the fennel seeds and dried herbs into the scored lines. Sit fat-side up in a roasting pan. Tuck the fresh herbs and the garlic cloves underneath. Preheat the oven to 450°F. Rub the skin all over with sea salt at the last minute and bang in the oven.

COOK Roast for 15 minutes. Reduce the heat to 350°C/Gas 4. Cook for another 1 hour 40 minutes. Add the halved apples, cut-side down. Start to check the meat for doneness with a skewer or meat thermometer—it should be white with clear juices (it may need another 20 minutes). Remove when done. Let rest in a warm place for 10 to 15 minutes.

Meantime, remove the apples, garlic, and herbs from the pan and arrange on a plate. Put the pan on the stove. Add the cider, stock/water, and star anise. Stir well, scraping up all the caramelized bits. Bring to a boil and simmer, whisking, until reduced by a third. Remove the star anise and season to taste. Add lemon if it needs a little acidity.

PLATE Using a sharpened carving knife, cut the crackling neatly away from the meat and remove it in once piece. Cut the meat away from the bone and carve into slices. Arrange on a plate with the roasted apples and serve with the gravy, onion sauce, red cabbage, cauliflower cheese, roast potatoes, or mustard mashed potatoes (p109).

SIDES

RASPBERRY VINEGAR
RED CABBAGE

Preheat the oven to 350°F. Remove the core and strip the outer leaves from 1 red cabbage and slice into thin strips (¼ inch thick). Core, peel, and slice 2 apples. Peel and slice 1 onion, and crush two garlic cloves. Layer the cabbage, garlic, onion, and apple in an ovenproof dish, sprinkling with a little mixed spice and 1 tablespoon brown sugar as you do so. Dot with butter and pour over 2 tablespoons raspberry vinegar. Put in the preheated oven and cook for 20 minutes. Stir and season to taste before returning to the oven for another 20 minutes.

ONION SAUCE

Peel and mince 1 large mild onion. Melt a little bit of butter in a heavy pan. Add the onion, cover with wax paper, and leave over very low heat for a few minutes until soft and translucent without a hint of color. Whip the paper off and stir in ⅔ cup whipping cream. Let it bubble gently to reduce by half. Season with salt and white pepper. Blend with a stick blender or in a food processor. Add 1 teaspoon of minced sage, cover, and keep warm until serving.

CAULIFLOWER CHEESE

Preheat the oven to 450°F. Peel an onion and place in a pan with a bay leaf and 2½ cups milk. Bring it to the point of boiling and turn it off immediately. Leave for at least 30 minutes for the flavors to infuse. Meantime, cut the leaves and base from a cauliflower and break into florets. Bring a pan of water to a boil. Add the cauliflower and cook for 10 minutes or until just turning tender. Drain into a colander.

Melt 4 tablespoons butter gently in a heavy-bottom pan. Add generous ⅓ cup all-purpose flour and stir with a wooden spoon on low heat for 2 minutes as the mix cooks into a paste (or roux). Remove from the heat, take the onion and bay leaf out of the milk, and add it to the roux a bit at a time, whisking to incorporate it smoothly. Return the pan to low heat. Whisk or stir for 8 minutes until thickened. Throw in 1⅓ cups grated strong Cheddar, 1 teaspoon mustard, the juice of ½ a lemon, and a dash of Worcestershire sauce/mushroom ketchup. Season. Throw the cauliflower into one big dish or small ones, pour the sauce over and top with scant ¼ cup more cheese. Bake for 20 to 30 minutes until golden.

CRISP CHINESE PORK BELLY

FEEDS 4 TO 6

INGREDIENTS

1 x 3¼ pounds piece of boneless pork
   belly

MARINADE

3 garlic cloves, peeled and crushed

a pinch of sugar

1 tablespoon peanut oil

½ teaspoon sesame oil

2 teaspoons fine salt

1½ teaspoons Chinese five spice

RUB

1 teaspoon fennel seeds

1 teaspoon Chinese five spice

1 teaspoon sea salt

—— BONUS BITE ——

ROAST PORK BELLY AND WALNUT SALAD

Preheat the oven to 425°F. Score and stab
your pork belly all over. Press 2–3 teaspoons
fennel/cumin seeds, some dried rosemary/
sage/thyme, and sea salt into the cracks. Bang
it into the oven and blast for 20 minutes.
Reduce the heat to 300°F. Roast for 3 to 4
hours until the meat's meltingly tender and
the crackling crisp (slip under the broiler for
a quick final crisp if needed).

To make the dressing: put 2 teaspoons
Dijon mustard into a bowl. Whisk in 2
tablespoons white wine vinegar, drop by
drop. Add ½ cup walnut oil, whisking drop
by drop until creamy. Season. Set aside. Boil
11 ounces baby potatoes for 10 minutes
until tender. Assemble: Arrange a mix of
lettuce/watercress/chicory in a bowl. Add the
drained potatoes. Toss in dressing. Carve the
meat into ribs (if boned) or lengths. Scatter
over the salad pieces of crisp American
bacon or caramelized walnuts (p194).

Pork belly absorbs Chinese flavors beautifully. Follow the ritual to get the skin good and crisp. It's delicious eaten warm, though I also like it cold, dipped in soy or hoisin sauce.

PREP Score the skin for crackling (p97). Stab it all over with a sharp knife. Pour a bit of boiling water into a large dish. Invert the meat and stick a fork into either side. Hold the top of the joint (the fat and skin only) in the water for 5 minutes. Remove and pat dry.

Mix the marinade ingredients in a large dish. Sit the pork in it, skin-side up. Let chill, uncovered, for 3 hours or overnight. Remove and return to room temperature before cooking.

COOK Preheat the oven to 425°F. Rub the fennel seeds, five spice, and salt into the cracks. Put the meat in a pan and cook, skin-side up, for 20 minutes. Lower the oven to 400°F and cook for another 50 minutes until crisp and tender. Remove.

Preheat the broiler to high. Sit the meat under it for 2 to 3 minutes to crisp. Let rest for 15 minutes.

PLATE Carve or break into chunks with a cleaver. Eat on bowls of rice drizzled with hoisin sauce.

LAMB

Sheep have everything going for them. They're cute and tasty. Joking aside, lamb's a wonderful meat full of unique, powerful flavor. Yet again it's all about breed and sourcing if you want to avoid the tough old garbage that can hit the market. Start by getting your hands on young spring lamb. It's the most tender. Check out salt marsh lamb too—it's got a unique salty tang that, as with all lamb, reflects the taste of the environment it's lived in. Rare breed lamb is actually on the increase. If in doubt about where to start, have a chat to your local butcher and hopefully he/she will hook you up with some fantastic produce. Let's also not forget the older ladies and gents. Hogget, a sheep of 9–18 months old, has a beautiful, deeper flavor. It needs a longer cook but is well worth the wait. Mutton, older than 18 months, has an even richer, gutsy flavor and is great when cooked nice and slow. From the humble stew to exotic curries, the sheep really gives you its all while retaining its own robust identity. Get stuck in (and don't make any baaaaa-d jokes—sorry).

WHICH LAMB IN THE PAN?

NECK A bargain cut to grind up for **BURGERS**, **MEATBALLS** etc. or slow **BRAISE** in stock with vegetables to bring out its flavor.

SHOULDER Richly sweet flavored meat, good for **ROLLING**, **STUFFING**, and **ROASTING**.

DICED SHOULDER The obvious choice for **STEWS** and **CURRIES**, nice and juicy, don't rush it.

RACK OF LAMB A rack of small cutlets in a single sweet piece makes a really fast **ROAST**. Lean, so needs well oiling or protecting with a crust.

CUTLETS Sweet and tender chops which are great for fast suppers. Versatile and lovely—**GRIDDLE**, **PAN-FRY** or **OVEN ROAST**.

LOIN Like beef fillet, it's tender, expensive and likes a fast **ROAST**. Eat it pink.

NOISETTE A cut from the loin and a neat eat. **BROIL** or **PAN-FRY**. It loves a good sauce.

LOIN CHOP A leaner chop, **GRIDDLE**, **BROIL**, **PAN-FRY**, **BRAISE**. Eat pink.

BREAST Cheap and sweet, but fatty. Cook **WHOLE ON THE BONE** or get it boned, roll it up, **STUFF** it, and slap in the oven. Or chop and use as a **STEWING** meat.

LEG OF LAMB Perfect for **ROASTING**, bone in or out. Stuff it if you like. Open it up, spice it up and butterfly it for a **BARBECUE**. Whole or half-leg works for a medium-fast roast to eat pink, or a long slow roast to get it falling off the bone.

DICED LEG Good for faster **STEWS** and **CURRIES**.

LEG STEAKS Versatile. **GRIDDLE**, **BROIL**, quick cook in the **OVEN**, **SKEWER**, **BBQ**, or **STIR-FRY**.

SHANKS The tip of the leg. Great sweet meat when given a very long **BRAISE** with wine or stock.

CHILL prepackaged lamb in vacuum packs, etc. in original sealed containers.

LOOSELY WRAPPED or bagged meat needs to be taken out of its packaging.

PLACE it on a dish/plate that's large enough to contain any drips/liquids.

COVER it loosely in foil or wax paper. Store away from cooked and raw foods.

FREEZE individual portions by tightly wrapping them in plastic wrap before putting into freezer bags, so you can grab them easily as you want them.

REFRIGERATE roasts, steaks and chops for 3 to 5 days; diced meat for 2 days; grind for 1 day.

If you want to **MARINATE** lamb; store roasts, steaks, and chops in the mix for up to 4 days. Diced and stewing meat can be marinated for 2 days.

Lamb roasts, steaks, and chops can be **FROZEN** for 9 months; ground meat for 3 months.

WHAT TO LOOK FOR
in your LAMB

LOOK FOR:

GOOD MARBLING

FIRM-TEXTURED MEAT WITH A PINKISH HUE

WHITE AND FIRM FAT

AVOID:

DARK AND WET MEAT

YELLOW AND SOFT FAT

TOO MUCH FAT

LAMB ACTION

BUTTERFLYING

This is a nice, relaxed way with a leg of lamb. Get it boned out (ask the butcher to "tunnel bone it") then marinate, barbecue, oven-cook, or broil it.

1. Lay the leg on a board.

2. Stick your filleting or sharp chef's knife into the cavity left from the bone.

3. Cut it open from top to bottom

4. Open the joint out (it looks like a butterfly). Turn upside down.

5. Make a slight cut through the center, like the hinge in a book, to keep it flat.

6. Turn it over. Make some light crisscross cuts to take any rubs, spices, etc.

7. Cook as per your chosen recipe.

SUPERMARKET SHEEP SHOPPING

Supermarkets keep the most common cuts —easy roasts and lots of useful quick-cook chops and steaks. Their butcher counters can tell you about provenance (good ones are hot on this) and will cut joints, etc. to the size you want. Plus, they save their best meat for the counter. The best lamb is aged for 8 days for flavor. If you're in a hurry and can't go through the detective work, use your eye and judgment. Lamb freezes better than other meats. So, save yourself cash and pick up bargains from the freezers. Better, buy spring lamb in season and freeze your own. If you're after rare breed lamb, check out what's available on the internet.

SHEEP DOCTOR

LAMB PROVIDES...

AMINO ACIDS

WHICH YOUR BODY NEEDS TO BUILD AND KEEP STRONG

PROTEIN

JUST **90g** PROVIDES **43%** OF YOUR DAILY RECOMMENDED DOSE

That's support for healthy hair, skin, eyes, bones, muscles

B VITAMINS

to help fight depression, maintain a healthy nervous system, and SUPPORT GOOD MENTAL AND PHYSICAL HEALTH

IRON

necessary to get you performing at peak, physically and mentally.

ZINC HELPS PREVENT INFECTIONS, AID

healing, and knock off colds.

Omega 3s

found in grass-fed lamb help with mental agility.

VITAMIN D

A KEY VITAMIN WHICH HELPS STRENGTHEN BONES, BATTLE

S.A.D *(seasonal affective disorder)*

and is now thought to be a useful tool to help battle cancers

COOKING TIMES FOR LAMB

I like my lamb just pink, not raw and never overcooked.
Times depend on heat and size so are approximate.
Always test it. Rest cuts for 5 minutes. Roasts for 15.

FAST CUTS

PER SIDE [CUTLETS / CHOPS / STEAKS]

1 LAMB = 1 MINUTE

KEBABS

RACK OF LAMB

1 LAMB = 1 MINUTE

BIG ROASTS

Cook your roasts at 425°F for 10 minutes. Reduce to 350°F.

RARE
18 minutes per 1 pound

MEDIUM
25 minutes per 1 pound plus 20

WELL-DONE
30 minutes per 1 pound plus 25

TESTING, TESTING
Is it done yet?

SKEWER TRICK —poke it into the thickest bit of meat. Avoid the bone. Count to 5.

HOLD IT ON YOUR WRIST.
COLD (rare)
WARM (medium)
SCALDING (well-done).

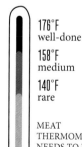

176°F well-done
158°F medium
140°F rare

MEAT THERMOMETER NEEDS TO READ...

FLAVOR IT UP

Lamb can take really strong flavors, so treat your chops, roasts, and cutlets to some creative herb and spice mixes. Leg and shoulder joints can be changed completely by stuffing. Spread the mix over your unrolled shoulder or into your boned leg, then tie it up to flavor from the inside out.

Marinate with...

1. Olive oil, lemon juice, or white wine vinegar, Dijon mustard, garlic, and thyme
2. Yogurt, cumin, garlic, coriander, turmeric, cinnamon, and lemon
3. Smoked paprika, lime, chili powder, and yogurt
4. Chinese wine/vinegar, soy sauce, garlic, oyster sauce, and coriander

RUB WITH...

1. Pesto and oil and lemon
2. Harissa paste, garlic, and lemon
3. A bit of your favorite curry paste, oil, and apricot jam
4. Tapenade, oil, and lemon

STUFF WITH...

1 Salsa verde or tapenade mixed with bread crumbs
2 Softened onion, chopped mint, pine nuts, and cooked couscous
3 Cubed dried apricots, bread crumbs, garlic, softened shallot, lemon juice, and rosemary

COVER WITH...

1. HERB CRUST Blitz up 6 ounces white bread with 2 garlic cloves, 2–3 tablespoons minced herbs, 4 tablespoons soft butter, and season with salt and pepper. Mix it up. Spread Dijon mustard over your lamb and press the crust into it.
2. MUSTARD AND GARLIC BREAD CRUST Blitz bread with garlic, dried mint, lemon zest, and mustard powder. Brush melted red currant jelly over lamb. Add the crumb.

A SHEEP *(carving)* TRICK

Instead of faffing about here's a quick carving trick. Sit the joint on a board, fat end down. Hold the shank. Cut straight down one side as close to the bone as you can. Do the same with the other side. Cut the meat across into thick slices. Done...

FRIENDS
ALMOND, ANCHOVY, APRICOT, BEANS, BULGUR WHEAT, BALSAMIC VINEGAR, BUTTERNUT SQUASH, BLOOD SAUSAGE, CARDAMOM, CHESTNUT, CHICKPEAS, CHILE, CINNAMON, CORIANDER, CUCUMBER, CUMIN, COUSCOUS, DRIED FRUITS, EGGPLANT, FETA, GARLIC, HARISSA PASTE, HUMMUS, LEMON, MINT, NUTMEG, ONION, OREGANO, PARSLEY, PEAS, POTATO, RED WINE, RHUBARB, ROSEMARY, RUTABAGA, STAR ANISE, THYME, TOMATO, YOGURT, ZUCCHINI

GRIDDLED CUTLETS
WITH HOT BREAD AND FRESH HERB SALSA

 HEALTHY FAST FEEDS 2 TO 3

No fancy tricks: it's simply sweet meat teamed up with a saucy herby concoction. To mix it up a bit, slap on a marinade (p117). Eat your salsa rough or blitz it into a smooth sauce.

INGREDIENTS

3–4 cutlets per person, whatever size
  you want (at room temperature)
a little olive oil
sea salt and pepper
4–6 slices of bread (coarse-textured
  white or sourdough)
FRESH HERB SALSA
½ ounce mint (leaves only)
½ ounce fresh cilantro
½ tablespoons small capers, drained
  and roughly chopped
5 anchovy fillets, finely chopped
juice of ½ a lemon
4 tablespoons olive oil
1 teaspoon Dijon mustard

TIP
Team the salsa with lamb steaks/roasts/
griddled chicken. The smooth version's good
with cheese soufflé (for dipping) or spread
in an omelet.

········ **TIME SAVER** ········
Make up the salsa ahead and chill in a
covered bowl until ready to use. The smooth
one stores for up to 2 weeks.

——— **CHANGE IT UP** ———
1. Rub a bit of mint sauce and balsamic
vinegar into the meat to flavor before oiling
the pan and griddling.
2. For sweet griddled cutlets, brush a mix
of honey, mint, and lemon juice onto plain
cutlets 2 minutes before they're done.
3. Try baking your cutlets: marinate for at
least 30 minutes, then bake at 350°F for 10
minutes per side.

PREP Make the salsa: Wash and dry the mint leaves and cilantro. For a rough salsa, mince the herbs on a board with a sharp chef's knife. Place in a bowl with the chopped capers, anchovies, lemon juice, oil, and mustard. For a smooth salsa, blitz everything in a food processor or handheld blender until smooth.

Prep the cutlets: Trim off any excess fat if necessary, and rub a few drops of oil into the meat with your fingers (or use a pastry brush, if squeamish). Season lightly with pepper and a tiny bit of salt.

COOK Heat a griddle or stovetop grill pan until it's almost smoking hot. Slap the meat down and cook for 2 minutes without shifting. Flip. Repeat for 2 minutes to color well and flavor up. Turn each cutlet onto its fatty back with tongs and hold for a few seconds to brown up. For well-done, give the meat another minute per side. Test to see it's done as you like it (p116). Rest it on a plate and sprinkle with sea salt.

Griddle the bread in the hot pan for 30 seconds per side, or until crisp and marked by the lamb juices.

PLATE Pile the cutlets and bread on a plate and let people grab. Serve the salsa in a bowl for dipping. Enjoy with tabbouleh (p128) or couscous salad, any griddled vegetables, and mezze dips such as hummus (p38), cucumber tzatziki (p40), and yogurt mixed with crushed garlic.

BONUS BITES

A RACK OF CUTLETS
Preheat your oven to 425°F. Sear the rack on both sides in a very hot pan with a bit of oil. When cool, spread the fat side with 1 tablespoon smooth salsa/pesto/Dijon mustard. Blitz up 2 handfuls of fresh herbs, 2 handfuls of crustless white bread, 1 garlic clove, and press on top of the lamb to form a crust. Roast for 15 to 20 minutes. Combine a little red currant jelly and red wine in a pan and simmer for a minute. Drizzle over the cutlets to finish.

STICKY SPICED CUTLETS
Rub the cutlets in a mix of 1 teaspoon grated ginger, 1 teaspoon cumin, ½ teaspoon coriander, ½ teaspoon turmeric, 2 crushed garlic cloves, and 3 teaspoons peanut/vegetable oil. Griddle as before. Eat with rice and raita (p130).

CUTLETS AND BEANS
Rub the cutlets with a bit of olive oil, lemon juice, crushed garlic, and dried oregano. In a pan warm a glug of olive oil, 1–2 diced garlic cloves, a sprig of rosemary, and 1½ cups drained canned cannellini beans for 5 minutes. Griddle the cutlets as before and serve on the beans with crunchy bread.

GREEK LAMB PIE

FEEDS 4

INGREDIENTS

1–2 eggplants (roughly 1 pound)
salt and pepper
olive oil
1 teaspoon dried oregano/thyme
2–3 mealy white potatoes
2 medium onions, peeled and chopped
2–3 garlic cloves, peeled and crushed
grated zest of 1 lemon
a handful of fresh oregano/thyme/
    parsley
1½ pounds best ground lamb
¼ teaspoon ground cinnamon
scant ¼ cup red wine
1 x 14-ounce can chopped tomatoes or
    squashed plum tomatoes
2 tablespoons tomato paste
1 teaspoon sugar
4½ ounces feta cheese, cut into cubes
a handful of freshly grated Parmesan

—— CHANGE IT UP ——

For all-Greek moussaka, use two-thirds
eggplant, one-third potato. Finish with a
layer of eggplant and cover with a béchamel
sauce (p185) made with
feta cheese instead of Cheddar.

—— BONUS BITE ——

ALL-LANCASHIRE HOTPOT

Coat 1½ pounds cubed stewing lamb (or 2
lamb shoulder chops, bone in and excess fat
removed, per person) in flour, seasoning,
and dried rosemary. Brown it off in a pan.
Sweat 3 thickly sliced large onions in oil
and butter for 10 minutes. Peel and thinly
slice 2 pounds mealy potatoes. Layer up
the lamb, onion, and potato, finishing with
a final layer of potato. Add ¾ cup chicken
stock, but don't submerge it. Dot with butter,
cover with foil and bake at 400°F for 1½ to 2
hours, uncovering for the last 10 minutes.

Lancashire in the north of England goes to Greece in this great concoction: you've got layers of gorgeous eggplant in a tasty lamb moussaka sauce topped with crunchy, succulent golden potatoes.

PREP
Preheat the oven to 425°F.

EGGPLANTS: Slice into ½-inch circles. Sprinkle with a little salt and let sweat (degorge) on a board in a single layer for 15 minutes. Pat the salt off and blot dry using paper towels. Sit on a nonstick baking sheet, brush with oil, and sprinkle with the dried oregano/thyme. POTATOES: Peel and slice into ⅛-inch circles. Pat dry. Sit in a single layer on another baking sheet. Brush with oil. Put the 2 baking sheets into the oven. Bake for 10 minutes or until the eggplant is softening and the potato is starting to turn golden. Remove and set aside.

Meantime, make the sauce. Heat a glug of oil in a large sauté pan or casserole dish. Add the onion, garlic, lemon zest, and fresh herbs. Fry the mix gently without coloring for 5 minutes or so, or until the onion is translucent. Keep stirring so it doesn't catch. Increase the heat a bit. Crumble the meat in. Stir to color for a minute or two. Add the cinnamon. Increase the heat, add the wine, and let it bubble. Add the tomatoes, paste, and sugar. Reduce to low heat and simmer for 10 minutes, stirring occasionally, until the sauce is reasonably thick but not at all dry. Taste and add seasoning.

Spoon a little sauce into the bottom of one large or 4 small ovenproof dishes. Cover with a single layer of eggplant. Scatter over a few feta cubes. Add more sauce. Add a layer of potato. Scatter over some Parmesan. Add more sauce, eggplant, and feta, finishing with potato arranged in slightly overlapping circles on top.

COOK
Cover with foil and bake in the oven for 20 minutes. Remove the foil and cook for another 5 to 10 minutes, or until the potatoes are golden and the insides are bubbling away. Remove and let settle for 5 minutes.

PLATE
Bang individual pies onto small plates. Sit a large pie on the table and spoon it out. This is perfect with spoonfuls of cool tzatziki (p40) and dressed tomato salad.

MINTED SHEPHERD'S PIE

FEEDS 4

INGREDIENTS

⅛ ounce porcini or other dried
    mushrooms
scant ½ cup boiling water
1 medium onion, peeled and minced
3 garlic cloves, peeled and crushed
2 medium carrots, diced
1 tablespoon olive oil
a little bit of butter
salt and pepper
4 American bacon slices, sliced
    and diced
1½ pounds best ground lamb
scant ½ cup red wine
scant ¼ cup chicken stock (p49)
2 tablespoons tomato paste
½ teaspoon dried thyme
½ teaspoon dried oregano
a handful of fresh parsley
1–2 tablespoons mushroom ketchup
    (optional)
a squeeze of lemon (optional)
1–2 teaspoons good mint sauce/jelly
TOPPING
2½ pounds mealy potatoes, peeled
salt and pepper
2 tablespoons butter
2 teaspoons mustard
juice of ½ a lemon
a splash of milk (optional)
a handful of freshly grated Parmesan

TIP
Boil whole unpeeled potatoes if you have
time, for a drier, finer result. Put them
through a ricer or peel to mash once cooked.

---

*A shepherd's pie can be predictable; this on the other hand is not.
Adding just a few extras makes all the difference. Beautiful...*

PREP Pour the boiling water over the dried mushrooms and leave for 10 minutes. Prep the veg. Heat a large sauté pan, wide shallow pan, or casserole dish. Add the oil, butter, and a pinch of salt. Slap in the onion and garlic and cook gently for 5 minutes, or until transparent. Add the carrot. Cook for 3 to 4 minutes. Add the bacon and cook until the fat starts to run.

Drain the porcini over a bowl (saving the water). Chop them and add to the pan. Raise the heat a bit. Crumble the ground meat into the pan, breaking it up with your fingers. Stir it around to brown for a few minutes. Add the wine, mushroom soaking water, and stock. Increase the heat and boil for a few seconds. Reduce to a very low simmer.

Add the tomato paste, thyme, oregano, parsley, and mushroom ketchup, if using, and season with salt and pepper. Cook until you get a thick, rich sauce. Add more stock if it's too dry. Taste and adjust the seasoning, adding a squeeze of lemon, if you want.

Meantime, add the potatoes and a pinch of salt to a pan of cold water. Boil for 10 to 15 minutes until done (test with a knife). Drain, return to the pan, and shuffle on the heat for a few seconds to dry. Put the dried potatoes into a potato ricer, or use a masher/fork to break them down. Add the butter, mustard, and lemon juice and season with salt and pepper. Beat until smooth (don't use a processor). Add a drop of milk if stiff, but it mustn't be a sloppy mash. Taste, season, and set aside.

COOK Preheat the oven to 400°F. Spoon the sauce into 1 large dish or 4 small ovenproof dishes until three-quarters full. Dribble a subtle amount of mint sauce/jelly over the top. Add the mash. Use a fork and spoon to blob it over then bring it to the edges and ensure the meat is fully covered. Make ridges/peaks for a crunchy finish. Sprinkle over the Parmesan and sit the dish on a baking sheet. Cook for 30 minutes, or until crusty and bubbling.

PLATE Spoon from the large dish or eat straight from your own. Serve with ketchup and brown sauce.

A LAMB
IN A PAN

FAST

FEEDS 2

INGREDIENTS

2 medium potatoes, peeled
1 shallot/small onion, peeled
2 good-sized lamb steaks (leg or other
    lean cut), at room temperature
olive oil, for frying
salt and pepper
a bit of chopped fresh rosemary (or a
    pinch of dried rosemary/thyme/sage)
2 garlic cloves, peeled and crushed
5 tablespoons white wine
1½ teaspoons Dijon mustard

—— BONUS BITES ——

LAMB IN A DISH
Preheat the oven to 350°F. Boil a handful of new potatoes for 10 minutes until just soft. Drain, crush them a bit, and throw into a roasting pan with quartered onions, cherry tomatoes, and chunks of zucchini and eggplant. Fry the steaks in hot oil for 2 minutes until browned. Sit them on the veg. Add a bit of oil, dried herbs, salt, garlic, lemon juice, and pesto/smooth fresh herb salsa (p118). Roast for 20 to 30 minutes. Remove the lamb early if the veg needs longer.

BATTERED LAMB
Bash your lamb steaks to thin them out. Coat in seasoned flour then dip into an egg beaten with 1 teaspoon mustard and 1 tablespoon chopped basil. Coat in 2 handfuls of fresh bread crumbs (p201) mixed with a little grated Parmesan. Fry for 1 to 2 minutes per side until golden and cooked to your taste. Sprinkle with salt. Serve with lemon chunks.

Sometimes you want to save on the cleaning up. So, slap some beautiful lamb steaks on top of soft potatoes to share their juices and eat straight from the pan. Why not?

PREP Preheat the oven to 350°F. Cube the potatoes: Using a sharp vegetable knife, slice off their ends to square them up, then cut into ¾-inch wide slices. Cut the slices into ¾-inch batons. Cut those into ¾-inch cubes. Dry them on paper towels. Dice the shallot/onion.

Prep the lamb: If fat's an issue, trim the edges with a sharp knife (though you'll lose flavor). Rub or brush your steaks with a little oil on both sides. Season with pepper.

COOK Heat an ovenproof skillet over medium/high heat. Slap the steaks down. Sizzle and sear for a minute per side or until golden brown. Lift with tongs and hold any fatty edges of the meat down on the skillet to brown up. Remove and set aside.

Add a splash more oil to the skillet. Add the potato cubes and fry off for a few minutes, turning, until lightly golden. Add the herbs, shallot/onion, and garlic. Fry a few minutes more. Increase the heat. Add the wine and stir in the mustard. Sit the lamb steaks on top.

Transfer the skillet to the oven. Roast the lamb in the skillet for 5 minutes, or until the potatoes are soft. (Be careful not to overcook the meat: test it with a knife and lift it off early if need be.) Remove. Sprinkle with sea salt. Rest the pan in a warm place for 3 minutes before serving.

PLATE Go rustic. Slap the pan (on a mat) in the middle of the table and help yourselves: eat with salad, fresh greens, a good dollop of mustard, and bread for mopping up the juices.

THREE LAMB SKEWERS
WITH BEET TZATZIKI

FEEDS 3 TO 4

INGREDIENTS

TURKISH KEBABS
1 pound good lamb (leg or steak)
1 small onion, peeled and grated
a glug of olive oil
milk
KOFTA
1 pound 10 ounces good ground lamb
4 garlic cloves, peeled and crushed
3½ ounces onion, peeled and grated
grated zest and juice of 1 lemon
1 teaspoon ground cumin
1 teaspoon ground coriander
a small bunch of cilantro, chopped
KIBBE
1 x kofta mix (above)
scant 1 cup bulgur wheat
1 teaspoon dried red pepper flakes

✱✱✱✱   CASH SAVER   ✱✱✱✱
Alternate the cubes of lamb kebab with
oil-brushed quartered onions, chunks of
zucchini, mushrooms, and cherry tomatoes.

········   TIME SAVER   ········
Prep skewers ahead for your BBQ, but give
them time to return to room temperature.

——— BONUS BITES ———
LAMB BURGER
Divide the kofta mix into 4 and shape into
burgers. Fry in oil or broil for 4 minutes a
side until cooked. Stack in pita/buns/wraps
with dollops of hummus and yogurt mixed
with crushed garlic, arugula leaves, a bit of
crumbled feta, and some slices of tomato.
FETA MEATBALLS
Divide the kofta mix into 8 balls. Flatten
each in your hand. Put a cube of feta in the
center of each and pinch the meat into a
ball around it. Fry in oil for 3 minutes until
browned. Poach for 10 minutes in a pan of
easy tomato sauce (p176). Crack an egg in
per person and cover until cooked. Pile onto
pasta and enjoy.

*Forget your late-night van kebab: you can serve these up to the most
discerning customers. Cook all three on the BBQ to celebrate summer days
with mates or have your favorite skewer inside anytime; enjoy with healthy
beet tzatziki.*

PREP KEBABS: Chop the meat into bite-size pieces with a chef's knife. Add
it to a bowl with the onion, olive oil, and cover the lot with milk.
Chill and let marinate for at least 1 hour. Remove from the marinade. Blot dry.
Thread onto metal or presoaked wooden skewers.

KOFTA: Mix all the ingredients in a bowl using a fork. Break off and fry a nut-
sized piece in hot oil. Taste to check the seasoning's right. Adjust if you need
to. Use damp hands to scoop up a quarter of the mix and gently shape it into a
long sausage around the skewer. Repeat with the remainder. Chill the mix for
10 minutes.

KIBBE: Tip the scant 1 cup bulgur into a pan with 2½ cups cold water. Bring
to a boil. Reduce. Simmer on low for 15 minutes or until tender. Drain in a
strainer. Spread to dry or twist it in a dish towel. Fluff with a fork. Let cool.
Make up a batch of kofta mix. Lightly mix the two with a fork, adding the red
pepper flakes. Test for seasoning and shape it onto skewers as for kofta.

Get your skewers to room temperature. Brush them lightly with oil. Season
lightly with salt and pepper.

COOK KEBABS: Heat up a griddle or stovetop grill pan. Lay the skewers
down and cook quickly for 1 to 2 minutes, turning, until browned
on the outside, a bit pink and tender on the inside. Alternatively, cook on a
medium BBQ. KOFTA/KIBBE: Preheat a broiler. Broil the skewers for a few
minutes, turning regularly, until cooked right through. Don't overcook or
they'll toughen up.

PLATE Stack your skewers up on a plate. Eat with beet tzatziki, couscous,
and griddled vegetables, or as part of a mezze platter (p38–40).

••••••••••••••• TO GO WITH   ••••••••••••••••

BEET TZATZIKI
Peel 2 small (uncooked) beet and grate them thickly into a bowl. Stir
in 4 tablespoons Greek yogurt, the juice of ½ a lemon, a small bunch
of minced mint, 1 teaspoon horseradish sauce, and season to taste.
Leave for 30 minutes to infuse.

SLOW ROAST
LEG OF LAMB WITH BAKED EGGPLANTS AND DAUPHINOISE POTATOES

FEEDS 6

INGREDIENTS

1 large leg of lamb on the bone
   (4½ pounds plus)
6 fat garlic cloves
a small bunch of fresh rosemary
8–10 anchovy fillets
1 lemon
1 tablespoon olive oil
salt and pepper
a few sprigs of fresh thyme/
   2 pinches of dried oregano
generous 1 cup red wine
1 cup water/chicken stock (p49)
a bit of lemon juice (optional)
1 teaspoon red currant jelly (optional)

——— BONUS BITE ———
FASTER ROAST SPRING LAMB WITH LEMON

Preheat the oven to 425°F. Stab a piece of spring lamb (on or off the bone) and insert sprigs of rosemary and 6 sliced garlic cloves into the cuts. Rub with oil and seasoning. Roast in a pan without any liquid for 20 minutes. Pour the juice of 1 lemon over the lamb and reduce the heat to 350°F. Cook until done to your taste (p116). Rest it. Carve it traditionally and serve with gravy made from white wine.

Here's one for a Sunday dinner in fall or winter. Don't fuss about the anchovies. They add a sweet, salty richness but your lamb won't taste of them. Team with gloriously rich dauphinoise potatoes and silky eggplants baked with cheese.

PREP Start the night before or first thing. Dry the lamb with paper towels. Sit it on a board. Slice the garlic cloves into sticks. Pull the leaves off the rosemary stalks. Cut two-thirds of the anchovy fillets into halves. Thinly peel a third of your lemon and slice the zest into thin strips.

Stab the meat randomly with a sharp chef's knife to make defined cuts of about 1 inch depth. Slot bits of garlic, anchovy, lemo, and rosemary into them with bits of herb showing. Chill until needed (remembering to return to room temperature before cooking), or cook now.

Preheat the oven to 400°F. Rub the oil into the lamb, working around the herbs. Season lightly and sprinkle with the thyme/oregano. Sit the meat on top of the remaining anchovies in a roasting pan or dish. Pour the wine and water/stock into the pan. Put it into the oven.

COOK After 20 minutes, reduce the temperature to 266°F. Roast for 4 hours or more, basting every 20 minutes, until you can see the meat is done—it should look soft and be practically coming away from the bone. Do the skewer test (p116). The meat won't be pink like young, faster-cooking spring lamb but it will be very sweet and tender. Remove from the oven and rest the meat, foil covered, for at least 20 minutes.

Make the gravy: Spoon off any excess oil from the meat juices. Put the pan on the stove. Add water/stock or a bit more wine. Boil it up and stir with a wooden spoon to reduce the mix a bit. Taste and adjust the seasoning. Add a bit of lemon juice if it needs it or a teaspoon of red currant jelly for sweetness.

PLATE Carve the lamb the easy way (p117) by cutting into lovely thick slices. Serve with dauphinoise potatoes and baked eggplants for a real event or with peas, mint sauce, and parsley and lemon potatoes.

TO GO WITH
BAKED EGGPLANTS

Slice and degorge 3 large eggplants (p16) and fry in olive oil until just softening. Make up 1 quantity of easy tomato sauce (p176) or mix a jar of good strained tomatoes with 3 crushed garlic cloves. Slice 2 balls of mozzarella and grate 5 ounces Parmesan. Spread a little tomato sauce over the bottom of an ovenproof dish. Add a layer of eggplant and a bit of the sliced mozzarella and Parmesan, seasoning. Layer it up and finish with eggplants on top. Add what's left of the mozzarella and Parmesan. Cover with a domed bit of foil. Bake with the lamb for an hour then remove the foil and stick the heat up to finish or cook under the broiler. Alternatively, bake for 30 minutes at 400°F, removing the foil for the last 5 minutes.

DAUPHINOISE POTATOES

Preheat the oven to 350°F. Mix 1¼ cups heavy cream, scant ½ cup lowfat milk, 6 crushed garlic cloves, seasoning, and a pinch of dried thyme and nutmeg in a pitcher. Butter an ovenproof dish. Peel and slice 2 pounds mealy potatoes very thinly, using a knife or mandolin. Layer half into the dish and pour over half the cream mix. Layer up the rest and pour over the rest of the cream. Cover with foil. Bake for 1 hour. Uncover and dot with 2 tablespoons butter. Bake for 30 minutes until tender (test with a knife).

MINT SAUCE

Put 4 tablespoons minced mint leaves into a bowl with 2 tablespoons boiling water, 1½ teaspoons superfine sugar, 1½ tablespoons white wine vinegar, and 2 pinches salt. Leave for 30 minutes. Taste and adjust seasoning.

SLASHED ROAST LAMB AND YOGURT FLATBREADS

FEEDS 3 TO 4

INGREDIENTS

1 x 2-pound half leg of lamb (on the bone)
scant ½ cup yogurt
4 garlic cloves, peeled and crushed
1 tablespoon harissa paste
juice of ½ a lemon
salt and pepper

FLATBREADS
scant 2 cups all-purpose flour
1 teaspoon cumin or fennel seeds
1 cup plain yogurt
a pinch of salt

✶✶✶✶ CASH SAVER ✶✶✶✶
Slash a lamb shoulder all over and sprinkle with salt and paprika only. Rub with olive oil and roast at 325°F for 3 hours plus.

········ TIME SAVER ········
Substitute warm tortilla wraps or pita breads for the flatbreads.

—— BONUS BITE——
FAST BUTTERFLY LAMB FOR THE OVEN OR BARBECUE
Get your butcher to butterfly a boned lamb leg or do it yourself (p115). Slash the underside and rub with a mix of 1 tablespoon paprika, juice of 1 lemon, olive oil, and 6 crushed garlic cloves. Let marinate for a few hours or overnight in a large sealed plastic bag. Preheat the oven to 400°F. Cook in a pan until done and still pink inside (p116). To barbecue, sit over medium heat on a rack that's 10 inches from the coals. Baste regularly and turn once.

A Moroccan take on lamb: this meat takes to yogurt and spices.

PREP Sit your lamb on a board. Use a sharp chef's knife to slash 1-inch deep cuts into the top of the joint in a crisscross diamond pattern. Mix the yogurt, garlic, harissa, and lemon juice together to form a paste and season with salt and pepper. Rub into the top of lamb. Put it in a pan/dish and let come to room temperature. Preheat the oven to 350°F.

COOK Put the lamb in the oven to cook. Test after 30 minutes. Once done to your taste (p116), let the meat rest for at least 10 minutes.

Meantime, make the flatbreads. Sift the flour into a bowl. Add the rest of the ingredients. Mix with a fork or your hand to form a dough and bring together into a ball. Transfer to a lightly floured board. Divide into 8 pieces. Roll each one out into a thin circle, quarter turning the dough with each roll as you go to get it even. Heat a large flat skillet/crepe pan. Cook the flatbreads individually for a minute or so until browning, then turn over to cook for another few seconds. (Don't overdo it as you want them soft.) Keep the cooked wraps in a dish towel to stay warm/soft as you repeat.

PLATE Carve the meat by cutting down each side of the bone (p117). Slap it straight onto the fresh, warm flatbreads and wrap with arugula, tomato, red onion, hummus, and yogurt mixed with crushed garlic or lay it on top of a big pile of couscous salad or tabbouleh.

········· TO GO WITH ·········

TABBOULEH

Tip scant 1 cup bulgur wheat and 2½ cups water into a pan. Bring to a boil, reduce the heat, and simmer for 15 minutes. Drain through a strainer and spread it out on a large plate to dry, or tip into a strainer/colander lined with a dish towel, bringing the ends of the towel together and twisting to squeeze moisture from the bulgur. Drop it into a bowl and fluff it with a fork. Mix in a pinch or two of salt, 2 tablespoons each of minced mint and Italian parsley, 2 seeded diced tomatoes, ½ a cucumber, seeded and diced, ½ diced red onion, 2–3 tablespoons good fruity olive oil, and 3 tablespoons lemon juice. Mix lightly with a fork. Top with a handful of pomegranate seeds and your choice of extras: a few crumbled walnuts/pistachios; a handful of lightly toasted pine nuts; crumbled feta; griddled slices of halloumi cheese; chopped dried/fresh apricot, or cubes of beet.

AROMATIC LAMB MADRAS WITH NAAN AND SIDES

FEEDS 4

INGREDIENTS

1½ pounds lamb leg/shoulder
2–3 green chiles
2 large onions, peeled
4–5 tablespoons vegetable/sunflower/
   peanut oil
4 cloves
6 cardamom pods
salt and pepper
4 fat garlic cloves, peeled
   and crushed
a thumb-sized piece of fresh ginger,
   peeled and grated
1 teaspoon red chili powder
½ teaspoon ground cumin
½ teaspoon ground coriander
1 teaspoon turmeric
scant ¼ cup water
½ x 14-ounce can of chopped tomatoes
1–2 tablespoons tomato paste
2 teaspoons tamarind paste
½ x 14-ounce can of coconut milk
a handful of fresh cilantro leaves,
   chopped

—— CHANGE IT UP ——

1. Blanch a handful of green beans in a pan
of boiling water for a few minutes. Drain.
Add to the pan with a handful of spinach
leaves for the last few minutes of cooking
before serving.
2. Chop up 2 large tomatoes and add to the
mix before serving. 3. Use mutton in place
of the lamb. It will take longer to cook but
has a lovely rich flavor.

········ TIME SAVER ········

1. Make this a day or even two days ahead—
the flavors will continue to develop.
2. If you don't have time to make the spice
mix yourself, use 2–3 tablespoons of a good
curry paste instead.

Nothing like a takeout: here's a gorgeously soft, aromatic lamb curry. Fresh spices tenderize the meat and give it a subtle range of flavorings. Try this mix out on beef and chicken too.

PREP If in one piece, cut the lamb (across the grain) into 1½-inch cubes. Organize your spices so you can throw them into the pan as soon as you need. Mince the chiles. You can seed or leave them in for extra heat. Finely dice the onions.

Put a large heavy-bottom skillet/casserole dish onto heat. Add the oil. Toss in the cloves and cardamom and cook for a minute, so the spices release their fragrance.

Add the onions and a bit of salt. Cook over medium/high heat, stirring, for 10 minutes or so. Let them brown up to create a rich curry base (without burning). When good and colored, add the garlic, ginger, and chiles. Cook and stir. Add the chili powder, cumin, ground coriander, and turmeric. Cook and stir for 2 minutes.

Add the lamb. Stir and mix well to coat. Add the water, tomatoes, paste, and tamarind paste. The mix will look quite dry but it will loosen up as the meat releases its juices.

COOK Cover the pan and simmer on very low heat. Bang it into the oven at 350°F if the heat on your stove is too fierce. Check to see it's not too dry and stir every so often.

After 45 minutes, add the coconut milk and a bit of fresh cilantro. Stir well. Return to simmer for another 45 minutes, or for as long as your cut of lamb needs. Taste the sauce and adjust the seasoning.

PLATE Serve this up in a good-looking dish topped with lots of fresh cilantro. You'll want a bowl of raita to sooth the chili effect. Eat with naan bread or wraps, spinach dhal, and bombay crush potatoes.

TURN OVER
FOR SIDES

HONEY MINT RAITA

Mix together generous 1 cup Greek yogurt, 1 teaspoon good-quality mint sauce, ½ teaspoon salt, ½ teaspoon sugar, 3 teaspoons thin honey and a small handful of minced cilantro. Serve.

MADRAS SIDES

SIMPLE SPINACH DHAL

Wash ½ cup split red lentils in a strainer. Tip 1¾ cups water into a pan. Add the lentils and bring to a boil. Cook for about 10 minutes, or until soft. Drain well. Put 4 ounces spinach leaves into a pan with 1–2 tablespoons water and heat until the leaves wilt. Drain immediately and squeeze a bit of the water from the leaves. Heat 1 tablespoon sunflower oil in a clean pan. Add 1 teaspoon each of turmeric and chili powder and 1 crushed garlic clove. Add the lentils, spinach, 3 teaspoons lemon juice/2 teaspoons tamarind paste, 2 teaspoons tomato paste, and salt. Simmer for 15 minutes. Taste and adjust seasoning. To serve: Fry 3 sliced garlic cloves, a pinch of mustard seeds, and a few cilantro leaves. Bang them onto your dhal.

BOMBAY CRUSH

Scrub 1 pound waxy new potatoes to remove most of the peel. Cut into smallish pieces. Add to a pan of cold salted water with a few pinches of turmeric. Boil until a knife passes into them easily, 10 to 15 minutes. Drain. Spread on a plate and crush them a bit with a fork. Add a pinch of salt. Heat 3 tablespoons oil in a pan or wok. When hot, add 2 dried curry leaves, ½ teaspoon dried red pepper flakes, and 2 pinches each of cumin seeds, onion seeds, and black mustard seeds. Cook for a minute. Add 2 minced onions, 2 crushed garlic cloves, 1 teaspoon tamarind paste, 2 minced fresh green chiles, and a handful of chopped cilantro. Cook until the onions are soft and everything's melting together. Add the potatoes and 1 tablespoon water, stir well, and heat through. Season with salt and the juice of ½ a lemon. Top with torn cilantro.

NAAN BREAD

Put ⅔ cup lowfat milk and 2 teaspoons superfine sugar into a pan. Heat gently until lukewarm, stirring to dissolve the sugar. Pour into a bowl. Add a ¼-ounce sachet of active dry yeast, stir, cover, and let froth for 5 to 10 minutes, until it has developed a good head. Sift scant 3¼ cups all-purpose flour into a bowl. Add a pinch of salt, 1 teaspoon baking powder, and 1–2 teaspoons onion seeds. Add the yeast mix, 2 tablespoons vegetable oil, 1 beaten egg, and ⅔ cup yogurt, and mix together into a dough. Shape into a ball, sit on a lightly floured board, and knead for 10 minutes or knead in a machine for 8 minutes.

Sprinkle with flour, cover, and let rise in a warm place for an hour or so until doubled in size. Put a large baking sheet in your oven and preheat to its highest setting. Put your broiler onto high. Slap your dough back onto the board. Knead for a minute then divide into 8 bits. Roll each into a long, teardrop shape. Brush with a little melted butter and scatter with a few more onion seeds. Remove the hot sheet from the oven, cover with half your naan, and bang back into the oven for 3 to 4 minutes until they've puffed up. Broil for a few seconds ntil golden. Remove. Cover with a dish towel while you finish the rest.

Fish and Shellfish

My tasty relationship with fish began with my grandad. A keen fisherman, he taught me how to value it for what it is—versatile eating and brilliantly nutritious. If you're not catching your own, get to a good fish supplier (or even the fish counter in a supermarket) and treat yourself to some fishy banter. These guys will tell you what's freshest and in season, will do all the tricky descaling, butterflying, and cleaning as well as advising you on how to cook your chosen fish. Most importantly though they can tell you what's sustainable, as many fish and shellfish stocks are seriously depleted these days. Sourcing sorted, it's down to your skill set. Don't overload your delicate fish with heavy sauces, try and keep it simple so the fresh fish flavors shine through. Doneness is all: fish is at its very best when it's only just cooked. Don't rely on cooking guides—trust your eye.

Is it fresh?
WHAT TO LOOK (AND SNIFF) FOR...

WHOLE FISH:

EYES Fish eyes should sparkle brightly and look lively.
GILLS The undersides should be bright red (oxygenated) and clean.
SKIN Should be glistening, with shiny scales intact and undiminished natural patterning.
GENERAL The whole fish should look stiff, firm, and moist, with a stiff tail as though it's just posing before swimming off. If it looks sad, soft, dull, don't buy it.
SMELL IT Sea fish should have a faint but refreshing and pleasant tang of the sea. If fish smells unpleasant it will taste that way—don't be ripped off. Don't buy it.

FILLETS/STEAKS Harder to tell, but white fish should be white and translucent.

SMOKED FISH Choose glossy-looking fish.

SHRIMP Raw shrimp should be firm and glistening with no black age spots.

MUSSELS go for cleaner, undamaged shells (not shells caked in mud/covered in barnacles).

— ONCE HOOKED — –BEST STORAGE

Fish spoils fast (oily fish faster than white) so **EAT** fresh fish within 24 hours of buying.

Get it home **FAST** and into the refrigerator. Store it at 32–41°F.

RINSE whole fish, pat dry, sit on a plate, and seal with plastic wrap before storing at the bottom of the refrigerator.

LEAVE prepacked fish in its packaging until you cook it.

KEEP smoked fish well-sealed, so it doesn't flavor other foods.

LET fish return to room temperature for 30 minutes before cooking.

DEFROST frozen fish in the refrigerator, then drain and pat dry before using.

CATCH OF THE DAY

Always try and get hold of sustainably caught fish where possible. The asterisked fish in this list are those that have been overfished and are the ones where you should do your best to make sure you are buying from a sustainable source. For advice on sustainable buying, check the Marine Conservation Society website (www.mcsuk.org)

OILY FISH

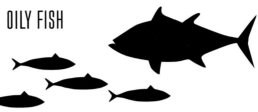

SALMON A hugely nutritious, affordable, versatile pink fleshed fish. Get steaks, fillets, or whole. Avoid Atlantic (over-fished). Organic farmed is best. Pan-fry, griddle, broil, BBQ, roast, bake, poach, steam, or stir-fry. Cook in foil or paper packages. Good in fishcakes and pies. Bake or poach whole. Smoked salmon is convenient but can be expensive. Get cheaper offcuts to throw into pasta dishes, salads, sandwiches, or bagels with cream cheese.

TROUT Brown or rainbow, whole or filleted. Go for organic farmed. Cook as salmon.
MACKEREL Super-food on a budget with a distinctive taste and fast cook. Buy whole or fillets. Pan-fry, broil, or BBQ. Smoked mackerel is vacuum-packed and its long shelf life makes it a good buy.
SARDINES Abundant, richly nutritious, cheap, chic, and sleek. Broil and BBQ over high heat for a crispy skin. Canned sardines are great on toast.

ANCHOVIES Get marinated from delis for salads and baking into casseroles/pasta dishes/fish pies. Canned/bottled are salty and need soaking in milk for an hour before using. Sophisticated, cheap, and nutritious—a brilliant ingredient for beefing up your cooking.
HERRING Kipper (the smoked version) is very cheap, highly nutritious, and easy to cook. Bang one or two, head down in a deep pitcher. Cover with boiling water. Leave for 2 to 3 minutes. Remove. Eat with bread and butter.
TUNA Expensive and threatened. Best left alone for now.

WHITE FISH

COD* An overfished delicious full-flaked fish. It comes as loin, fillets, or whole. Buy sustainable line-caught and try substitutes. Pan-fry, griddle, broil, poach, batter, bread crumb, or bake. Makes perfect fishcakes/pie/fish and French fries/fish fingers.
HADDOCK* Sweeter than cod but good flakes. Get fillets, steaks, or whole and use as cod. Smoked haddock is great added to pies, fishcakes, kedgeree, or omelets for character.
HAKE* A cod cousin with a more subtle, but meaty, flavor.

FLOUNDER* Fine-textured and delicate. Get it whole or filleted. Fast pan-fry or coat it in bread crumbs or batter.
SEA BASS Popular fish with a fine texture, and really good flavor, which can be baked whole or stuffed. Fillets are great for fast cooking.
LEMON SOLE Thin and delicate. Fry the fillets simply.
SEA ROBIN A cheap, meaty white fish to use in stews/curries/soups.

TILAPIA A firm white fish which takes strong marinades. Broil/fry/bake/BBQ.
BREAM A sweet firm fish. Good baked whole and barbecued with garlic/lemon.
MONKFISH Sold as steaks from the tail and cheeks. It's lean, expensive, bone-free, and works with strong flavors. Marinate raw (ceviche), wrap, bake, or BBQ.
SOLE* Expensive and delicate. A fish supplier will skin the dark side for you. Fry or broil whole with the white skin on.

SHELLFISH

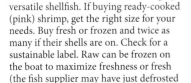  

MUSSELS Sweet, cheap, and nutritious. Buy live part-cleaned rope-grown mussels by weight or in neat nets.
SHRIMP Nutritious, delicate, and highly versatile shellfish. If buying ready-cooked (pink) shrimp, get the right size for your needs. Buy fresh or frozen and twice as many if their shells are on. Check for a sustainable label. Raw can be frozen on the boat to maximize freshness or fresh (the fish supplier may have just defrosted

them so ask). They will be gray/black/blue and of varying sizes. Uncooked shrimp need to be deveined. Pan-fry/griddle/stir-fry/BBQ/broil/poach/steam/bake, or add to curries/pies/bakes/tapas/salads/sandwiches/shrimp cocktails.
OYSTERS A sensual treat and best eaten raw. Shells need to be closed tight and undamaged. Get native/rock/pacific. Farmed native are available all year.

CRAB Filled with delicate white and rich brown meat. Get freshly boiled crabs or ready-dressed to eat with mayo, etc.
LOBSTER Hugely expensive. Freeze then boil or steam in the shell, or split and broil/BBQ.
SCALLOPS Sold in the shell or ready-shucked (look for plump, sweet smelling specimens with a pink coral). They're expensive, versatile, and good pan-fried or steamed.

FISH SKILLS

DESCALE A good crisp bit of fish skin is delicious but it usually needs descaling. Ask your fish supplier or do it yourself. Fish like flounder or mackerel have fine scales so leave them on, but larger fish like salmon, cod, haddock, and bass need attention. Do so before cleaning (if necessary). Snip off the gills with scissors and hold the fish by the tail in a plastic bag (or scales cover everything). Working from the tail toward the head, scrape down smoothly but firmly with the back of a chef's knife. The scales will pop off.

CLEAN Most fish is sold cleaned. If it hasn't been, ask the fish supplier to do it for you, or do it yourself (it's easy). Set up next to the sink. Snip the gills off with scissors. Use the scissors or a sharp knife to snip or slash along the belly line from the tail toward the head, stopping short of the gills. Pull the inner bits out with your fingers and discard. Rinse the cavity of your fish under running water, using fingers or a teaspoon to scrape out any stubborn bits. Drain and pat dry.

FILLET Ask your fish supplier. Or…

FLAT FISH

1. Sit it on a board.

2. Feel for the central bone. Insert the blade and cut the fish from head to tail just to the left of the bone, cutting down to it.

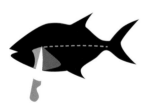

3. With the knife almost flat and working from the bone to the edge, use big long smooth strokes to cut the first fish fillet away from the bones, separating them cleanly. Keep it neat with as little wastage as possible.

4. Turn the fish and separate the second fillet.
5. Turn over and repeat. Trim the fillets.

ROUND FISH
1. Sit it on a board

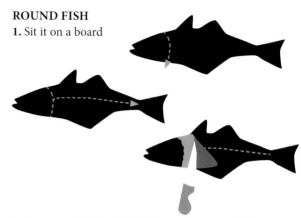

2. Cut around the back of the head down to the bone. Cut the skin from the head to the tail along one side of the backbone. Using the knife flat as above, cut long even strokes to separate the flesh and bone, pulling the fillet away as you cut. Turn and repeat.

SKIN Sit your fish fillet, skin-side down, on a board. Using your flexible knife, tuck the sharp blade edge between the skin and the flesh. Hold the skin in one hand (salt your fingers) and, holding the knife at a 45 degree angle, use a sawing action to separate the two.

DEBONE Check every bit of fish you cook for pin bones. Run your fingers over the flesh and nip out any offenders with tweezers.

CLEANING MUSSELS Start by discarding any that don't close when tapped sharply and any cracked/damaged mussels. Scrape away any barnacles using the back of a knife. Scrub and scrape them under running water. Rinse several times. Pull out the beards (threads) just before cooking.

Shelling and deveining shrimp
Pull the heads off. Peel the shells off smoothly. Use a sharp knife to cut along the black vein running along the back. Remove it with your fingers or the top of the knife. Rinse and pat dry. To butterfly, cut through the back and splay open without cutting all the way through. Rinse again and pat dry.

DOCTORS FISH & SHELLFISH

Fish and shellfish are stacked with **SUPER-NUTRIENTS** eat at least twice a week and keep it varied. They're high in

PROTEINS

for essential growth and development and are very low in fat, so suit weight watchers. SHRIMP, MUSSELS, AND SARDINES CONTAIN →**IRON** which protect against anemia, **ZINC** WHICH STRENGTHENS THE IMMUNE SYSTEM AND *Selenium* WHICH SUPPORTS THE LIVER. Crab, oysters, lobster are hot on

COPPER

which is great for the skin, hair, vision, teeth, bones, and heart, while mackerel is packed with **VITAMIN D** essential for healthy teeth and bones.

LINOLEIC ACID

in salmon helps with nerve repair and is good for hair and skin. OILY FISH IS UNIQUELY RICH IN FATTY ACIDS **OMEGA-3 & OMEGA-6** balancing good/bad cholesterol, boosting heart health, memory, protecting against blood clots, soothing arthritis, and helping with skin and nerve problems.

FRIENDS

WHITE FISH
BACON, BUTTER, CABBAGE, CHEESE SAUCE, CORIANDER, DILL, GARLIC, HUMMUS, KETCHUP, LEMON, LIME, OLIVES, ONIONS, PARSLEY, PEAS, POTATOES, SCALLIONS, TAPENADE, TOMATO SAUCE, VINEGAR, WINE

SMOKED FISH
BACON, CHEDDAR CHEESE, CREAM, MILK, MUSTARD, POACHED AND BOILED EGGS, ONIONS, PARSLEY, POTATOES

FISH IS HIGH IN KEY *B vitamins* INCLUDING **B12** ESSENTIAL for growth and blood health and **B6** WHICH AIDS insulin production, boosts blood health, and helps to counter PMT, diabetes, asthma, and depression. BONE-BUILDING

CALCIUM

can be found in fish bones of sardines, whitebait, anchovies.

OILY FISH
BEET, CUCUMBER, CHILE, CUMIN, CURRY PASTE, GARLIC, GINGER, HARISSA PASTE, LEMON, LIME, MUSTARD, OLIVES, ONION, POTATOES, RHUBARB, WASABI

SHELLFISH
BACON, BREAD CRUMBS, CAPERS, CHEESE SAUCE, CHICKEN, CHILES, CIDER, COCONUT MILK, CORIANDER, CUCUMBER, DILL, EGGS, GARLIC, GRUYERE AND CHEDDAR CHEESE, LEMON, LIME, MAYONNAISE, NOODLES, OLIVES, PARSLEY, THYME, WHITE WINE

IS IT DONE YET?

Raw fish is translucent. It becomes **OPAQUE** as it cooks (or sets) and starts to look obviously **FLAKY**.

So, **POKE IT** in the thickest part with a sharp knife to check. You'll quickly learn the right feel and look. Fish will continue to cook when you take it off the heat, so factor that in. If it's not done, bang it back.

POACHED SHRIMP WITH MAYO AND SHALLOT VINEGAR

 HEALTHY FAST **FEEDS 2**

INGREDIENTS

1 x essential mayonnaise (p153) or
   6–8 tablespoons store-bought mayo
generous 3½ quarts cold water
3 tablespoons salt
8 peppercorns
2–3 celery stalks (optional)
¼ of a lemon (optional)
8–16 raw North Atlantic/king/jumbo
   shrimp, shells on
SHALLOT VINEGAR
2 shallots, peeled
4–6 tablespoons malt vinegar
2 teaspoons superfine sugar

——— CHANGE IT UP———
Switch the mayo for aioli (p100).

Speedy preparation for a lovely, lazy lunch: enjoy yourself with the cracking and dipping ritual. If you're feeling flush, switch the shrimp for Dublin bay prawns. The mayo/vinegar combo here is great with stacks of crab, mussels, and other shellfish. Shrimp aren't just delicious—they're brilliantly good for you.

PREP Start with the dips. If you are making your own mayo, do so at least an hour ahead and chill. Make the shallot vinegar: dice the peeled shallots. Mix with the vinegar and sugar in a bowl.

Make up a court bouillon (poaching liquid): Measure the cold water and pour into a large pan. Add the salt, peppercorns, and optional celery/lemon and bring to a boil on high heat.

COOK Add the shrimp to the boiling water. Cook for 1 minute or a little longer for larger shrimp. Test. They should rise as they're done, feel firm, and turn pink. Remove, drain, and cool in a single layer.

PLATE Spoon mayo onto the side of your plates. Serve the vinegar in two small bowls for spooning onto the shrimp. Pile the shrimp onto the plates and serve with slices of buttered brown bread/soda bread muffins (p205) and lemon wedges. To eat: pull the heads off the shrimp and peel and crack the outer shells and legs off with your fingers. Devein (p134), if necessary. Alternatively, peel the cooked shrimp before plating.

BONUS BITES

BROILED FRESH SHRIMP
Heat the broiler to high. Thread as many raw shrimp as you fancy (shells on) lengthwise head through to tail onto small metal skewers. Broil them for 3 minutes per side, or until firm and pink. Sprinkle with salt. Dip into mayo or garlic butter (p138).

BBQ SHRIMP
Defrost as many frozen peeled jumbo shrimp as you like and marinate in a mix of chopped garlic, grated lemon zest, and olive oil for 2 hours. Skewer them lengthwise. Season and cook on a lightly oiled rack for 1 to 2 minutes per side, or until firm but still juicy.

SALT AND PEPPER SHRIMP IN CRISPY BREAD CRUMBS
Shell, devein, and butterfly 8 large raw jumbo shrimp (p134). Toss them in a mix of generous ⅓ cup all-purpose flour, 1 teaspoon fine salt, 1 teaspoon crushed Sichuan/black peppercorns, and ¼ teaspoon Chinese five spice powder. Dip in beaten egg then roll on a plate of panko/homemade dried bread crumbs (p201). Deep-fry in a pan one-third full of peanut oil (hot enough to cook a cube of bread in 30 seconds) and cook for 1 to 2 minutes, or until golden-crisp but pink inside. Drain on paper towel. Dip in a mix of 2 tablespoons superfine sugar, juice of ½ a lime, 2 tablespoons soy sauce, 2 tablespoons rice wine, and 1 tablespoon black rice/malt vinegar.

MUSSELS IN CIDER AND BACON WITH A MUSTARD CREAM SAUCE

 HEALTHY FAST   FEEDS 2

Seafood, cider, and smoky bacon (or use real ale for a darker sauce); team these nutritious fast-food beauties with crisp frites for a luxurious classic on a budget.

INGREDIENTS

2¼ pounds mussels
3 ounces smoked bacon
4 shallots/1 onion, peeled
2 garlic cloves, peeled
a few tarragon leaves/thyme sprigs
1 tablespoon olive oil
generous ¾ cup cider/real ale
1 tablespoon lemon juice (only if using cider)
scant ¼ cup heavy cream
¾ teaspoon Dijon mustard
a handful of Italian parsley, chopped

—— CHANGE IT UP ——

1. Switch the frites for shallow-fry fries (p78) or sweet potato wedges (p82)
2. For simple mussels, chuck a small wineglass of water/white wine/beer/cider to the pan, add the mussels, and cook until opened.

—— BONUS BITE ——

MUSSELS BAKED IN GARLIC BUTTER
Cook the mussels simply (see above) until all opened. Drain. Separate the shells and discard the tops. Sit the remaining halves on an ovenproof dish. Preheat the oven to 375°F. Cream ¾ cup soft butter with 3 crushed garlic cloves, 1 tablespoon minced onion/shallot, and 1 tablespoon minced parsley/tarragon and spoon evenly over the mussels. Sprinkle with 2 tablespoons dried bread crumbs (p201) and grated Parmesan/Cheddar/Gruyère cheese. Bake for 10 minutes. Eat straight from the oven with bread to soak up the garlicky juices.

·········· TIME SAVER ··········

The frites can be prepared and given their first fry up to 24 hours in advance of eating. Cover and chill until needed.

PREP

MUSSELS: Select, scrub, and clean the mussels as per the detailed process on p134, discarding any that are cracked, damaged, or refuse to close when tapped. Scrub them several times and tug out any black fibrous beards. SAUCE: slice the bacon into strips. Mince the shallots/onion. Crush the garlic. Finely slice the tarragon or strip the thyme.

COOK

Heat a wide sauté pan/casserole dish large enough to take all the mussels. Add the oil. Throw in the bacon and fry gently for 5 minutes. Remove with a slotted spoon. Add the shallots and garlic. Stir and fry very gently in the bacon oil for 5 minutes, or until soft and translucent. Increase the heat. Add the cider and lemon juice or the real ale and bring the mix to a boil. At that moment, whack the mussels in. Cover the pan immediately and cook for 3 to 4 minutes, shuffling the pan a few times to keep it even. Turn the mussels once and check progress. Once they're opened, drain the pot into a colander over a bowl. Keep the mussels warm. Return the liquid to the pan. Add the tarragon/thyme and boil for a minute to reduce and intensify the flavor. Add the cream and mustard. Stir, boil taste, and season it. Add the bacon. Pile the mussels into bowls. Pour over the sauce and scatter over parsley.

PLATE

Serve with warm bread to soak up the juices and frites (below) or French fries to dip into mayo.

TO GO WITH

FRITES

First fry (an hour before needed): Peel 2 large mealy potatoes (1¼ pounds). Cut across into ¼-inch slices. Stack and slice into ¼-inch sticks. Soak in cold water for 30 minutes. Drain. Dry thoroughly. Heat peanut oil to 320°F in a deep fryer or flat-bottom wok or pan no more than one-third full until a cube of bread will brown in 60 seconds. Add the frites gradually, in batches if you have to—don't overfill and don't leave the pan at any time—and cook for 6 minutes or until soft but still pale. Drain in the fryer basket or use a slotted spoon to lift onto paper towels. Set aside. Final fry: reheat the oil in the fryer to 350°F. A cube of bread browns in 30 seconds. Fry frites for 1 to 2 minutes until golden. Lift onto paper towels. Keep warm in a preheated oven at 350°F until needed.

THAI-STEAMED MUSSELS

 FEEDS 2

INGREDIENTS

a thumb-sized piece of fresh ginger
1 lemongrass stalk
4 scallions
1 large red chile
1 large handful of cilantro
1 lime
1 tablespoon peanut oil
1¾ cups coconut milk
1¼ pounds mussels, cleaned and
    debearded (p134)
salt or a shake or two of fish sauce
    (optional)

PREP Peel the ginger and cut into thin sticks. Crush the thin end of the lemongrass to bruise it. Cut off a 1¼-inch piece. Mince it. Slice the scallions thinly. Seed and chop the chile (p16). Chop the cilantro roughly. Halve the lime.

COOK Heat the oil in a wok or large, wide skillet. Add the ginger, lemongrass, scallions, and chile. Stir continuously over medium heat for 2 minutes, or until soft and fragrant. Add the coconut milk and the juice of half of your lime. Stir and let it bubble for 2 to 3 minutes to integrate the flavors. Add the mussels. Raise the heat a bit and cover. Cook for 3 to 4 minutes, stirring once or twice, until the mussels have opened.

Scoop the mussels into bowls using a slotted spoon. Taste the sauce. Season with a little salt or fish sauce if you think it needs it and add half the cilantro. If you'd rather have the sauce a little thicker, cook it for a few minutes longer.

PLATE Pour the sauce over the mussels and top with the remaining cilantro. Cut the remaining lime half into wedges and serve on the side. Eat with good bread for soaking up the juices.

MUSSEL AND TOMATO LINGUINE

 FEEDS 2

INGREDIENTS

4 tablespoons olive oil
4 shallots/1 onion, minced
½ red chile, seeded and diced
4 garlic cloves, 3 of which chopped
⅔ cup dry white wine
1 x 16-ounces can of chopped tomatoes
1 tablespoon tomato paste
a pinch of superfine sugar
1 teaspoon capers, drained
salt and pepper
6 ounces linguine
2–3 tablespoons torn Italian parsley/
    basil
1 pound fresh mussels, cleaned
    and debearded (p134)
a little bit of butter

PREP Make the sauce. Heat 2 tablespoons of the oil in a deep, wide skillet, add the shallot/onion and chile, and fry on low heat for 5 minutes. Add the chopped garlic and cook for a few minutes until soft but not colored. Increase the heat and pour in half the wine. Let it bubble for a few seconds, then add the tomatoes, tomato paste, sugar, and capers and season. Reduce the heat after 30 seconds. Simmer on low for 20 minutes, stirring occasionally and checking that the sauce doesn't dry out. Set aside.

COOK Boil a large pan of salted water. Add the linguine and cook for 7 to 8 minutes from when the water reboils or as the package directs. Meantime, put the tomato sauce onto reheat. As it begins to simmer, add the herbs, the rest of the oil, and the remaining wine. Let it bubble for 1 minute. Taste and adjust the seasoning. Bang the mussels into the pan. Slam the lid on. Cook on medium/high heat for 3 minutes, covered, turning once or twice. Taste and adjust the seasoning.

Drain the pasta. Return it to the pan. Crush the remaining garlic clove and stir through the pasta with the butter. Season with salt and pepper.

PLATE Divide the pasta between 2 large plates or wide shallow bowls and spoon the mussels and sauce on top, or mix everything together in one big bowl if you prefer it that way.

FAST SHALLOW-FRY FISH WITH DRESSED PEAS
AND HERB AND GARLIC POTATOES

HEALTHY

FEEDS 2

Beautifully simple: enjoy it for what it is. Use whatever type of white fish fillet you like—flounder, lemon sole, sea bass, cod, haddock, or hake—it's up to you.

INGREDIENTS

*2 x 4–6 ounces good fresh/defrosted
    white fish fillets, skins on
2–3 tablespoons all-purpose flour
salt and pepper
olive/peanut oil and
    butter, or clarified butter
1 lemon*

DRESSED PEAS

*1 cup frozen/fresh peas
2 teaspoons white wine vinegar
½ teaspoon Dijon mustard
1 teaspoon superfine sugar/honey
4 teaspoons olive oil*

HERB AND GARLIC POTATOES

*2 large potatoes
1 tablespoon olive oil
1–2 tablespoons fresh rosemary
    needles (or a good sprinkle of dried)
2 garlic cloves, peeled and crushed
a little bit of butter*

—— CHANGE IT UP ——

Make a maître d'hôtel butter by mixing 4 tablespoons soft butter with 1 tablespoon chopped parsley/dill/tarragon/basil, 2 teaspoons lemon juice, salt, and pepper. Add to your fried fish for an instant sauce.

PREP Organize your fish: If your fish supplier hasn't done so already, descale it (p134). Then feel it all over to check for large or smaller pin bones (they're often not visible) and remove them with tweezers. Pat the fish dry and set aside until needed.

Potatoes: peel and cut the potatoes into ½–¾-inch cubes. Put a heavy-bottom skillet on medium heat. Add a good coating of oil. When hot, add the potatoes, rosemary, and garlic. Fry them gently for 15 to 20 minutes, checking and turning for even cooking, until the potatoes are crispy and golden.

Mix the dressing for the peas: Beat the vinegar, mustard, sugar/honey, and a pinch of salt in a bowl until amalgamated. Beat the oil in very slowly. Taste and adjust for balance and seasoning. Boil the peas in a little salted water for 3 minutes. Drain and add to the bowl.

Fetch the fish. Spread the flour on a plate and season with salt and pepper. Turn the fish in the flour to coat.

COOK Heat a skillet that's large enough to take both bits of fish (or fry them in turn). Add a bit of oil and butter or use clarified butter. When it's pretty hot, add the fish fillets, skin-side down. Cook for 2 minutes, until the skin is very crispy and the upper edges look opaque. Press down with a spatula if it arches up. Turn and cook for another 1 to 2 minutes or until done. It's best moist, not dry. Don't overcook it.

PLATE Lay your magnificent fish on a warm plate, skin-side up so it stays crisp. Add the peas in dressing. Serve the potatoes in bowls with mayo and ketchup or tartare sauce.

HOW TO
CLARIFY BUTTER

Butter burns at low temperatures; clarify it (lose the salt/milk solids/impurities) and it manages much greater heat, adds gloss to a sauce, and keeps for much longer. Use it to pan-fry fish, shellfish, omelets, and sauté meats without browning/burning.

Sit generous **1 CUP BUTTER** (or the amount you need) in a heavy-bottom pan. Leave to **MELT VERY GENTLY** on very low heat. **DON'T STIR/TOUCH/DISTURB IT**. Remove from the heat. It will have split into **3 LAYERS. SKIM THE FOAM** from the top using a large metal spoon; discard it. **POUR OFF** the middle layer to keep—store it in the refrigerator or freeze. **DISCARD** the bottom **MILKY LAYER**; or stir it into a sauce or soup if there's one going.

GRIDDLED MACKEREL WITH PICKLED CUCUMBER AND BEET AND POTATO SALAD

FEEDS 2

How to magic a piece of regular oily fish into something pretty special? It's all about the contrasts, as ever. Beet and mackerel's a classic combination. The pickle adds a bright note.

INGREDIENTS

4 small mackerel fillets
  (see p134 if prepping your own)
scant ¾ cup all-purpose flour
salt and pepper
a little bit of softened butter
a handful of corn salad or watercress
1 tablespoon lemon juice
½ teaspoon sugar
3 tablespoons olive oil

BEET AND POTATO SALAD

11 ounces waxy salad potatoes
5 ounces cooked beet
4 tablespoons crème fraîche
2–3 teaspoons horseradish sauce
a squeeze of lemon juice
4 tablespoons chopped chives

CUCUMBER PICKLE

1 tablespoon cider vinegar
1 tablespoon superfine sugar
2 shallots, peeled and finely sliced
½ cucumber

PREP Start with the potato salad: Boil the potatoes in salted water until tender. Peel and cut them into ¾-inch cubes. Cube the beet similarly. Mix the crème fraîche, horseradish, lemon juice, and some seasoning together, tasting and adjusting until it's got a bit of a kick to it. Add the cubed veg and chives and turn them through. Set aside.

Mix the pickle: Stir the vinegar, sugar, shallots, and a pinch of salt together. Slice the cucumber very thinly. Add to the liquid and set aside.

Check the fish for pin bones, removing any you find with tweezers. Spread the flour on a plate and season with salt and pepper. Turn the fish to coat it, patting gently between your hands to remove any excess flour. Spread softened butter evenly over the fleshy top of each fillet.

Wash the salad greens. Put the lemon juice and sugar in a bowl with a good pinch of salt and a bit of pepper. Whisk/beat the oil in drop by drop until combined. Set aside.

COOK Put a griddle or stovetop grill pan onto high heat. Sit the fish, buttered-side down, onto the pan to sear. Cook for 2 to 3 minutes until the skin is crisp. Turn and cook for 1 minute until done. Remove at once.

PLATE Sit the cooked mackerel on plates and season with salt and pepper. Dress the salad greens in lemon dressing and heap those on. Add a pile of drained, pickled cucumber and the potato salad. Enjoy with soda bread (p205) and butter.

BONUS BITES

GRIDDLED HARISSA MACKEREL (OR TROUT)
Stuff 2 cleaned, descaled mackerel/trout with a bit of cilantro, 2 sliced garlic cloves, the juice of 1 lemon/lime, a little salt, and 1 small, seeded sliced chile. Slash the outer skin 3 times diagonally. Push a little extra sliced garlic into the slits then rub the fish all over with a mix of 2 tablespoons harissa paste and 1 tablespoon olive oil. Chill for 30 minutes. Cook on a searing hot griddle or stovetop grill pan for 3 minutes per side, or until cooked through. Serve with a pile of well-seasoned couscous tossed with cilantro, lemon juice, and olive oil.

A BIG PIECE OF PAN-ROASTED WHITE FISH WITH CHAMP

HEALTHY

FEEDS 2

Let the fish shine through: never rely on timing guides with this delicate ingredient. It's all about eye, touch, and building up your judgment. Here's a truly glorious taste-fest.

INGREDIENTS

2 x 9 ounces good fresh firm thick white fish fillets (sustainable haddock/cod, etc.), skin on
salt and pepper
2 tablespoons olive oil
CHAMP
3 garlic cloves
2 scallions
1 pound mealy potatoes
5 tablespoons butter
3–4 tablespoons heavy cream/milk

TIP

If you don't have an ovenproof pan, just slide the fish onto a metal baking sheet before transferring to the oven.

········ **TIME SAVER** ········

Frozen white fish fillets come ready-skinned and deboned. Defrost a few hours ahead to cut your prep time down. Pour off any excess water and pat dry before flouring.

——— **BONUS BITE** ———

TASTY FISH KEBABS

Chop 4 x 4-ounce pieces of white fish/mackerel into bite-size chunks. Marinate in a mix of the juice of 1 lemon/lime, 2 crushed garlic cloves, 2 tablespoons olive oil, 2 tablespoons chopped cilantro, and a bit of salt and pepper, for 30 minutes. Thread onto metal skewers. Broil under a preheated broiler for 3 to 4 minutes, turning, until the fish is cooked through. Eat with paprika mayo (⅔ cup mayo mixed with 1 teaspoon smoked paprika) and shallow-fry fries (p78).

PREP Make the champ: Peel the garlic and slice the scallions. Boil the potatoes and garlic in a pan of lightly salted water for 20 minutes, or until tender when tested. Peel and press through a potato ricer into the warm pan or mash it in there. Add two-thirds of the butter, the cream or milk, and season with salt and pepper. Beat until smooth. Stir in the scallion. Add the remaining butter, cover with foil, and keep warm.

Meantime, prep the fish: If your fish supplier hasn't already done so, descale and debone your fillets, removing large bones and pin bones with tweezers. Pat the fish dry. Season with salt and pepper. Set aside until needed. Preheat the oven to 425°F.

COOK Heat the oil in a large ovenproof pan on high heat. Add the fish, skin-side down. Fry for 2 minutes, or until very crisp, then transfer to the oven. Roast for 6 minutes or until the fish is opaque but moist (check frequently as this is size-dependent).

PLATE Spoon champ onto plates. Sit the fish on top. Eat with onion marmalade (below) and lemon wedges. Or fresh herb salsa (p118). Or a mixture of diced cherry tomatoes and black olives in balsamic dressing.

TO GO WITH

ONION MARMALADE

Thinly slice 1½ pounds red and 1½ pounds white onions. Heat 4 teaspoons olive oil and 2 teaspoons butter in a large heavy-bottom pan. Add the onions, ¼ teaspoon black pepper, 1 cup dark brown sugar, ¼ cup white sugar, and an (optional) cheesecloth-wrapped stem of rosemary. Simmer on low heat for 40 minutes to reduce, checking and stirring regularly. When soft and amalgamated, remove the rosemary, if using, and add 2 cups red wine, scant ¼ cup water, scant ¼ cup balsamic vinegar, ⅔ cup red wine vinegar, 4 crushed garlic cloves, 2 teaspoons lemon juice, and 2 pinches of sea salt. Boil fiercely. Reduce and fast cook (checking it doesn't burn) for 20 to 30 minutes, or until the mix is sticky. Taste and adjust seasoning. Remove and spoon into a clean sterilized jar. Seal until airtight.

CLASSIC SEASIDE
FISH CAKES

FEEDS 3 TO 4

Simple but delicious: a bit of very lightly poached white fish with just a taste of smoked fish folded into the driest of mashed potato with some Italian parsley, then fried off. A luxury budget meal.

INGREDIENTS

1 pound mealy potatoes
salt and pepper
1 x 12-ounce fillet of fresh/defrosted
*   white fish (sustainable haddock/cod,*
*   etc.), skin on*
4 ounces smoked haddock
*   (undyed if you can get it)*
1 plump shallot, peeled and grated
milk, to cover
4 tablespoons torn Italian parsley
2–3 tablespoons all-purpose flour
olive/peanut oil and a bit of butter, for
*   frying (or use clarified butter p141)*

PREP Boil the whole, unpeeled potatoes in salted water for 20 minutes, or until tender. Drain well. Strip the skins away. Press through a ricer for the smoothest mashed potato or use a fork/masher to bash out the lumps. Season lightly with salt and pepper.

Poach the fish: bang it into a large skillet/pan in a single layer with the shallot and season. Cover with the milk. Bring to the point of boiling, then reduce the heat and simmer for 3 minutes, until the fish is barely cooked (white outside, still a bit gelatinous inside). Remove with a slotted spoon. Remove any skin and tweeze out stray bones without breaking the fish pieces up too much. Cool before mixing carefully into the potato with the torn parsley, trying to keep the chunks of fish nice and large. Chill for 1 hour or until firm.

Sprinkle the flour on a plate and season with salt and pepper. Shape the fish and potato mixture into 4–6 cakes with damp hands. Turn the fish cakes in the flour to coat and protect them well. Chill until needed or cook now.

COOK Preheat the oven to 400°F. Heat the oil and butter in an ovenproof pan. Fry the cakes on medium heat for 2 minutes per side until golden, then finish in the oven for 10 minutes. Or fry, turning once, until crisply golden outside and piping hot all through.

PLATE Enjoy these crisp, fishy beauties with a heap of peas or a bit of steamed broccoli drizzled with Caesar dressing (p29); or eat with shallow-fry fries (p78) and tartare sauce (p150).

BONUS BITES

CRUNCHY SALMON AND BLACK OLIVE FISH CAKES
Make up 8 ounces mashed potato as above, adding ¾ cup minced onion fried in 1 tablespoon olive oil until soft. Mix in 2 tablespoons torn cilantro and 8 chopped black olives and season. Poach 2 x 4-ounce pieces salmon for 3 minutes as above but using water, not milk. Remove from the water, strip off the skin, and break up into rough chunks. Cool before mixing into the mash and chilling as above. Shape into 4 cakes and turn in seasoned white flour. Dip into beaten egg then roll in a few good handfuls of panko or homemade dried bread crumbs (p201) to coat. Fry for 5 minutes per side (or fry/bake as above)until hot and golden.

CHILI AND LEMONGRASS BABY CAKES
Chop and drop 12 ounces deboned, skin-free white fish into a processor. Add 1 cup fresh white bread crumbs, 2 teaspoons minced lemongrass, 3 fat chopped garlic cloves, the sliced whites of 5 scallions, 1–2 seeded red chiles, the juice of 1–2 limes, 2 teaspoons fish sauce, 2–3 tablespoons chopped cilantro, and a little salt. Pulse for a few seconds until processed but not too finely. Shape into 6–8 little cakes. Turn in seasoned flour to coat and dip in beaten egg. Fry in peanut oil for 2 to 3 minutes per side or until cooked through. Dip into chili or other sauce or serve on top of noodle salad.

A VERY PROPER
FISH PIE

FEEDS 4

INGREDIENTS

1 pound 2 ounces thick fresh white fish fillets, skin on
5 ounces smoked haddock
4 ounces hot-smoked salmon
1 onion, peeled and halved
a few black peppercorns
2 garlic cloves, peeled
1¾ cups milk
salt and pepper
5 ounces cooked shrimp
2 hard-boiled eggs
a squeeze of lemon juice
SAUCE
2 heaping tablespoons butter
scant ¼ cup all-purpose flour
scant ½ cup dry white wine
scant ½ cup heavy cream
1 tablespoon chopped fresh dill
   (or parsley/tarragon)
TOPPING
3 pounds mealy potatoes
2 tablespoons butter
a good squeeze of lemon juice
a handful of grated Gruyère cheese
2–4 tablespoons milk
salt and pepper

—— CHANGE IT UP ——

1. Add mussels to the pie. Add a dozen or so cleaned mussels to a pan with 2 tablespoons white wine or water and cook (p138). Extract the mussels from their shells and add to the fish when assembling. Strain the juices and add to the sauce to boost the flavor.

2. Replace the mashed potato with a puff pastry topping. Assemble the pie as far as the topping, putting a pie funnel in the center of the dish if you have one. Thinly roll out a piece of bought all-butter puff pastry to fit your pie dish, cover, and crimp the edges. Brush with a mix of beaten egg and milk and bake for 30 minutes, until crispy and golden.

This is fish pie done properly. No shortcuts, and building layers of texture and flavor. If you're not into shrimp use extra white fish. For real depth of flavor, add the mussels (below).

PREP Make the topping: Peel the potatoes and bring them to a boil in a large pan of cold, lightly salted water. Lower the heat and simmer for 15 to 20 minutes, or until tender when pierced with a knife or skewer. Drain then bang them back into the pan and shuffle over low heat for a minute or so to dry them. Put them through a ricer if you have one or mash them. Add the butter, lemon juice, Gruyère, and half the milk and beat well. Add the remaining milk only if needed (don't let it get too wet—you'll want it to hold texture and crisp up) and season to taste.

Sit the white and smoked fish in a large skillet/roasting pan. Add the onion, peppercorns, and garlic. Cover with the milk and add a pinch of salt. Simmer over very low heat until the fish is just cooked. This may take as little as 3 minutes depending on thickness. Scoop each piece out as it's done and put it on a plate. Set the milk aside. Peel any skin off the fish, trying not to break it up. Feel for any bones and remove. Set aside. Preheat the oven to 400°F.

Make the sauce. Strain the reserved milk through a strainer. Put it into a pitcher and add any juices from the fish plate. Melt the butter in a large heavy-bottom pan. Add the flour. Stir over low heat for 2 minutes to form a thick paste (roux). Remove from the heat and beat in the wine to form a smooth sauce. Return to the heat and cook, stirring, for another 5 minutes or so. Pour the milk into the sauce very gradually off the heat, beating as you go, return to the heat, and cook for 2 minutes. Add the cream, dill or other herb, season to taste, and set aside.

Assemble the pie: Spread a bit of the sauce into a baking dish (an oval 11 by 2 inches is perfect) or 4 small ones. Break the fish into big bits. Scatter over the bottom, mixing the types up. Add the shrimp. Squeeze lemon juice over them. Season. Peel, slice, and lay the eggs evenly over the top. Cover the lot with white sauce. Use a fork and spoon to arrange the mashed potato over the sauce in peaks. Sit the dish on a baking sheet.

COOK Bake the pie in the oven for 20 to 30 minutes, or until browned and crisp on top and piping hot inside (pierce the center with a skewer to test for heat). Remove from the oven and let settle for 5 minutes.

PLATE Serve at the table with a choice of fresh herb salsa (p118), aioli (p100), or a chicory and green leaf salad in honey mustard dressing (p26). Or go traditional and eat with peas.

SALMON NIÇOISE

FEEDS 2

An Asian restyling of a French classic: it's unusual but extremely good.

INGREDIENTS

2 eggs
salt and black pepper
2 tablespoons soy sauce
1 teaspoon superfine sugar
1 tablespoon rice vinegar
1 star anise
2 x 5–6 ounces salmon fillets
SALAD
3 ounces fine green beans
4 handfuls of green salad leaves
6 scallions
¼ of a cucumber
4 radishes
6 cherry tomatoes
2 bundles of somen noodles
8 black olives
MARINADE
½ red chile, seeded and diced
a small handful of torn cilantro
a thumb-sized piece of fresh ginger
1 tbsp soy sauce
1 garlic clove, peeled and crushed
1 tablespoon lemon/lime juice
2–3 tablespoons homemade (p153) or
   store-bought mayonnaise
ASIAN DRESSING
4½ teaspoons white wine vinegar
a pinch of superfine sugar
1 tablespoon soy sauce
1 shallot, peeled and sliced
1 garlic clove, peeled and crushed
5 tablespoons sunflower/peanut oil
1 teaspoon sesame oil

·········· TIME SAVER ··········
Use teriyaki sauce to marinate the salmon in
place of the suggested marinade

PREP Fill a small pan with enough water to cover the eggs. Bring it to a boil. Add a pinch of salt and reduce to a simmer. Lower in the eggs and cook for 9 minutes until hard-boiled. Sit the eggs under cold running water until cool. Roll on a board to crack and peel neatly, starting from the air pocket at the rounder end. Mix the soy, sugar, vinegar, and star anise together in a bowl, add the eggs, and set aside for 3 hours to flavor and color. Turn once.

Mix the marinade ingredients together in a dish. Turn the salmon pieces in it and chill for at least 30 minutes, fish skin-side up. Mix the dressing ingredients together in a bowl and set aside.

Prep the salad: trim the beans then boil in lightly salted water for 4 minutes or until tender. Drain and refresh in cold water. Drain again. Wash and dry the leaves. Finely slice the scallions at an angle into long diagonal strips. Peel, halve, and seed the cucumber, then slice widthwise. Slice the radishes and halve the tomatoes. Cook the noodles in lightly salted boiling water for 5 minutes or until just soft. Drain and rinse in cold water, then toss in 1 tablespoon of the dressing.

COOK Pat the salmon dry then brush lightly with oil. Put a griddle or stovetop grill pan onto high heat until almost smoking. Transfer the fish to the pan and cook skin-side down for 3 minutes or until it's good and crispy. Lower the heat a bit, turn, and cook for another 2 minutes or until the salmon is firm, opaque, and juicy with just a trace of pink in the center. Remove immediately.

PLATE Toss the noodles in the remaining dressing, setting aside a little for finishing. Toss the salad ingredients separately. Sling the noodles onto plates. Arrange the salad and olives on top. Cut the eggs in half. Perch a piece of salmon on each plate (or break them up into pieces if you prefer) and give the whole thing a final drizzle of dressing before serving.

BONUS BITES

FAST EGG, BACON, AND SALMON SALAD
Hard-boil 2 eggs as above. Cool in cold water and peel. Fry 3 slices of bacon in a pan until crisp, setting aside the fat in the pan. Cut 2 skinless salmon fillets into bite-size chunks and roll in the juice of ½ a lemon, 1 tablespoon olive oil, 1 crushed garlic clove, 1 tablespoon minced dill/tarragon/cilantro, and season. Add the salmon to the pan and fry in the bacon fat, turning with tongs, for 3 minutes or until cooked through. Throw a handful each of green leaves, cherry tomatoes, and croutons into a bowl and toss with a honey mustard dressing (p26). Crumble over the crispy bacon and top with the salmon pieces and halved eggs.

SALMON SASHIMI
Using a sharp knife, slice a chilled 9 ounces top-grade fresh salmon fillet across the grain at a 45 degree angle into pieces ¼ inch thick. Wipe the blade between cuts. Arrange in slightly overlapping single lines on 2 plates and serve with a small bowl of soy sauce, a heap of wasabi paste/strong English mustard, and a few bits of pickled ginger. Eat with chopsticks.

FISH AND FRIES WITH HOMEMADE TARTARE SAUCE

FEEDS 2

INGREDIENTS

2 large mealy potatoes
peanut/sunflower oil/beef dripping for
    frying
12 ounces white fish fillet
4 tablespoons all-purpose flour
salt and pepper
BATTER
1¼ cups self-rising flour
1½ teaspoons baking powder
2 egg yolks
1¼ cups lager or soda/mineral water
TARTARE SAUCE
1 tablespoon tarragon
1½ tablespoons Italian parsley
1 ounce gherkin or cornichons
3 tablespoon homemade (p153) or
    store-bought mayonnaise
3 tablespoons sour cream/plain yogurt
1½ tablespoons capers, drained
2 tablespoons lemon/lime juice

—— CHANGE IT UP ——

1. If you don't want to deep-fry, fill a deep skillet with ¾–1¼ inches oil and cook the fish over medium/high heat for 3 minutes per side. **2.** Shallow-fry fries (p78) and sweet potato wedges (p82) also work well with this fish and don't need deep-frying.

—— BONUS BITE ——

FISH IN GOLDEN CRUMBS
Prep the fish as before. Coat in flour, dip into beaten egg, then panko/homemade dried bread crumbs (p201). Shallow-fry for 3 minutes per side, or until crisp and golden.
DIY FISH FINGERS
Cut a couple of skinned white fish fillets into fingers. Dip in flour, beaten egg, and panko/ dried bread crumbs as above. Shallow-fry, then eat on a plate with ketchup or in a sandwich.

Succulent white fish sealed in crisp golden batter with delicious fries and herby tartare sauce: a few smart skills and it's yours on a plate. Go for smaller bits of fish here as they make for easier deep-frying.

PREP Start by making the fries and giving them their first fry: Peel the potatoes and cut into ½-inch slices. Stack these up and slice into ½-inch sticks. Soak in cold water for 30 minutes. Drain, then dry thoroughly on paper towels or a dish towel.

Fill a deep-fat fryer with your chosen oil or use it to one-third fill a deep saucepan or wok. If you have a cooking thermometer, heat it to 266°F. Otherwise, drop a bread crumb in—if it's golden after 1 minute, the oil is ready. Add the fries gradually and fry for 5 to 6 minutes until tender but pale. Drain on paper towels and set aside.

Sort the tartare sauce: Mince the tarragon, parsley, and gherkin. Mix everything together and divide between two small ramekins. Chill.

Prepare the fish: Check for bones by feeling for them with your fingers. Remove any skin using a sharp, flexible knife (p134). Cut larger fish into smaller portions (about 4 by 2 inches is good but it depends on thickness). Dry it.

Sprinkle the white flour on a plate with a little salt and pepper. Roll the fish in it to coat thoroughly. Set aside. Preheat the oven to 350°F.

Finish the fries: Reheat the fries oil, raising the temperature to 375°F (a cube of bread will crisp up in 30 seconds). Slip the fries gently into the hot oil. Cook for 1 to 2 minutes or until golden and crispy. Scoop out onto a baking sheet covered with paper towels using a slotted spoon. Sit them in the oven while you cook your fish. Don't salt them.

Make the batter just before you fry: Sift the flour, baking powder, and a pinch of salt into a bowl. Make a well in the center and drop in the egg yolks with a glug of the beer, if using. Break the yolks up with your balloon whisk or wooden spoon then start to incorporate the flour, pouring the beer or water in as you do until you get a totally smooth batter the thickness of light cream.

COOK Reheat the oil to 375°F. Dunk two floured fish pieces into the batter and coat well, letting any excess drip off. Lower each piece into the hot fat very gently. Let it fry for 4 minutes (or 5 to 6 for thicker pieces) until golden, crispy, and puffed up. Remove to paper towels. (I like to sit it on a rack in a preheated oven so it retains its crunch). Repeat with remaining fish.

PLATE Bang the fish bits onto plates with the fries and tartare sauce. Serve with lemon wedges for squeezing, malt vinegar, and ketchup, salting at the table so fries and fish stay crisp.

EGGS AND DAIRY

I don't know about you but my shopping list always includes "eggs," "cheese," "other dairy bits" written in automatic scribble. Maybe I'm guilty of taking them for granted: something I'm not proud of given how much my cooking and diet depends on them. Just imagine a world without the perfectly poached egg; the same goes for a chunk of Cheddar or a slice of mellow Stilton or a cool slick of butter on a good bit of bread. Of course these guys aren't just great in their own right, we're talking here about some of the most useful ingredients on the planet. Without them, so many dishes just wouldn't be possible—think soufflés, tarts, sauces, ice creams, cakes, crepes, and meringues—and then there's the excitement and skill-set involved in cooking them. It's easy enough to bang a home-roasted chicken on the table but a perfect eggs benedict and impeccable omelet, a butter that doesn't burn as soon as you turn your back on it, or a custard that doesn't curdle—now that's confident cooking.

LAYING IT OUT
EGG OPTIONS

HEN'S EGGS: at their freshest these are unbeatable. Boil, scramble, poach, fry, and bake: use in omelets, batters, sauces, custards, mayonnaise, ice cream, pasta, pie dough, baking, coatings, soufflés, meringues, and mousses. They come in four sizes: medium, large, XL, jumbo. Always get large for baking. Consider free-range or organic.

DUCK'S EGGS: richer and creamier, these supersize statement eggs are now widely available. Excellent soft- and hard-boiled, poached, bread crumbed/deep-fried, or scrambled. They make richer yet lighter cakes and desserts. The whites take longer to whisk but hold air brilliantly.

QUAIL'S EGGS: delicious mini-eggs with a sweet, delicate taste and a larger proportion of yolk to white. Hard-boil to eat with salt. Add to fish pies. Bang onto salads (soft- or hard-boiled). Poach, fry, or deep-fry wrapped in sausage meat for Scotch eggs. They have a very long shelf-life (tough shells), look cute, and are increasingly available.

CRACKING EGGS:
What to look for

Eggs vary wildly in quality and welfare: shop around for the best you can get. Deli, grocery store, farm gate, supermarket, street market, here's what to look for.

SHELLS: color: white, brown, pastel, speckled, it's cosmetic— they'll taste the same.

CONDITION: must be undamaged/crack-free. Lift each egg to check before you buy.

STATE: shells are porous so go for clean shells.

FRESHNESS: the fresher the better. Check the box (or egg—they're often date stamped) for the "best before" date and stick to it. If the egg isn't stamped or you're in doubt test them. Sit the whole egg in its shell in a bowl or glass full of cold water. Fresh eggs will sink and settle horizontally. Slightly older eggs will rise up at the round end—they're still good for baking. Old stale eggs float to the top—don't use.

LOOK: a good egg has a plump upright yolk which is yellow/orange and sits on a compact, firm, jelly-like white. Blood spots are normal so leave or remove with a knife tip.

HOW TO
SEPARATE EGGS

1. Get 3 bowls.

2. Crack the egg sharply on the side of a bowl or counter edge.

3. Hold it over a bowl. Pull the two halves apart with your thumbs, letting the yolk settle in one half of the shell as the white spills down.

4. Pass the yolk backward and forward between the halves until the white has gone.

5. Drop the yolk into the second bowl. Tip the white into the third.

6. Separate your next egg into the first bowl and repeat the process.

OR DO IT BY HAND: Crack the egg and drop it into a bowl. Tip it into your clean cupped hand which is held over another bowl. Let the white drip down through your fingers. Place the yolk in another bowl.

EGG STORE

KEEP IN THE BOX

For protection, to remind you of their expiration date and to stop porous shells absorbing other tastes and smells

KEEP COOL

Sit the box away from any heat source in the kitchen so you can use them directly (always use eggs at room temperature) or keep them in the refrigerator.

HOW TO MAKE
ESSENTIAL MAYONNAISE

Sit a large bowl on a dish towel. Add **2 EGG YOLKS**, a pinch each of **SALT** and **SUGAR**, 1 good **TEASPOON MUSTARD,** and beat together using a balloon whisk. Measure **¾ CUP PEANUT OR SUNFLOWER OIL** and **SCANT ¼ CUP MILD OLIVE OIL** into a pitcher. Start to drip-trickle it over the yolks, beating constantly, adding it in a very slow drizzle so it emulsifies. Once it starts to thicken properly, stop and add **1 TABLESPOON WHITE WINE VINEGAR** or lemon juice. Continue to beat, adding the oil a little more steadily. Once it's all in, add a further **1 TABLESPOON VINEGAR** or juice and **1 TABLESPOON HOT WATER**. Give it a final beat and adjust the seasonings. Flavor with garlic, wasabi, mustard, ketchup, or dill.

MAYO TIPS Make sure all your ingredients are at room temperature. To save a mayo that splits, tip another yolk into a bowl and add the split mix ½ a teaspoon at a time, whisking all the while.

EGG AND DAIRY DOCTOR

EGGS AND DAIRY PACK THEIR FAIR SHARE OF BONE-STRENGTHENING **CALCIUM AND PROTEIN** MAKING THEM PRIME FOODS FOR VEGETARIANS. Eggs, hard, and semi-hard cheeses are high in *Vitamin A* WHICH SUPPORTS VISION, SKIN, AND IMMUNE SYSTEM, **VITAMIN B2** which is good for the skin, eyes, and nervous system, and **VITAMIN B12** which supports the immune system and the manufacture OF RED BLOOD CELLS. EGGS, YOGURT, AND MANY CHEESES CONTAIN **PHOSPHORUS** for healthy teeth and bones. EGGS CONTAIN **ZINC** which boosts fertility and *Iron* WHICH HELPS TRANSPORT OXYGEN ROUND THE BODY. The level of SATURATED FAT in eggs is LOW so ignore previous advice about restricting consumption on health grounds WATCH HIGH LEVELS OF SALT AND SATURATED FAT in cheese; luckily it's a rich food so you don't need a lot.

CHEESE BOARD

Cheesemaking is an ancient art enjoying a revival; work out what's best for a cheeseboard or for cooking. Buy and store it well.

HARD

These are sharp cheeses which have a hard dense texture and which vary in strength from mild to palate-scorching. Varieties include **VINTAGE CHEDDAR**, **AGED GOUDA** and **GRUYÈRE**, **EMMENTHAL,** and **MANCHEGO**. **PARMESAN** and **PECORINO** are the driest and have a very long shelf-life. They're expensive but you don't need a lot: grate them into your cooking and over finished dishes.

SEMI-HARD

Here you've got a huge range of affordable, amiable cheeses which vary in strength, taste, and texture. Many melt well: some work best uncooked with fruit, bread, and celery, chutney, or with a bit of fruit cake or in a salad.

CHEDDAR: A tasty, versatile cheese which works for all manner of eating and cooking. Choose fully flavored or substitute with an alternative cheese like double gloucester or red leicester if you prefer it milder.
LANCASHIRE: A lovely, tangy English cheese which melts well and holds its flavor in cooking: get it creamy, tasty, or crumbly. It's good in risottos, burgers, and Welsh rarebit.
GRUYÈRE: A nutty Swiss cheese with a bit of an edge which melts well. It's great in fondues, tarts, soufflés, with eggs, and works in potato dishes.
CHESHIRE: Melts well, a crumbly milky tasting white English cheese.
RACLETTE: Swiss melting cheese; good with potatoes and for dipping.
WENSLEYDALE: A mild slightly tart English cheese which works best eaten as is or in salads.
EDAM AND GOUDA: Dutch cheeses, Edam is lower in calories. Gouda has a stronger flavor and is a better melt. Both are good in salads and for snacking.

BLUE

A distinctive style of cheese with a blue line and macho reputation. Varieties include **STILTON**—the king of English cheeses—and the cave-aged **ROQUEFORT**. Some, like **GORGONZOLA** can be quite palate-challenging but others, like **CAMBOZOLA** can be soft and subtle. Try before you buy…

SOFT

A range of seductive spreadable cheeses including brie, camembert, and taleggio with a bloom and ooze to them.
BRIE: A soft fruity creamy cheese which should ooze out onto the plate when ripe: its edible rind should be white and firm and the cheese itself pale yellow and creamy. Eat with wine and crackers. It does melt so experiment with it. Brie de Meaux is best.
CAMEMBERT: A crumbly soft item which gets creamier. Enjoy with a crunchy baguette and fruit and nuts, or try baked whole with wine and herbs, or bread crumbed and deep-fried.
TALEGGIO: Melts into a thick tasty cream without splitting. Slice it onto puff pastry tarts, over potatoes, and onto steaks and burgers.

FRESH

MOZZARELLA: Traditionally made from buffalo's milk, most mozzarella is processed and packaged in brine. Melted, it has a unique stringy quality. Serve with fresh basil and tomatoes or use it sliced or grated on pizzas, in pastas, or bakes. Get blocks of denser cooking mozzarella for grating into lasagnes, etc.
FETA: Cube or crumble it into Greek salad with chopped tomatoes, olives, cucumber, and a sharp dressing. Use to stuff peppers, tomatoes, zucchini.
RICOTTA: Made from the liquids of the cheese, it should be creamy. Use for desserts or stuffing cannelloni and pasta dishes.
MASCARPONE: Not really a cheese but a cream cheese-style cream. Use for sauces, in cheesecakes and for tiramisu.

GOAT

There are hundreds of different types out there ranging from mild to pungent, creamy to crumbly. It's shaped in logs, cones, wheels, crottins. Get it fresh or rolled in herbs, ash, mixed with herbs and garlic. Crumble into salads. Slice it to melt on tarts, pizzas, use to stuff vegetables, or bread crumb and deep-fry.

CHEESE ETIQUETTE
WHERE TO GET IT, WHAT TO LOOK FOR & HOW TO STORE

THE SPECIALIST CHEESE STORE: get free samples and advice on what's best. Find out what's in season (cheeses have them). Expect a range of artisan cheeses from home and away; can get expensive…

THE GOOD SUPERMARKET: caters for great value cooking cheeses; try before you buy only works at the cheese counter. Check labels for cheese information.

Cheese checklist

◄ look for fat/sodium levels if it matters to you;
◄ strength of flavor should be graded (key for cooking cheese);
◄ check sell-by date;
◄ check suitability for vegetarians (rennet-free is the way forward);
◄ and the type of milk used (anyone who is pregnant, ill, very young must avoid cheese made with unpasteurized milk).

Looking for the best

It's best to get cheese freshly cut from a whole piece rather than pre-packed. The outer rind of the hard and semihard cheeses should be intact. The paste should look calm and pleasant, neither dry nor sweaty; the rind of soft cheeses should be evenly colored—surface mold is normal on some cheeses.

STORAGE

Cheese hates extremes: it's best kept in a box in the larder, cellar, windowsill, or the warmest part of the refrigerator (salad drawer or butter section). Chill fresh cheeses. Rewrap any cheese sold in plastic wrap: replace with baking/wax paper and then plastic wrap to preserve. Hard cheeses can last for weeks but don't let them dry out. Soft cheese may need an extra few days to ripen—use your judgment. Always give eating cheese a couple of hours to return to room temperature.

FRIENDS

EGGS
ANCHOVY, ARUGULA, ASPARAGUS, BACON, BASIL, BEET, BREAD, CHEESES, CHILE, CHORIZO, CHUTNEYS, CINNAMON, CREAM, CRESS, CUCUMBER, DILL, HAM, HONEY, LEMON, LETTUCE, MAYONNAISE, MUSHROOMS, MUSTARD, ONIONS, OLIVES, PARSLEY, PASTA, PICKLES, PEAS, POTATOES, SHRIMP, SOY, SMOKED HADDOCK, SMOKED SALMON, SAUSAGE, SPINACH, TARRAGON, TOAST, TOMATOES, WATERCRESS

CHEESE
APPLES, ASPARAGUS, AVOCADO, BACON, BEEF, BREAD, CABBAGE, CARROT, CAULIFLOWER, CELERY, CHICORY, CHICKEN, CRACKERS, CREAM, CUCUMBER, EGGPLANT, GARLIC, GRAPES, LEMON, LETTUCE, LIME, MANGO, MUSHROOM, NECTARINE, ONION, ORANGE, PASTA, PEACH, PEAR, PORK, POTATOES, SHRIMP, SCALLION, TOMATO, WALNUTS, WATERCRESS, WHITE WINE, WHITE FISH

1 BOILED

BOILED EGG AND TOASTED SOLDIERS

FAST

FEEDS 1

INGREDIENTS

2 large hen's eggs (at room temperature)
a pinch of salt for the water
2 slices toast
softened butter, for spreading
salt and pepper

—— CHANGE IT UP ——

Switch the toast for asparagus spears. Snap the woody ends from a few bits of seasonal English asparagus and peel the stalks. Boil for 3 to 4 minutes. Dip as per toast.

TIPS

1. If eggs crack in the water, add a tablespoon of any vinegar to seal them.
2. To hard-boil a hen's egg, cook in boiling water from cold for 10 minutes. Cool under running water to stop the yolks discoloring.

Enjoy your egg in its purest form; boil simply for a set amount of time to create one of the most delicious and indulgent ready-meals ever. Thin strips of toast are compulsory.

PREP Fill a small pan with enough water to cover the eggs. Bring it to a boil. Add the salt.

COOK Lower the eggs into the pan using a large spoon or a pair of tongs. Increase the heat so the water returns to a boil. As soon as it does, reduce it to a gentle boil. Set your timer. For a very soft egg, cook for 4 minutes; for medium, cook for 5; for a firm white, and moist still runny yolk, cook for 6. Adjust the timing if using smaller eggs. If cooking eggs from chilled allow 30 seconds extra. Remove immediately at the end of your chosen cooking time.

PLATE Spoon the eggs into cups on a plate. Bang the top of the first egg with a spoon to crack it. Peel the shell off. Or cut it across with a knife. Repeat with the second or it will continue to cook. Spread butter on the toast. Cut it into thin strips or slices. Put a little salt and pepper on the plate. Get dipping.

BONUS BITES

LUXURY DUCK'S EGGS AND FRIED SOLDIERS
Bring a pan of water to a boil as above. Lower 2 duck eggs into it. Set the timer for 6 minutes once it returns to a boil. Meantime, melt a little butter in a skillet. Cut 2 slices of firm white bread into sticks as wide as they are deep. Fry them, turning, until crisp and a bit smoky. Sit the eggs in cups. Serve as above with the fried bread sticks for dipping.

SWEET SOFT-BOILED QUAIL'S EGGS AND SOLDIERS ON SALAD
Boil 5 ounces baby new potatoes for 10 minutes or until tender. Drain. Meantime, broil 2 American bacon slices until crisp. Make up a honey mustard (p26) or walnut dressing (p33). Remove crusts from a slice of white bread. Dice it into ¼-inch bits. Heat a little olive or walnut oil in a pan and fry the dice until crisp. Set a small pan of water to a boil. Add 6 quail's eggs. Boil for 2 minutes for soft-boiled or 3 to 4 minutes for hard-boiled. Cool in running water, crack at their rounded ends, neatly peel the shells off, and slice in half across. Throw the potatoes into a bowl with 2 handfuls of soft green salad leaves and toss with 1–2 tablespoons of dressing. Crumble the bacon on top. Add the soldier croutons and the sliced quail's eggs and drizzle over more dressing to finish.

GLORIOUS SCRAMBLE

 FAST **FEEDS 1**

INGREDIENTS

3 large hen's eggs (at room temperature)
a pinch of cream of tartar
2 tablespoons butter
salt and pepper

TIP
Soak your used pan in hot water immediately with a dash of vinegar so the egg remains don't stick.

2 *scrambled*

Here's an unusually gentle way to prepare your scrambled eggs: using the oven means you've got more control over the texture and more time to make toast. You can multiply this up pretty easily so if you've got loads to feed it's a good 'un.

PREP Preheat the oven to 340°F. Get an ovenproof bowl ready. Crack the eggs into a large mixing bowl. Add the cream of tartar. Beat with a balloon whisk for 30 seconds.

Meantime, put a heavy-bottom pan onto low heat (7–8 inches is good). Add the butter to melt.

Tip the eggs into the pan. Stir constantly with a wooden spoon for 30 seconds, or until lumps just begin to form. Transfer to the ovenproof bowl.

COOK Bake the eggs in the bowl for 8 to 9 minutes, or until as creamy as you like. Stir the mix once after 4 minutes. Keep an eye out and test it so it doesn't overcook.

PLATE Add salt to taste. Pile the egg immediately onto hot buttered toast, muffins, or bagels. Add black pepper. It's also perfect with the great full English breakfast (baked sausages, baked mushrooms, baked tomatoes, and baked beans).

BONUS BITES

SCRAMBLE IN A PAN WITH STIR-INS
Beat 3 large eggs in a bowl. Add 2 teaspoons cream, a pinch of salt, and a little pepper. Gently heat 3 teaspoons butter in a small heavy-bottom pan until melted. Add the eggs and reduce the heat to very low. Stir the eggs once every 20 seconds or so using a wooden spoon. The egg ribbons gently as it cooks. Remove from the pan the second it's done so it doesn't overcook. Sprinkle with a few grains of vanilla salt and a little thyme, ideally. For stir-ins: Just as your egg is almost set as you like it, stir in any of the following to melt or heat through: thin slivers of smoked salmon, crispy bacon pieces, a few drained capers, a tiny bit of grated Cheddar or Gruyère cheese, a little diced, fried chorizo, a couple of sliced mushrooms fried in garlic butter, a bit of shredded cooked mackerel, a sprinkle of chopped dill or tarragon.

3 FRIED

EGG BANJO

FAST · FEEDS 1

INGREDIENTS

2 slices good white bread
   (store-bought or homemade, p202)
softened butter, for spreading
tomato ketchup/brown sauce
1 teaspoon good olive oil
   (or flavorless oil of your choice)
1 teaspoon butter
1 large egg (at room temperature)

TIPS
1. For overeasy eggs, flip with a spatula after 1 minute and cook for another minute before serving.
2. For compact fried eggs, crack them low in the pan slowly.

CHANGE IT UP

1. For a bacon and egg banjo, fry 2 slices of Canadian bacon in the pan. Remove and keep warm in a preheated oven before adding the egg to the pan and cooking in the bacon fat until done. Slap into a roll with the bacon. **2.** For a veggie banjo, fry 4 button mushrooms in a little oil at the same time as the egg. **3.** To make egg banjo for a crowd, crack 4 eggs into 1 tablespoon hot oil. Cover with a lid. Reduce heat to medium/low. Cook for 3 to 5 minutes.

AKA the Fried Egg Sandwich. To enjoy the full banjo effect, take a good bite and strum the yolk off your front using one hand while you hold the sandwich up and out to the side with the other.

PREP Spread both your bread slices with butter (be liberal or restrained to taste) and one with sauce. Heat the oil and butter in a small pan over medium heat. It needs to be hot enough for your egg to bubble and spit as it hits the fat, but don't burn it.

COOK Get your egg in: tap it sharply against the side of the pan. Tuck both thumbs into the natural crack you've created and pull the shell apart so it slips neatly out into the hot fat. Or crack it into a cup and pour it in.

Let it settle for a few seconds. Tip the pan at an angle so the fat runs down. Using a teaspoon, spoon the hot buttery juices over the egg for 1 minute or until it's done: the white firm, the yolk cooked underneath but still runny on top with a very light transparent film over it. Whip it out with a spatula the second it's done. Bang it onto the sauced slice of bread. Sandwich it.

PLATE Get stuck in.

how to **BANJO...**

PERFECT POACHED EGGS AND PANCETTA ON POTATO CAKES
WITH HOLLANDAISE SAUCE

FEEDS 2

INGREDIENTS

2 large eggs
a little peanut or other flavorless oil
  for lining
4 strips of pancetta/American bacon
POTATO CAKES
2 medium potatoes
1 ounce onion
salt and pepper
1 tablespoon olive oil
a little bit of butter
HOLLANDAISE SAUCE
3 egg yolks
1 teaspoon superfine sugar
1 tablespoon water
1 tablespoon white wine vinegar
1 tablespoon lemon juice, plus extra
¾ cup clarified butter (p141) or soft
  butter
salt and pepper

TIP
Add minced tarragon/basil to leftover hollandaise and reheat gently over a pan of hot water. This sauce is also great with steak/griddled chicken/white fish/asparagus.

—— CHANGE IT UP ——
1. For eggs benedict, make the hollandaise sauce and keep it warm. Poach the eggs as above or use the skillet method below. Toast 2 sliced muffins/bagels. Spread with soft butter. Add a slice of ham, a poached egg, and cover with sauce.
2. For salmon benedict, use a slice of smoked salmon instead of ham.
3. For mushroom benedict, brush a portobello mushroom with olive oil and cook on a hot griddle or stovetop grill pan for 2 minutes per side. Lay on a toasted muffin and top with a poached egg and hollandaise.

Once you're down with the perfect poached egg and a silky sexy hollandaise you're well on your way to veteran status.

PREP Potato cakes: At least 1 hour before eating, boil the potatoes whole for 10 minutes or until just softening but still a bit firm. Remove. Drain. Cool. Just before cooking, peel and grate coarsely into a bowl along with the onion. Season and mix lightly with a fork. Set aside.

COOK EGGS: Line 2 cups/ramekins with large pieces of plastic wrap, leaving plenty to spare. Brush lightly with oil using a pastry brush and crack an egg into each. Pull the wrap up and twist to make them watertight. Plop into a pan of simmering water for 3 minutes to poach until the whites are set and yolks still runny. Untwist to touch and check (twist and return if you need to). Cool immediately in chilled water, still in the plastic wrap, so the eggs stop cooking.

HOLLANDAISE: Put a pan of water onto heat. Get a large heatproof bowl that can fit into the top without touching the water. Add the egg yolks, sugar, water, vinegar, and lemon juice. Sit it into the pan. Reduce the heat to a bare minimum (if it's too hot your sauce will scramble) and beat continuously with a balloon whisk. The mix will be thin at first but thicken to the point where the whisk leaves a trail on the surface. This will take 3 to 8 minutes. Be patient.

Take it off the heat. Add the butter while still whisking. For clarified butter, pour and whisk in a small steady trickle so the mix doesn't curdle. For soft butter, add ½ teaspoon at a time, whisking each bit in before adding the next. Season with salt and pepper and squeeze over a little extra lemon juice to finish. Keep the sauce warm; it can't be reheated. Sit it in a bowl, wrap covered over a pan of hot water off the stove. Stir it regularly. If it curdles, bang a new egg yolk into a clean bowl and whisk your sauce in bit by bit to pull it back.

Put a frying pan onto medium/high heat. Add the oil/butter. Get two large cookie cutters or chef's rings. Sit them on a board. Stuff each with potato cake mix. Carefully transfer to the pan to cook for 3 minutes. Turn with the help of a spatula. Fry until crisp and cooked through. (If you don't have any cutters don't worry, just go free-style instead). Remove from the pan and keep warm.

Fry the pancetta in the same pan for 1 to 2 minutes per side until crisp. Sit it on paper towels. Reheat the eggs: put a pan of water onto simmer. Plop the eggs in for 1 to 2 minutes. Remove with a slotted spoon and remove the plastic wrap.

PLATE Place the potato cakes on plates. Layer with the pancetta, sit the poached eggs on top, and spoon over a good dollop of hollandaise.

—— BONUS BITE——

SKILLET POACHED EGGS
Two-thirds fill a small skillet with water.
Add a pinch of salt, bring to a boil, and
reduce to a simmer. Crack the egg straight
in (or pour it in from a cup) and let cook
for 3 to 4 minutes, until the white is set
and the yolk runny. Lift it out on a slotted
spoon. Drain off water. Trim the white
with scissors if you need to. Sit on hot
buttered toast and season. Or team with
a griddled portobello mushroom, fried
vegetarian/pork sausage, and fried tomato
for an all-day breakfast.

A SIMPLE OMELET

FEEDS 1

INGREDIENTS

3 large free-range eggs
2 teaspoons water
   (optional, but makes it lighter)
1 teaspoon chopped Italian parsley
1 teaspoon chopped tarragon leaves
1 teaspoon chopped chives
3 teaspoons butter/olive oil/clarified
   butter (p141)
salt and black pepper

TIP

Using clarified butter (p141) means you can get your pan hotter for a faster and tastier result as it has a higher smoking point than regular butter.

CHANGE IT UP

1. For a cheese omelet, add 1 tablespoon finely grated Cheddar/Parmesan to the egg mix (with or without the herbs) and sprinkle another 2 tablespoons over the mix as you season it. Use a spatula to fold it over and slide it out onto a plate.
2. For a cheese and ham omelet, fill with a thin slice of good ham torn roughly and a good grating of Gruyère or Cheddar to taste.
3. For a mushroom omelet, make up some hot mixed mushrooms (p25). Spread over the omelet base and fold before sliding out.
4. For a blue cheese and onion marmalade omelet, crumble 1¼ ounces Stilton or other blue cheese and mix with 1 tablespoon warm caramelized onion (p80) or a good onion marmalade (p144). Fill the omelet just as it's ready.

You can measure a cook by their omelet. Keep it simple and the method fast. Get it out while it's still slightly underdone and be subtle with the filling.

PREP
Crack the eggs into a bowl. Add the water. Beat lightly with a fork for a few seconds to combine well but no more. Beat in the herbs. Put a plate on to warm.

COOK
Bang the butter into an omelet pan on high heat (6½–8 inches bottom for a 3-egg omelet). As soon as it foams, shoot the egg mix in and get to work.

Give the mix a quick stir with a fork so it spreads across the bottom. Then use it to draw the outer setting edges of the omelet up toward you so the liquid egg runs down to the edge and underneath to set itself. It helps if you tilt the pan away from you. Do this a few times, working very quickly around the pan until the omelet is done. It should have a softly set base, a soft top that's a bit runny still (it'll cook as you fold it) and should take less than a minute. Season it very lightly and quickly with salt and pepper (salting early can toughen the egg).

Roll it out of the pan for maximum softness. Take it away from the heat and tilt it down toward your plate. Tease the edge nearest the handle with the fork or a spatula so it flips over and rolls out.

PLATE
Omelets won't wait, so have a salad dressed and ready with maybe some French fries or fried garlic and rosemary potatoes, or just good bread.

BONUS BITE

CLASSIC OMELET ARNOLD BENNETT
Heat ⅔ cup milk in a pan with a peeled, halved shallot and a few black peppercorns. Add 5 ounces smoked haddock (undyed is best) and simmer for 5 minutes or until soft. Remove the fish. Use a fork to break it into flakes and check for bones. Set aside. Make up a hollandaise sauce (p160). Preheat the broiler. Make a 3-egg omelet following the method above, making sure it's still very soft. Cover it with flakes of fish and spoon the hollandaise over the top. Bang under the broiler for a few seconds until it glazes and browns a little and sprinkle with chives to finish.

CREPE COMPLET

FEEDS 4

INGREDIENTS

generous ¾ cup all-purpose flour
a pinch of salt
1 large egg
1¼ cups milk
1 tablespoon melted butter, plus extra
for frying
YOUR CHOICE OF FILLING

—— CHANGE IT UP——

1. Mix your crepe up by filling it with the following ingredients ... **Savory:** torn ham and grated Gruyere, fried mushrooms, and tarragon, smoked trout, dill, and sour cream. **Sweet:** maple syrup, sugar, and lemon juice, hot blueberries, strawberries, and ginger cream, raspberries and ice cream, sliced banana, and Nutella.
2. To up the nutrients, replace scant ¼ cup of the white flour with buckwheat flour.

TIP

It's common for the first crepe to stick. Throw it away if it happens. No shame.

········ TIME SAVER ········

Make the batter up to 24 hours ahead. Add a splash of water and rewhisk before using.

—— BONUS BITE——

BAKED CHICKEN & MUSHROOM CREPES
Make up a bèchamel sauce (p185) and the crepes. Shred 6 ounces leftover roast chicken. Slice and fry 1 pound mushrooms in ½ tablespoon oil and 1 teaspoon butter with a little garlic and tarragon until soft. Preheat the oven to 400°F. Lay the crepes flat out and grate a little Cheddar or Gruyère over each. Lay a mix of mushrooms and shredded chicken down the center, adding dabs of sauce. Roll and place seam down in a greased dish. Cover with remaining sauce and sprinkle with extra cheese. Bake for 30 minutes until golden.

Here's a French way with a classic British breakfast (wrap it in a crepe) and some other lovely fillings. Enjoy anytime. I made 200 of these for a party once.

PREP Sift the flour and salt into a bowl. Make a well in the center. Crack the egg into it with a good splash of milk. Start to beat the flour into the liquid using a balloon whisk or wooden spoon. Add the remaining milk slowly, beating as you go, to get a smooth batter. Add the melted butter. Pour the batter into a pitcher. Set aside.

COOK Put a crepe pan or large shallow skillet onto high heat. Coat with melted butter using a silicone brush (or put a bit in and swirl to coat) so your crepe won't stick. Working fast, add 2–3 tablespoons of batter to the pan or pour the equivalent from a pitcher or ladle. Swirl the pan to coat evenly and achieve a thin crepe. Cook for 1 minute or until the base browns up. Turn it with a metal spatula (run underneath to loosen first) or stand back from the stove and toss it high into the air with a forward movement so it turns. Catch it in the pan. Cook for another minute. Slide it, flat, onto a sheet of wax paper. Make the rest and layer them up with more paper. Make up your filling of choice and fill and fold as described.

PLATE Get stuck into these as they are or team with a salad of your choice.

═══ FILLINGS ═══

1 EGG AND BACON
Broil 4–8 bacon slices for 2 minutes per side. Keep warm. Fry 4 large eggs in 2 teaspoons each of butter and oil as per egg banjo for a crowd (p158). Put crepes onto warm plates. Tear the bacon into small pieces. Divide and scatter down the middle of each crepe. Top with an egg. Add a dollop of ketchup. Flip the sides over to cover.

2 SAUSAGE AND APPLE
Bake 4 good fat pork (or vegetarian) sausages at 400°F for 20 minutes or until done. Core and slice 2 small eating apples into sixths and fry as per filling 3. Fill the center of each crepe with sausage and apple and fold the edges in.

3 CARAMELIZED APPLE AND BLOOD SAUSAGE
Fry 2 slices of blood sausage in a little oil for 1 to 2 minutes per side until cooked. Keep warm. Core and slice 2 small eating apples into sixths. Fry in 2 teaspoons butter for 1 minute per side. Sprinkle with 1 teaspoon sugar. Cook 1 minute per side longer. Alternate crumbled blood sausage and apple down the middle of each crepe. Fold the edges in. Serve with maple syrup.

4 HAM AND CREAM CHEESE
Spread a thin layer of cream cheese over each crepe. Add a thin slice of ham to the center of each and flip the sides over to cover.

FAST FRITTATA WITH BUTTERED SPINACH AND INSTANT TOPPINGS

 **FEEDS 1 TO 2**

A frittata is a flat Italian omelet; this one packs layers of flavor.

INGREDIENTS

3½ ounces baby spinach
1½ tablespoons butter
2 ounces Parmesan/vegetarian
   equivalent
3 large free-range eggs
1 tablespoon olive oil

INSTANT TOPPINGS

1. 2 ounces feta cheese, crumbled
2. a handful of arugula and a few
   shavings of Cheddar/Parmesan
3. 6 chopped cherry tomatoes in a few
   drops of dressing
4. 3 slices of air-dried ham/crispy
   pancetta

—— BONUS BITES ——

EGGPLANT, FETA AND DILL FRITTATA

Fry 8 x ¼-inch slices of eggplant in a little olive oil, turning once, until brown and soft. Remove. Add a sliced shallot to the pan and cook until it just softens. Crumble and semi-mash 3½ ounces feta cheese in a bowl, adding 5 beaten eggs, a handful of torn dill, ½ teaspoon dried mint, and a pinch of pepper. Heat olive oil in an omelet pan and add half the mix. Layer the eggplant in and cover with the rest. Cook on very low heat for 10 minutes or until the base is set but the top is slightly runny. Drizzle 1 tablespoon oil over the top and sit under a hot broiler for 2 minutes or until just set and lightly golden.

ROASTED BROCCOLI FRITTATA

Toss 300g broccoli florets in 1 tablespoon olive oil with 2 pinches each of sea salt and cumin and a pinch of red pepper flakes. Roast in a preheated oven at 400°F for 10 minutes. Beat 5 large eggs, a pinch of pepper, and scant ¼ cup finely grated Parmesan/Cheddar together. Add the egg and broccoli to a heated omelet pan with 1 teaspoon oil. Fry on low heat for 5 minutes or until the base is set but the top is still a bit runny. Sprinkle with ⅓ ounce extra Parmesan, dab with butter, and sit under a hot broiler for 2 minutes until set and golden.

PREP Prep your choice of topping so you're good to go. Preheat a broiler.

COOK Cook the spinach: empty it into a pan with 2 tablespoons water. Stir to wilt it for 2 minutes. Drain it into a strainer. Press any excess moisture out with a spoon. Tip it into a bowl, season lightly. Stir in 1 teaspoon of the butter. Set aside. Finely grate the Parmesan or other hard cheese.

Mix the frittata: crack the eggs into a bowl and beat with a fork. Add half the cheese and all the buttered spinach. Put your 6½–8-inch bottom omelet pan onto high heat. Add the oil. Once it's hot, add the egg/spinach mix. Reduce the heat to low after 20 seconds.

Let cook on low for 1 to 2 minutes or until the base is just set and the top still runny. Sprinkle with the rest of the Parmesan and dot with butter. Finish under the broiler for 1 to 2 minutes until browned at the edges with the top glazed, golden, and puffy.

PLATE Slide it onto a plate and add your choice of toppings. Eat with bread, piles of dressed green salad, and a plate of sliced tomato dressed with oil, lemon juice, and sliced shallots.

CHEESE SOUFFLÉS WITH
ONION MARMALADE

FEEDS 6

INGREDIENTS

2 tablespoons butter, plus extra
1 tablespoon grated Parmesan
    (optional)
7 ounces Cheddar
¼ cup all-purpose flour
1¼ cups milk
1 tablespoon cider
3 very large eggs, separated (p153),
    plus an extra white
1¼ teaspoons Dijon mustard
2 teaspoons lemon juice
a shake of Worcestershire sauce
a good pinch of cayenne
salt and pepper
4 chives, snipped (optional)
1 x onion marmalade (p144)

Add an extra egg white or two to the mix if
you like to make for a lighter soufflé.

—— CHANGE IT UP ——

For a mixed cheese soufflé, replace a third
of the Cheddar with either Gruyère or
Parmesan.

—— BONUS BITE ——

ONE BIG SOUFFLÉ: For one big soufflé for
sharing, grease a 1.5-quart soufflé dish with
melted butter as above. Sprinkle and coat
with grated Parmesan, if you like. Spread
1–2 tablespoons of onion marmalade, a
bit of homemade tomato sauce, or cooked
buttered spinach across the bottom of the
dish. Fill with the basic soufflé mix and
sprinkle with grated cheese. Bake for 40 to
45 minutes until ready as above.

*Special; but don't let the word soufflé put you off. They're easy enough
to make. As for taste they're lovely, light, and cheesy with a delicious
sweet onion base. Get them onto the table straight from the oven:
perfect for dinner parties.*

PREP Organize 6 x 2¾-inch individual soufflé dishes. Grease them well
with a little melted butter. Apply with a pastry brush using upward
strokes so the soufflés rise well. If using Parmesan, divide between the dishes.
Shake and tap it around to coat them well. Finely grate the Cheddar.

COOK Make a thick white sauce: Melt the butter to foaming point in a
heavy-bottom pan on gentle heat. Add the flour and stir to make
a paste using a wooden spoon. Stir for 2 minutes as the paste cooks. Remove.
Use a balloon whisk to beat the milk and cider into the paste very gradually so
the sauce you create is ultra-smooth. Return to low heat and stir until the sauce
thickens. Set aside for 1 minute. Preheat the oven to 400°F.

Beat the egg yolks straight into the white sauce with the mustard, lemon juice,
Worcestershire sauce, cayenne, salt, black pepper, and chives if using. The base
mix has to be well seasoned to counteract the bland white. Add the grated
Cheddar, saving enough to sprinkle over the tops later. Combine well.

Whisk the 4 egg whites with an electric hand whisk or balloon whisk. (If you've
used the latter for your sauce, dunk it into boiling water and dry it well.) Once
the whites can stand in stiff peaks, stir one heaping tablespoon into the egg
yolk mix to loosen it, using a spatula. Tip the rest on top and fold them in
gently with as few cutting, scooping movements as you can get away with. If
the odd bit of white remains, that's fine, but don't overmix it.

Spoon 1 teaspoon of the onion marmalade quickly into the bottom of each
dish. Use a larger spoon to fill each dish with the soufflé mixture to within
¼ inch of the rims. Run a clean thumb tip around the edge of each to help
shape traditionally. Top with the remaining cheese.

Bake for about 10 minutes without opening the oven door. The soufflés should
be well risen, golden, pretty firm on top but soft in the center. (To be honest,
you need to wobble them a bit to test and you probably won't know if they're
just right until you get your spoon in.)

PLATE Sit the soufflés on small plates, with teaspoons on the side. Tell
everyone to get their spoons down to the oniony bit at the bottom
so they can mix it up.

EASY LEMON SOUFFLÉS AND APRICOT SAUCE

FEEDS 6

INGREDIENTS

2 tablespoons melted butter
1–2 tablespoons sifted confectioners'
  sugar, for dusting
1½ teaspoon good apricot jam
5 large free-range eggs (at room
  temperature)
¾ cup superfine sugar or vanilla sugar
1 large juicy lemon
scant ⅔ cup ground almonds
APRICOT SAUCE
6 tablespoons apricot jam
water
1 teaspoon butter
a good squeeze of lemon juice

—— CHANGE IT UP ——

Replace the apricot jam with homemade
lemon and passion fruit curd (p216) or
store-bought lemon or
orange curd.

✱✱✱✱ CASH SAVER ✱✱✱✱

Bang used vanilla beans into superfine sugar
to store for instant vanilla sugar.

TIPS

If the egg whites collapse because you
overwhisk them, just whisk in another egg
white to save them.

These go fast, believe me. Within 3 minutes of getting them out of the oven during first testing, all six had disappeared and there were very burned but happy mouths all round.

PREP Coat 6 x 2¾-inch individual soufflé dishes lightly with melted butter using a pastry brush with upward strokes. Dust the insides with a little confectioners' sugar. Spoon the jam into the bottom of each one. Preheat the oven to 350°F.

Bang and roll the lemon on a counter to soften it a bit for better juicing. Wash and dry it well. Grate finely. Cut in two and squeeze as much juice out as possible.

Using clean hands, separate the eggs into two grease-free bowls. Using a balloon or an electric hand whisk, whisk the egg yolks until fluffy. Start to add the sugar, a bit at a time, whisking, until you have a thick mousse. Still whisking, add the zest, juice, and ground almonds. Stop as soon as they're in. Boil a kettle.

Remove the blades from your whisk. Dunk them or the balloon whisk into boiling water to remove the grease then dry well. Whisk the egg whites to the stiff peak stage.

Stir a tablespoon of whites into the mousse to loosen. Tip the rest in. Fold in very gently with a spatula to preserve air. Divide the mix between dishes, coming to within ¼-inch of the tops. Shape with your thumb around the edges.

COOK Cook for 20 minutes or until very well risen and golden on top. Wobble to judge it as for cheese soufflés. Meantime, melt the jam in a pan on very gentle heat with the butter and as much water as you need to thin it a little. Add lemon juice to taste. Pour into a pitcher.

PLATE Serve soufflés on a plate with a teaspoon and a pitcher of sauce to pour into the centers at the table.

FRENCH EGG, CHEESE, AND BACON TART

FEEDS 6

In other words, quiche lorraine, and made the proper French way. It's rich and sumptuous so please make it.

INGREDIENTS

scant 1⅔ cups all-purpose flour
½ teaspoon fine salt
½ cup (1 stick) chilled butter or ¼ cup
    (½ stick) butter/¼ cup lard
2 tablespoons chilled water
1 tablespoon soft butter for greasing
FILLING
5½ ounces Canadian bacon slices
1 tablespoon butter
4¾ ounces Gruyère cheese
6 egg yolks
1¾ cups heavy cream
salt and pepper
a pinch of nutmeg

TIPS

1. To reduce the chance of breaking the pie dough as you shape it into the pan, break off a spare bit and use to press the shell gently into place.
2. To remove the tart from the pan, carefully break off any overhang clinging to the rim. Sit the tart on top of a jar. Holding the pan firmly, push down so the rim is released. Slide the tart onto a plate or board to take to the table.

········ TIME SAVER ········

Reheat extra the next day or take into work and microwave. Freeze any extra. Defrost before reheating thoroughly.

PREP Sift the flour and salt into a large bowl. Cube the butter/lard and rub into the flour between your fingertips until it resembles fine bread crumbs. Add the water gradually, mixing together with a fork, until you have a pliable dough that's neither dry nor sticky. By machine: pulse the flour, salt, and butter until fine. Pour in the water gradually, pulsing between additions. Roll the dough into a ball, flatten into a disk, wrap in plastic wrap, and chill for 1 hour.

Preheat the oven to 425°F. Rub a tablespoon of soft butter over the bottom and sides of a 9 by 1¼-inch loose-bottom tart pan to help the dough cook/prevent sticking. Remove the dough from the refrigerator. Let it soften a little before rolling it out on a lightly floured board and fitting it to your tart pan, leaving an overhang (p201). Prick the base of the dough very lightly all over with a fork so it won't rise as it bakes.

Filling: Lay your bacon slices on a board. Remove any rind with a sharp chef's knife. Cut it into thick crosswise strips on the diagonal or snip with kitchen scissors. Melt the butter in a skillet on medium heat. Once it's foaming, scatter the bacon bits in. Fry for a few minutes, turning, until they're cooked but not crisp. Spoon onto paper towels and set aside.

Slice the cheese thinly and spread it evenly across the pie dough base. Scatter the bacon pieces evenly over the top so every slice will get some. Beat the yolks in a bowl with a fork, adding the cream, seasoning, and nutmeg until well incorporated. Pour the mix over the cheese and bacon.

COOK Bake for 20 minutes then reduce to 350°F for another 20 minutes, or until the filling has set and is browned on top. Remove. Cool for 10 minutes.

PLATE Slice the tart into portions at the table using a cake slice or very sharp knife. Serve with boiled new potatoes, a carrot and orange salad, or boiled new potatoes and a green salad with honey mustard dressing.

TO GO WITH

CARROT AND ORANGE SALAD

Coarsely grate 12 ounces peeled carrots. Mix with 1 peeled, chopped orange and 3 chopped dates. Toss in 3 tablespoons olive oil, 1 tablespoon lemon juice, and a pinch each of salt and sugar. Sprinkle with a few chopped cashews.

LEEK, TARRAGON, CHEDDAR, AND SOUR CREAM TART

FEEDS 6

INGREDIENTS

scant 1⅔ cups all-purpose flour
½ teaspoon fine salt
½ cup (1 stick) chilled butter or ¼ cup
  (½ stick) butter/¼ cup lard, plus
  extra for greasing
1 ounce strong Cheddar
2–3 tablespoons chilled water
1 egg white for sealing
FILLING
1 pound 2 ounces leeks
2 tablespoons butter
1 tablespoon olive oil
scant ¼ cup water
8 ounces strong Cheddar
scant ½ cup heavy/whipping cream
generous ⅔ cup sour cream
½–1 tablespoon chopped tarragon
4 large eggs
salt and pepper

TIP

Use uncooked rice or dry beans instead of
pie weights for baking blind.

My favorite tart; sweet, soft leek works a treat in the creamy cheese base. Using lard in your basic pie dough gives it a crumblier texture than all-butter. A top eat with friends and family.

PREP Make the pie dough. By hand: Sift the flour and salt into a large bowl. Cube the butter or butter/lard mix. Rub it lightly into the flour between your fingertips until it resembles fine bread crumbs. Finely grate the cheese. Stir it into the mix with a fork. Add the water gradually, mixing with the fork for pliable dough that's neither dry nor sticky (add more flour or water to get it right). Don't overhandle the pastry at any stage as it spoils the texture. Roll the dough lightly into a ball then flatten it into a disk. Wrap in plastic wrap and chill for 1 hour. By machine: Pulse the flour, salt, cheese, and butter until fine. Add the water gradually, pulsing between additions until a dough forms. Stop and test with your fingers to check it's not too dry. Roll, wrap, and chill.

Preheat the oven to 350°F. Sit the pastry on a floured board and let soften a little. Grease a 9 by 1¼-inch loose-bottom fluted tart pan. Roll the dough out in a circle to fit the pan plus 2 inches extra. Without stretching the dough, roll the pin under it and lift it over and down into the pan. Support the edges with one hand. Press into the bottom and sides for a close fit without it cracking. Use spare dough to fill any holes/breaks, leaving an overhang on the edges in case it shrinks. Prick the surface lightly with a fork.

COOK Cut a piece of wax paper and lay it into the dough to protect the base and sides. Fill it with pie weights and bake blind for 10 to 20 minutes, until the sides are hard and lightly colored. Remove the paper and weights and brush lightly with egg white. Bake again for 4 minutes. Cool.

Meantime, make the filling: Trim, wash, and dry the leeks. Slice the white and palest green parts across in ½-inch slices, discarding the tough dark green leek. Melt the butter with the oil in a large skillet on low heat. Add the slices of leek and let sweat for 2 minutes. Add the water, cover with a lid, and sweat for another 3 minutes or until soft but not browned, turning carefully if you need. Season to taste and let cool.

Grate the cheese finely and spread half of it evenly over the tart bottom. Tip the rest into a bowl with the cream, sour cream, and tarragon. Mix with a fork. Beat the eggs. Stir them into the mix. Arrange the softened drained leek evenly over the cheese, cut side down. Pour the cream mix evenly over the top and carry it carefully to the oven. Bake it for 40 minutes or until the filling is puffy and golden brown. Remove. Let it settle for 10 minutes.

PLATE Sit the tart on a plate or board. Cut it into slices at the table. Serve with cooled baby potatoes tossed in mayonnaise, a green salad with honey mustard dressing (p26), or a carrot and orange salad (p169).

PASTA, NOODLES, RICE, AND *Couscous*

Everyone remembers their first cooking disaster. Mine was a batch of pasta dough. Too many eggs died in vain that day, escaping from the well of flour I'd made, ending up splattered all over the kitchen floor. I was nine. I sulked for a bit and then got over it. Now I've got the method sorted it's a slicker operation and every so often I'll make ravioli (store-bought ones are too dry) or a lovely dish of homemade pasta. But I won't lie. I use the dried stuff for every day. A lot of the produce out there is excellent and, like all the other staples in this chapter, it's easy to cook and so fast. The key to the basics is to get the cooking method right: pasta needs to boil in loads more water than you'd think to stop it sticking. Some varieties of rice need rinsing before they cook to keep them fluffy, while others want to hold onto their starch to keep the grains glutinous. Couscous needs a little bit of help once it's prepped. The very simplicity and blandness of these basics means they will play a key supporting role in your cooking—pile in the flavors and enjoy yourself.

BAGGING YOUR PASTA
A Buyer's Guide

FRESH FROM THE DELI An expensive delicious treat and fast-cooking. FROM THE SUPERMARKET Hmm ... "fresh" prepacked is a bit faster to cook than dried but costs more and often thickens in cooking and so eats heavily.

DRIED FROM THE DELI Get the best artisan brands and adventurous shapes and varieties (squid ink/beet, etc.). These cost a bit more but eat well.
FROM THE SUPERMARKET Brilliant range and value in most. Dried pasta can be better than fresh and it's the ultimate convenient fast food. It's fast to cook (ok, a bit longer than "fresh") and cheap. Try out store-own brands (some are excellent) or get a good readily available artisan variety.

VARIETIES Pastas (dried and fresh) are made with or without egg. Pasta with egg takes a bit longer to cook and is richer, so you don't need so much per person. Brown pasta is healthier (more fiber and magnesium) but a heavier eat. Buy buckwheat, corn, rice, or soy based pastas to avoid gluten. Filled pasta is expensive to buy and is often dry, heavy, and disappointing. So make your own (p182).

PASTA STASH

Fresh pasta lasts 2 to 4 days in the refrigerator.

Dried pasta lasts 2 years or 1 year if made with egg (it's brittle, so store carefully).

Prepared pasta dishes for baking freeze well. Defrost then cook.

Toss ⅓ cup pine nuts in a dry pan to toast very lightly for 2 to 3 minutes until golden (not brown). Blitz in a processor with 1 garlic clove, 2 ounces basil, 3 ounces Parmesan, and the juice of ½ a lemon for just a few seconds. Add ½ cup good olive oil in a steady trickle for a thick green sauce.

SHAPES

Long pastas (spaghetti, linguine, angel hair, etc.) work best with light sauces.

Short pastas (penne, farfalle, fusilli, macaroni, etc.) work best with heavy sauces.

Ridged and hollow pastas are better at holding onto a sauce.

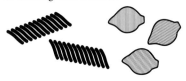

Baby pastas are designed to bang into soups for balance, difference, texture, and value.

PASTA COOKING ACTION

TIMING Cook it just before serving (don't precook and reheat). Fresh pasta cooks in 1 to 2 minutes. Fresh stuffed 2 to 6 minutes (filling- and size-dependent) Dried 8 to 15 minutes. Check the package for exact timings.

BIG PAN Get one with a lid (catering/hardware/Asian stores have bargains).

WATER Boil up at least 4 cups of water per 3½ ounces of pasta in a covered pan. Pasta needs lots of room to spread or it sticks. The water must be boiling before you add the pasta.

SALT Add 1½ heaping teaspoons per 4 cups of water to bring out the flavor just before you add the pasta.

OIL If you're cooking lasagna, add a bit to the water to prevent sticking.

STIR Stir the pasta once as you add it to the pan to prevent sticking.

TESTING Cook for the designated cooking time but test minutes before it's due. Fish a bit out and bite it. It should taste tender but not mushy. Italians call it "al dente" but get it as you like it. If it's to be baked into a dish (lasagna/macaroni) give it a bit less time at this stage.

DRAINING Tip into a colander or strainer to drain. Save a bit of pasta water to loosen your sauce if it needs it. Tip the pasta back into the warm pan.

DRESSING Add a little oil, butter, or reserved pasta cooking water. Add some or all of your sauce to coat or pile it onto the served pasta.

ALMOST INSTANT PASTA DRESSINGS

Stir the following into freshly cooked pasta…

butter, grated Parmesan, and black pepper

grated lemon zest and juice, cream, or crème fraîche

hot olive oil flavored with sliced garlic and diced chile

oil-based salad dressing

a good pesto sauce

PASTA FRIENDS

ANCHOVIES, BACON, BASIL, BUTTER, CHEESE SAUCE, CHILE, CREAM, CRÈME FRAICHE, EGGS, GARLIC, LEMONS, MASCARPONE, MOZZARELLA, MUSHROOMS, NUTMEG, OLIVE OIL, OLIVES, ONIONS, PANCETTA, PARMESAN (OR VEGETARIAN EQUIVALENT), PARSLEY, RAGU, RICOTTA, ROASTED VEGETABLES, SAUSAGES, SPECK, SPINACH, TOMATOES, WINE, ZUCCHINI

Noodle FRIENDS

BEAN SPROUTS, BLACK BEAN SAUCE, BROCCOLI, CHICKEN STOCK, CHILES, CHINESE LEAF, CILANTRO, FISH SAUCE, GARLIC, GINGER, GREEN BEANS, HOISIN SAUCE, LEMONS, LIMES, MALT VINEGAR, MINT, MISO, MUSHROOMS, ONIONS, OYSTER SAUCE, PEPPERS, PLUM SAUCE, RICE VINEGAR, RICE WINE, SESAME OIL, SCALLIONS, SOY SAUCE, SWEET CHILI SAUCE, SWEET BLACK VINEGAR, TERIYAKI SAUCE, TOFU, WATER CHESTNUTS

USE YOUR NOODLE
—WHAT TO GET FOR THE JOB—

You'll find a brilliant range of dried noodles in your local supermarket. Asian stores, and Chinese supermarkets stock a huge range and at good prices.

EGG NOODLES Found in the chilled cabinet or dried into nests or sheets. Get them thin, medium, or thicker to taste. Boil noodles (following package directions) and add to stir-fries or bang in soups. Fresh are wok-ready but more expensive and have a shorter shelf-life.

RAMEN NOODLES Thin Japanese egg noodles good for stir-fries/soups/salads.

SOBA NOODLES Taste nutty and are darker than normal noodles. Cook and serve cold in a dressing for salad.

UDON These wide, white noodles are great for soups and Asian stews.

CELLOPHANE NOODLES (aka Chinese vermicelli/glass noodles) Pretty bland, fine shreds of noodle designed to absorb flavors. Don't boil but soak for a few minutes (see the package) before using in soups, salads, and stir-fries. You can also deep-fry without soaking for crispy noodles.

RICE AND GRAINS

Store grains in airtight containers in a dark cupboard. Use within a year.

EASY-COOK RICE Not the nicest but the fastest. It's steamed before milling so long grains will stay separate during cooking.

AMERICAN ALL-PURPOSE RICE Your standard white or brown long-grain rice.

BASMATI RICE Top choice for curries and pilaf and a finer aromatic grain.

THAI FRAGRANT/JASMINE Good with Chinese, Thai, and curry dishes and great for salads.

STICKY RICE Traditional with Thai dishes served in the bowl or rolled into small balls. Sticky rice needs soaking overnight or for as long as you can before cooking.

RISOTTO RICE Supermarkets and delis stock a range of different varieties (vialone nano/carnaroli/arborio) of this short grain to make creamy risotto. Never rinse it.

COUSCOUS Shelved with grains in the store but actually a precooked pasta that just needs soaking in liquid to prepare it. Eat hot with vegetable and meat stews (tagines) or flavor and spice it up for salads.

BULGUR WHEAT Great with Eastern salads.

QUINOA A nutritionally perfect, gluten-free, supergrain, and complete protein which can be used instead of rice and couscous.

POLENTA Great either served wet (like mash) with flavors like herbs/butter/grated cheese/garlic added or set and brushed with oil, then broiled and served with a tomato or meat sauce or roast griddled vegetables. Instant cornmeal cooks in 5 minutes (check pack for directions).

|||||||||||| THE RICE COOKER |||||||||||||

FREESTYLE METHOD Bring a large pan of lightly salted water to a boil. RINSE easy cook/American/basmati rice in a strainer to prevent sticking. Add to boiling water. Stir once. Cook it, uncovered, on a rolling boil. Test a few grains to check they're tender. Easy-cook, test at 5 minutes. American and basmati, test at 8. Brown rice takes 15 to 20 minutes. Rinse just-tender rice in a strainer with boiling water from the kettle. Sit the strainer back on the pan. Cover. Leave for 3 minutes. Fluff it up.

ABSORPTION METHOD For Thai/jasmine/sticky rice. Add 2½ parts water to 1 part rice a pan with a little salt. Stir once. Cover. Simmer on very low heat for 10 to 15 minutes until swollen and tender. Leave for 10 minutes before decanting.

RICE SPECIALS

1 STIR-FRY RICE
Cook basmati, jasmine, or American rice following your method of choice (see above). Cool rapidly and chill immediately so it's safe to use. Don't leave it around at room temperature. Stir-fry from cold so the grains stay separate.

2 STUFFED VEG
Mix cooked and cooled rice with spices/herbs/oils/grated cheese/cream/sautéed shallot/seasoning/lemon zest/meat ragu, etc. Stuff into hollowed out tomatoes, bell peppers, or zucchini, drizzle over olive oil, and bake in a preheated oven at 350°F until the veg are soft and the stuffing is piping hot.

3 *Pilaf* Tip basmati rice into a bowl and cover with cold water. Rinse and change 6 times over an hour or until clear. Fry 2 diced shallots and garlic in oil or butter until soft. Add the rice. Turn for 2 minutes or until colored. Add chicken or vegetable stock (twice the liquid to volume of rice) and simmer over low heat for 10 to 15 minutes. Season and add minced herbs. Eat with lamb kebabs (p124), griddled harissa mackerel (p142), or chicken in piri-piri sauce.

RICE FRIENDS

BACON, BEANS, BEEF, BROCCOLI, CHEDDAR, CHICKEN, CHILE, CHILI SAUCE, CREAM, EGG, EGGPLANT, GARLIC, GREEN VEGETABLES, HARISSA, HOISIN SAUCE, LAMB, LEMON, MINT, MUSHROOMS, OILY FISH, ONION, PARMESAN, PARSLEY, PEAS, PORK, RAGU, SHALLOT, SOY SAUCE, SCALLIONS, STOCK, WHITE WINE

STAPLES NUTRITION

GRAINS AND STAPLES SHOULD MAKE UP ⅔ OF YOUR PLATE. Whole grains are nutritionally superior to processed grains as they contain more fiber and other nutrients.

PASTA IS A COMPLEX **CARBOHYDRATE** It releases energy slowly, keeping blood sugar levels steady, making it ideal for athletes and for EVERYDAY ENERGY NEEDS. IT'S LOW IN FAT AND CONTAINS ADDED **FOLIC ACID** AND **IRON** WHICH TACKLES ANEMIA AND GIVES MENTAL FOCUS. It's easy to digest and the starch relaxes the body making it good for insomnia and a mood enhancer.

BROWN RICE IS A RICH SOURCE OF **PROTEIN** *for* GROWTH, **CARBOHYDRATE**, **FIBRE**, *Vitamin B1*, **NIACIN**, AND **IRON** —WHITE HAS LESS.

BULGUR WHEAT IS PACKED WITH **B VITAMINS**

QUINOA IS A PERFECT **PROTEIN** SO PARTICULARLY GOOD FOR VEGETARIANS AND WHEN CASH IS SHORT. Balance staples with loads of vitamin-rich vegetables and your choice of fish, meat, eggs, and cheeses.

SPAGHETTI WITH EASY TOMATO SAUCE

 HEALTHY FAST ## FEEDS 4

Simple as you like—and trust me you will like. This sauce is perfect on spaghetti (though it goes well with other pasta shapes too) and works in many different scenarios. Get the seasoning right to balance any acidity…

INGREDIENTS

5½ ounces dried spaghetti
salt and pepper
a glug of olive oil
a little bit of butter
a handful or two of freshly grated
    Parmesan (or vegetarian alternative)
a few basil leaves (optional)
EASY TOMATO SAUCE
3 tablespoons olive oil
2 garlic cloves, peeled and finely sliced
a pinch of red pepper flakes/crumbled
    dried chile
2 x 14-ounces cans of chopped/whole
    plum tomatoes
a good pinch of sugar
a squeeze of lemon juice or a drop of
    balsamic vinegar (optional)

—— CHANGE IT UP ——

1. Try tearing in a few fresh basil leaves as you finish the sauce, or swirling a teaspoon of pesto (p172) through it before serving.
2. For a chili tomato sauce, sweat off 1–2 finely diced red chiles for 3 minutes before adding to the sauce in place of the red pepper flakes.
3. For a thicker tomato sauce, sweat off a minced onion for 5 to 10 minutes before adding the red pepper flakes and garlic.
4. If you like it creamy, blitz the cooked sauce with a stick blender or in a food processor with 2 tablespoons mascarpone or cream cheese until smooth.

PREP Make the sauce: Put a heavy-bottom pan over gentle heat. Add two-thirds of the oil then the garlic and red pepper flakes. Let it warm through to soften the garlic for 2 minutes or so (coloring will turn it bitter). Add the chopped tomatoes directly. If using whole plum tomatoes, squish them in with your fingers or break them up with a wooden spoon. Add the sugar and season with salt and pepper. Stir well. Bring to a boil then lower to a simmer and cook for 10 to 20 minutes.

PREP Meantime, cook the pasta: Put a large, covered pan of water with a pinch of salt and a glug of oil onto boil. Add the pasta and cook until *al dente* (p173 or check your package for timings).

Finish the sauce: Season to taste, add a little more sugar if it's sharp or a drop of lemon juice or balsamic to brighten it. Add the remainder of the olive oil.

Drain the pasta into a colander. Tip it straight back into the pan and add the butter and a little black pepper. Stir in the sauce.

PLATE Stick a large fork into the pasta. Twirl to hook a reasonable amount. Lift and place onto plates or into warm bowls. Or grab it out with a pair of tongs. Scatter over some Parmesan, top with a few basil leaves, if you like, and serve with bread or garlic bread (p178) and a arugula salad with balsamic dressing (p28).

BONUS BITES

CHILI AND BACON TOMATO SAUCE
Blitz a can of chopped tomatoes. Fry a handful of diced bacon/pancetta with 1 diced small onion, a diced chile, and a diced garlic clove. Add the tomatoes and cook as before.

RAW TOMATO SAUCE
Chop a handful of good vine or cherry tomatoes. Spoon out the seeds and roughly chop. Marinate in a mix of 2 tablespoons olive oil and 1 tablespoon wine vinegar with a few torn basil leaves or a bit of chopped parsley to taste. Alternatively, toss with a few chopped olives, ½ teaspoon drained capers and a drizzle of olive oil. Leave for 30 minutes. Toss into spaghetti.

STIR-IN SPAGHETTI CARBONARA

FAST

FEEDS 2

Here the heat of the pasta cooks the egg yolks and pulls everything together into a beautifully creamy sauce. A must-have dinner.

INGREDIENTS

a pinch of salt
a glug of oil
2 large egg yolks
scant ¼ cup freshly grated Parmesan/
    pecorino cheese, plus extra for
    serving
1 tablespoon milk
7 ounces spaghetti
freshly ground black pepper
a few crispy garlic bread crumbs
    (optional, p201)

BACON AND MUSHROOM STIR-IN

3 ounces unsmoked bacon/pancetta
a little bit of butter
2 tablespoons oil
6 small white mushrooms

SMOKED SALMON STIR-IN

a little freshly chopped dill (or dried)
2–3½ ounces mild smoked salmon
lemon wedges

PREP Put a large pan of water onto boil for the pasta, adding the salt and oil. Now, prep your choice of stir-in. For the bacon and mushroom: cut the bacon/pancetta into strips. Heat the butter and oil in a skillet, add the meat, and cook until it releases fat and is lightly browned. Remove. Slice the mushrooms. Add to the pan and stir until soft but holding shape. Season lightly. Set aside. For the salmon: Mince the dill and slice the fish into strips. Make the garlic bread crumbs, if using.

Beat the egg yolks in a bowl. Add the grated cheese and milk.

COOK Add the spaghetti to the boiling water and cook until *al dente* or as you like it (see p173 or check your package for timings). Drain well. Throw the pasta back into the pan. Add the egg and cheese mixture immediately along with your choice of stir-in. Stir well to coat the strands.

PLATE Twirl spaghetti into bowls or plates. Add plenty of black pepper. Scatter with Parmesan and/or crispy garlic bread crumbs and serve with garlic bread. Serve the salmon with lemon wedges to squeeze over.

**** CASH SAVER ****
Substitute cubes of leftover post-roast ham for the bacon pieces.

• • • • • • • • • • • • TO GO WITH **• • • • • • • • •**

GARLIC BREAD

Preheat the oven to 425°F. Slash a baguette, diagonally, with a bread knife, but keep it intact. Mix ½ cup (1 stick) soft butter, a 4½-ounce ball of mozzarella cheese, ⅔ cup grated Cheddar, 3 crushed garlic cloves, a squeeze of lemon juice, a little pepper, and 2 tablespoons chopped parsley together in a bowl. Spread the mix into each slash, smearing any last bits over the top and wrap in foil. Sit on a baking sheet (or chill/freeze it until needed) and bake for 20 minutes, until hot and crisp but sticky inside.

SPICY SAUSAGE PENNE

FEEDS 4

INGREDIENTS

1 pound penne
a pinch of salt
a glug of oil
freshly grated Parmesan, for serving
SAUCE
1 tablespoon olive oil
4 good spicy sausages (ideally Italian
   but Toulouse or chorizo work)
2 onions, minced
6 garlic cloves, crushed
2 good pinches of red pepper flakes/
   1 red chile, finely diced
½ cup red wine
1 x 14-ounce can of chopped tomatoes
2 pinches of dried oregano
1 teaspoon sugar
1 tablespoon tomato paste
1–2 teaspoon chili sauce or harissa
   paste (optional)
2 ounces mozzarella cubes or 2–3
   tablespoons heavy/sour cream
   (optional)
a handful of fresh parsley, chopped
   (optional)

——— CHANGE IT UP———

For a vegetarian alternative, replace the
sausage with 1 large chopped eggplant. Cook
the onion until soft then add the garlic and
eggplant. Fry it gently for 15 minutes before
adding the wine and continuing as above.

TIP

If you've overestimated the amount of pasta
you need for any dish, transform it into a
salad for the next day. Toss it in a bit of oil
or salad dressing or stir some pesto (p172 or
a good store-bought one) in there and add
whatever else you fancy.

*Get yourself a few spicy sausages and crumble them up into a few
basic pantry ingredients; you've got yourself a punchy sauce in less
than half an hour. It's also great with ribbon pastas like tagliatelle.*

PREP Make the sauce: Put a large frying pan or casserole over medium
heat. Add the olive oil. Slice the sausage open, extract the meat, and
crumble into the pan. Cook, stirring, for a few minutes until colored on all
sides. Add the onions, garlic, and red pepper flakes/diced chile, lower the heat,
and cook, stirring, for 10 minutes. Add the wine, bring to a boil, and cook until
the wine has evaporated.

Add the tomatoes, oregano, sugar, and tomato paste, lower the heat, and
simmer for 15 minutes, stirring sometimes. Taste and adjust the seasoning,
adding the chili sauce/harissa, if using, to taste. Let simmer over very gentle
heat, adding a splash of water to the sauce if it is looking too thick. Meantime,
put a large, covered pan of water with a bit of salt and oil onto boil.

COOK Add the penne to the boiling water. Cook until *al dente* (p173 or
check your package for timings). Drain well.

If using cream, stir into the sauce. Stir the sauce into the pasta, adding
mozzarella cubes and parsley, if using.

PLATE Tong the pasta out onto plates or pasta bowls. Top with parsley.
Serve with Parmesan, red wine, good bread, and salad.

ASPARAGUS
RAVIOLI

Recipe on p182

ASPARAGUS RAVIOLI

FEEDS 4

INGREDIENTS

scant 2¼ cups strong white bread
*   *flour, plus extra for rolling out*
salt and black pepper
3 large eggs
1 tablespoon olive oil
2 tablespoons freshly grated Parmesan

FILLING

11 ounces fresh asparagus
3 teaspoons ricotta
3 teaspoons mascarpone
3 teaspoons freshly grated Parmesan
½ teaspoon finely grated lemon zest
½ garlic clove, peeled and crushed
3 teaspoons fresh bread crumbs (p201)
a squeeze of lemon juice

SAUCE

1 tablespoon butter
a good squeeze of lemon juice
a few sage leaves, finely sliced

—— BONUS BITE ——

TOMATO RAVIOLI

Blitz up ⅔ cup easy tomato sauce (p176) in a food processor and mix together with 6 teaspoons bread crumbs and 8 teaspoons grated Parmesan. Season to taste and use to fill the ravioli.

BUTTERNUT SQUASH RAVIOLI

Preheat the oven to 400°F. Cut, peel, and weigh out 11 ounces of butternut squash. Roughly chop into cubes, toss in oil, and roast in the oven for 15 minutes or fry gently until soft. Cool then blitz in a food processor until smooth. Add scant ½ cup grated Parmesan, ½ tsp nutmeg, the grated zest of 1 lemon, and a squeeze of lemon juice, and stir to combine. Season to taste and use to fill the ravioli.

A milestone on your journey to veteran status: making your own pasta dough does take a bit of time but the results are spectacular. Use a (not costly) hand crank pasta machine to get your pasta silk-thin.

PREP Make the pasta. By hand: Take a large bowl and sift the flour and half a teaspoon of salt into it. Crack the eggs into a hollow in the middle then add the oil. With your hand in a claw shape, move from the center outward in a clockwise motion, mixing everything together to form a soft dough. By machine: Mix and pulse the dry ingredients in a food processor adding the egg and oil gradually through the funnel. Sit the dough on a floured board and knead like bread (p200) for 10 minutes until silky smooth, adding a bit more flour if still a bit sticky. Cover and leave for 1 hour or wrap in plastic wrap and chill until needed.

Filling: Put a skillet of water onto boil. Bend the asparagus spears to break them off at their woody ends and discard. Add to the pan and boil for 2 to 3 minutes until just tender. Drain, roughly chop, and let cool, then put into a processor and blitz with the cheeses, lemon zest, and garlic until just blended. Stir in the bread crumbs and season for a stuffing that can just hold its shape (add more bread crumbs if too wet, or a little extra water or lemon juice if too stiff).

Roll the pasta. By machine: Divide the dough into 6 pieces. Cover 5 with a dish towel and flatten the remaining piece with your hand. Put the roller on your pasta machine onto its widest setting. Roll the piece through. Guide then catch it with your other hand as it emerges. Fold in two and repeat. Now, reduce the width setting on the machine. Lightly dust the pasta with flour to ensure smoothness then roll it through it again. It will thin out and become silky smooth. Repeat until you're on the tightest setting, flouring lightly between each rolling so it doesn't tear. Repeat with the rest. Leave for 10 minutes.

By hand: Cut the dough in two. Flatten into circles. Roll the first piece out and away from you with a rolling pin. As you pull it stretch it back with your other hand. Use the pin to flip it over and quarter turn. Repeat until paper thin.

Make the ravioli: Lay your first piece of pasta on a table or clear, clean counter. Place heaping teaspoons of filling down the center of the sheet to the halfway point, leaving a good space between each one. Brush a square around each mound using egg wash. Now, fold the other half of the pasta over the top. Press down gently around the mounds to seal and exclude the air. Cut around the mounds with a 2¾-inch cookie cutter or free-style with a knife. Repeat with the rest. Let them dry for 20 minutes if you have time.

COOK Bring a large pan of salted water to a boil and add a little oil. Meanwhile, melt the butter for the sauce gently in a pan. Add the lemon juice and sage, stir, and season to taste. Cook the ravioli a few at a time, for 2 to 3 minutes. Remove carefully with a slotted spoon and drain.

PLATE Divide the ravioli between warmed plates or bowls. Spoon over the sauce and scatter over the Parmesan. Serve with bread to mop up the juices.

CLASSIC OLD-SCHOOL MACARONI CHEESE

FEEDS 4

INGREDIENTS

1 small onion, peeled
6 black peppercorns
3¾ cups milk
8 ounces macaroni/penne
4 tablespoons butter, plus extra for
    baking
generous ⅓ cup all-purpose flour
1 teaspoon English mustard
a good squeeze of lemon juice
1¾ cups grated strong Cheddar
salt and black pepper
a shake of Worcestershire sauce/
    mushroom ketchup (optional)

TOPPING

2 ounces white bread
½ garlic clove, peeled
a bit of parsley
a bit of grated lemon zest

—— **BONUS BITE** ——

SWISS-STYLE BAKED MACARONI

Preheat the oven to 400°F. Boil 4½ ounces
potatoes for 5 to 10 minutes until just soft.
Drain. Meantime, fry 2 ounces bacon cubes
in a pan for 5 minutes, until they release
their fat and crisp up. Remove from the
pan then add the potatoes to cook until
just coloring. Cook 4¼ ounces macaroni
as before. Make up the béchamel sauce
following the technique above, but with
2½ cups milk, 2 tablespoons of butter, 3
tablespoons of flour, and scant ½ cup each
of grated Gruyère and Cheddar cheese.
Add a glug of white wine or Kirsch if you
like before adding the cheese. Stir the pasta,
sauce, bacon, and potato together, tip into
a dish, scatter with a little extra cheese
and bake for 20 to 30 minutes. Eat with
applesauce.

This old-school favorite is packed full of flavor. If you're short on time don't bother to infuse the milk. Use a strong cheese.

PREP Start your sauce: Put the onion, peppercorns, and milk into a pan and heat to the point of boiling. Remove from the heat and leave for 30 minutes for the flavor to infuse. Strain though a strainer and set aside.

Meantime, cook the pasta. Bring a large pan of salted water to a boil. Add the pasta. Cover. When it boils again, take the lid off and cook until *al dente* (p173 or check your package for timings). Drain. Preheat the oven to 400°F.

Melt the butter in a heavy-bottom pan. Add the flour. Stir rapidly with a wooden spoon over low heat for 2 minutes to cook out the flour. Remove from the heat.

Very gradually, beat the flavored milk into the paste with a balloon whisk or spoon until absolutely smooth. Return to the heat and stir until the mix boils and thickens, adding a splash more milk if necessary. Lower the heat and gently simmer for 5 minutes. Add the mustard, lemon juice, and cheese and season to taste, adding a dash of Worcestershire sauce/mushroom ketchup if you like.

COOK Mix the pasta and sauce together. Tip into a large buttered dish or a few small ones. To make the topping, blitz the bread with the garlic and parlsey. Add the lemon zest and scatter over the top. Dot with butter or a few drops of oil and bake for 20 to 30 minutes, until bubbling and golden.

PLATE Spoon into bowls and enjoy on the couch. Alternatively, serve up with roasted whole vine tomatoes (p78) or zingy tomato green beans (p51).

TOMATO AND OLIVE LASAGNA

  FEEDS 3

Lasagna's a great crowd pleaser; layer up ragu with lasagna and béchamel sauce and everyone's happy (p85). For something less obvious (but lovely), give this a go. The pungent sauce packs a delicious punch.

INGREDIENTS

6–10 lasagna sheets
  (dried/chilled/homemade)
⅔–scant 1 cup grated Parmesan
4 ounces mozzarella, diced
a few crispy garlic bread crumbs
  (p201, optional)

TOMATO SAUCE

3 tablespoons olive oil
a little bit of butter
3 pinches of red pepper flakes
4 garlic cloves, peeled and crushed
2 x 14-ounce cans of chopped tomatoes
½ teaspoon sugar
a good pinch of dried oregano
generous ¾ cup pitted black olives
3 teaspoons capers, drained
6–8 anchovies (optional)
fresh basil (optional)
salt and pepper

BÉCHAMEL SAUCE

2 tablespoons butter
3 tablespoons flour
2½ cups milk
1 teaspoon English mustard
a good squeeze of lemon juice
2 ounces strong Cheddar
1 ounce Parmesan
salt and pepper

TIP
Salted anchovies from a can or jar can be used directly. For a milder taste, soak them in milk for 30 minutes, then drain.

PREP If using fresh lasagna: Make, roll and cut the pasta to shape and size following the instructions for ravioli (p182). Cover with a floured dish towel. Dry for 1 to 2 hours before using.

For the tomato sauce: Put a medium pan onto low heat and add the oil and butter. Add the red pepper flakes and garlic and cook for 2 minutes before adding the tomatoes, sugar, and oregano. Simmer gently for 10 minutes. Add the olives, capers, anchovies, and basil, if using, and season to taste.

For the béchamel sauce: Melt the butter in a heavy-bottom pan. Add the flour. Stir rapidly with a wooden spoon over low heat for 2 minutes. Remove from the heat. Slowly pour the milk into the paste, bit by bit, with a balloon whisk or spoon until absolutely smooth. Return it to the heat and stir until the mix boils and thickens, adding a little extra milk if it needs it. Lower to a gentle simmer and cook for 5 minutes. Add the mustard, lemon juice, cheese, and season. If using dried pasta sheets, soak in cold water for 10 minutes. Drain well.

Preheat the oven to 400°F. Layer up your lasagna: Grease a shallow ovenproof dish. Smear a little of the béchamel sauce across the bottom. Cover with a layer of pasta, then a layer of tomato sauce. Add some grated Parmesan and diced mozzarella before layering up again in the same way. Finish with a layer of pasta and top with the béchamel sauce, a handful of grated Parmesan, a little extra grated mozzarella, or garlic bread crumbs, if using.

COOK Cover with foil and bake for 30 minutes, uncovering for the last 10, until the cheese has melted and the top is golden brown. Remove from the oven and let settle for 5 minutes before digging in.

PLATE Spoon onto plates or into bowls. Eat with a sharply dressed arugula salad and a bit of bread to mop up the juices.

BONUS BITES

EGGPLANT AND ZUCCHINI LASAGNA
Make the tomato sauce as above but omit the olives, capers, and anchovies. Slice 2 eggplants and 3 zucchini lengthwise into strips, brush lightly with oil, and griddle both for 5 to 10 minutes until softening. Add the veg slices to the lasagna when layering up as before.

MUSHROOM AND TARRAGON LASAGNA
Soak a handful of dried porcini in hot water for 20 minutes. Drain and cut into small pieces. Lightly fry 1 pound of mixed mushrooms (e.g. cremini/portobello/oyster) with 1 crushed garlic clove, a few tarragon leaves, and the porcini in a little butter and oil. Add 2 tablespoons heavy cream, a sprinkling of grated nutmeg, a squeeze of lemon juice, and season to taste. Layer béchamel, lasagna, mushrooms, Parmesan, béchamel, etc., and bake as above.

SPINACH AND RICOTTA CANNELLONI

FEEDS 4

INGREDIENTS

6–10 lasagna sheets
   (dried/chilled/homemade)
   or 12 small dried cannelloni tubes
4 tablespoons heavy/whipping cream
a few good handfuls of grated
   Parmesan/Cheddar/mozzarella
SAUCE
2–3 tablespoons olive oil
1 medium onion, peeled and minced
3 garlic cloves, peeled and crushed
a good pinch of red pepper flakes
2 x 16-ounce cans of chopped tomatoes
1 teaspoon sugar
1 teaspoon balsamic vinegar
salt and black pepper
STUFFING
9 ounces spinach leaves
1 x 9-ounce tub ricotta
2 small egg yolks
grated lemon zest, to taste
grated nutmeg, to taste (optional)
generous ⅓ cup grated Parmesan
salt and pepper

—— CHANGE IT UP ——

1. For a creamy cannelloni, top the bake
   with béchamel sauce (p185).
2. For a change of flavor, swap the balsamic
   vinegar for 1 teaspoon vodka instead.

TIP

Use the spinach mix to stuff ravioli (p182) or
whiz it up in a food processor and add it to
easy tomato sauce (p176).

Another classic baked pasta dish and a sophisticated blend of flavors. These pasta tubes are best made using either fresh or dried sheets of lasagna. Soften them up and roll them around the stuffing before saucing and baking. Skip the nutmeg if you're not keen on the flavor.

PREP For fresh lasagna: Make, roll and cut the pasta to shape and size (p182). Cover with a floured dish towel. Dry for 1 to 2 hours.

Make the sauce: Put a pan onto heat and add the oil. Tip in the onion, garlic, and red pepper flakes and cook on low heat until very soft, not colored, about 5 to 8 minutes. Add the tomatoes, sugar, and balsamic vinegar and season to taste. Bring to a boil, then reduce the heat to simmer over very low heat for 30 minutes, stirring occasionally. Set aside.

Make the stuffing: Wash the spinach but don't drain it. Bang it into a large pan with 2 tablespoons of water on very low heat. Turn with a spoon as it wilts right down over 3 to 4 minutes. Tip it into a colander to drain, and squeeze to remove excess moisture. Cool and roughly chop. Tip it into a bowl, add the remaining stuffing ingredients, and mix well, adjusting the seasoning to taste.

Preheat the oven to 400°F.

If using dried own or store-bought lasagna, put a large pan of salted water onto heat. When it boils, add the sheets and cook for 1 minute until just softening and pliable. Drain. Cut into large squares if you need. Otherwise, get your pliable store-bought sheets or nocook tubes for stuffing. Stuff or wrap-around: Divide the filling between your fresh lasagna squares. Roll up into tubes and sit seam-side down in a single layer in a greased ovenproof dish. Alternatively, spoon the mix into your cannelloni tubes. Pour your tomato sauce evenly over the lot. Drizzle with cream and sprinkle with grated cheese.

COOK Bang your cannelloni straight into the oven and bake for 20 to 30 minutes, or until hot all through and bubbling.

PLATE Spoon onto plates from the dish on the table. Enjoy with classic green salad, a plate of sliced tomatoes, and shallots drizzled in olive oil and some good bread for mopping the sauce up.

BONUS BITE

BIG MAC AND CHEESE
Sweat off 1 chopped onion and a crushed garlic clove in oil until soft. Add 11 ounces ground beef/pork, season with salt and pepper, then fry for 10 minutes. Cool. Mix with generous 1 cup ricotta, scant ½ cup freshly grated Parmesan, and 2 ounces mozzarella. Wrap into lasagna sheets or stuff into tubes before covering with tomato sauce and cooking as above.

CHAR SIU PORK
ON SOFT NOODLES
WITH BEAN SPROUTS

FEEDS 2

INGREDIENTS

1 x 14 ounces–1 pound 2 ounces
plump pork tenderloin
2 tablespoons thin honey
a splash of water

MARINADE

1 tablespoon granulated sugar
1 tablespoon yellow bean curd sauce
1 tablespoon oyster sauce
1 tablespoon Shaoxing rice wine
1 tablespoon red chili bean curd
a splash of sesame oil
a pinch of Chinese five spice

NOODLES

3 nests or sheets of egg noodles
2 tablespoons peanut oil
a splash of sesame oil
1 garlic clove, peeled and thinly sliced
a handful of bean sprouts
2 teaspoons soy sauce

—— **BONUS BITE** ——
PORK RAMEN

Mix 1 teaspoon superfine sugar, 1 tablespoon malt vinegar, 1 tablespoon sweet chili sauce, 2 tablespoons fish sauce, 1 teaspoon tomato ketchup, and a bit of finely diced red chile in a bowl to make a finishing sauce. Set aside. Bring 3¾ cups chicken stock to a boil with ¼ star anise, a peeled and finely sliced thumb-sized piece of ginger, and 3 garlic cloves. Cover and let simmer for at least 20 minutes. Strain the stock, season to taste (adding a dash of soy if you like), and return to the heat. Add a good handful of chopped Chinese cabbage/iceberg lettuce and simmer for a minute. Add a couple of bundles of ramen noodles to the stock and cook for 1 minute or until done. Divide the noodle broth between serving bowls and top with sliced char siu pork, a few bean sprouts, and 2 sliced scallions. Serve with the sauce.

Racks of barbecued char siu pork hanging from hooks in the windows of London's Chinatown are one of my earliest food memories. It's definitely worth a trip to your Asian grocery store to stock up on ingredients for this. You could get away without the red bean curd here but hold out for the yellow if you can. Try it on bowls of rice if you're out of noodles.

PREP Make the marinade: mix all the ingredients together in a large nonmetallic dish.

Remove the pork tenderloin from its packaging if necessary. Pat dry and trim off any fat/membrane with a filleting knife. Sit the meat in the dish, and turn it in the marinade so that it is coated. Chill overnight, or for at least 5 hours.

Remove the pork from the refrigerator at least 30 minutes before cooking to give it time to get to room temperature. Preheat the oven to 425°F. Boil a kettle.

COOK Pour the boiling water into a roasting pan and sit on a low shelf in the oven. Remove the pork from the marinade and sit on a metal rack on the shelf directly above the pan. Cook for 10 minutes. Lower the temperature to 350°F and brush the meat with marinade to stop it drying out. Give it another 5 to 10 minutes until cooked through, but not dry. Remove from the oven and set aside to rest for 5 minutes.

Preheat the broiler to high. Mix the honey and water to make a glaze. Brush it over the pork. Broil for 3 to 4 minutes, turning once, until the edges char very slightly. Remove and set aside.

Cook the noodles in boiling water according to the package directions. Drain. Heat the oils in a wok. Throw in the garlic and bean sprouts, tossing and stirring for 2 minutes, or until cooked. Add the noodles and toss until hot. Add the soy sauce.

To make a sauce, put the marinade into a pan with a few tablespoons of water from the pan in the oven. Boil thoroughly for 2 minutes.

PLATE Carve the pork into slices. Heap the noodles into bowls and lay the meat over the top. Drizzle with the sauce to finish.

ASIAN NOODLES AND STIR-FRY VEG IN SAUCE

HEALTHY FAST

FEEDS 2

INGREDIENTS

5 ounces egg noodles
3½ ounces broccoli
1 small onion, peeled
¾-inch piece of fresh ginger
2 garlic cloves, peeled
1 red chile
4 shiitake mushrooms
1 fat head of pak choi
2 ounces green beans
½ cup chicken/vegetable stock
    (p49/p15)
2 teaspoons cornstarch
1 tablespoon peanut oil
1 teaspoon sesame oil
1 tablespoon soy sauce
2 tablespoons oyster/black bean sauce
salt and pepper

—— CHANGE IT UP ——

1. For a chicken stir-fry, chop bits of chicken breast/thigh into bite-size bits. Toss in a bit of soy, rice wine, and a pinch of sugar. Leave for a bit. Stir-fry in 1 tablespoon each of peanut/sesame oil for 3 to 4 minutes until white all through. Remove. Cook the vegetables as before and stir in with the noodles to finish.

2. For a tofu stir-fry, marinade as above and throw on top of the cooked noodle dish.

A simple, fast, throw-together meal with some lovely flavors.

PREP Cook the noodles: put a large pan of water onto boil. Throw the noodles in. Turn off the heat and leave for 2 to 3 minutes until cooked (or follow the package directions). Drain well. Refresh in cold water. Set aside.

Prep the veg: Wash the the broccoli and divide into florets. Slice the onion into half moons roughly ⅛ inch thick. Peel and grate the ginger. Slice the garlic and seed (p16) and slice the chile. Slice the mushrooms. Wash the pak choi and separate the leaves. Wash and trim the beans.

Warm the chicken/vegetable stock in a small pan. Spoon two tablespoons of the stock out into a cup, add the cornstarch and stir it in.

COOK Stir-fry: Heat the peanut and sesame oils in a wok. Add the onion, beans, and broccoli, toss and stir-fry for 2 minutes. Add the garlic, ginger, and mushrooms. Stir-fry for 2 minutes. Add the pak choi and cook for 1 minute. Add the soy, chile, and chosen sauce. Cook for a minute. Add the stock and cornstarch mix and season. Let it bubble to thicken. Stir the noodles into coat and cook through.

PLATE Tip into bowls and enjoy as it is with cups of green tea, or serve alongside char siu pork (p187).

VEGETABLE KORMA
WITH BASMATI RICE

FEEDS 3 TO 4

INGREDIENTS

8 cardamom pods
1 teaspoon ground cumin
1 teaspoon ground coriander
1 teaspoon turmeric
1 small cinnamon stick
1½ cups basmati rice
3 garlic cloves, peeled and crushed
a thumb-sized piece of fresh ginger,
    peeled and grated
1 red chile, seeded (p16) and diced
1 tablespoon peanut oil
2 tablespoons butter
2 medium onions, peeled and sliced
1 small eggplant, chopped
7 ounces butternut squash, peeled and
    cubed
1 mealy potato, peeled and cubed
¾ cup canned chickpeas, drained
1½ cups water/vegetable stock (p15)
4 ounces ladies fingers, trimmed and
    sliced across
a small handful of green beans,
    trimmed and sliced
⅔ cup whipping/heavy cream
4 tablespoons yogurt
a handful of fresh cilantro, chopped
a good sprinkle of garam masala
salt and pepper
1 tablespoon ground almonds
a good squeeze of lemon juice

Here the delicate fluffy rice complements a subtle creamy korma. Prep everything up in advance and it's easy. If you don't do dairy, make up the tomato-based curry at the bottom of the page instead.

PREP Organize your spices: Bash the cardamom lightly and add to a dish with the cumin, coriander, turmeric, and cinnamon stick. Rinse the rice in a strainer under running water. Set aside. Put cold water into a pan ready to boil later. Set the garlic, ginger, and chile to one side on a plate. Prep the veg.

COOK Put a large pan onto heat. Add the oil and butter. Fry the onion for 5 minutes, or until soft but not colored. Add the garlic, ginger, and chile and cook, stirring, for 2 minutes. Tip in the spices and stir for 30 seconds as they release fragrance. Stir in the eggplant, squash, potato, and chickpeas.

Add the water/vegetable stock and bring to a boil. Reduce the heat and simmer on low for 10 minutes, or until the squash is just tender. If it's looking dry, add a splash more water.

Put the pan of rice water onto boil, covered. Add the rice. Reduce the heat. Cover and simmer for 10 minutes (p175) or as the package directs.

Meantime, add the ladies fingers and beans to the curry. Cook for 5 minutes or until tender. Stir in the cream, yogurt, chopped cilantro, and garam masala and season to taste. Simmer gently for 5 minutes. Taste again and adjust the seasoning if needed. Add a few ground almonds for a slightly thicker texture and/or a little lemon juice to get the right acidity.

Test the rice for doneness—it should be soft and plump. Drain into a strainer. Sit the strainer back into the pan and cover with the lid for 2 minutes.

PLATE Tip the rice into a bowl and fluff it up with a fork. Serve with the korma as is, or with poppadoms, naan bread (p130), mango chutney, honey mint raita (p130), and other meat curries.

BONUS BITES

TOMATO VEGETABLE CURRY
Fry 1 minced large onion, a little grated ginger, 3 crushed garlic cloves, and 2 seeded and diced red chiles until soft. Add 2 chopped tomatoes and the spices as above and cook for 3 minutes. Add 8 tablespoons strained tomatoes and 1 cup water with 7 ounces cubed butternut squash, a handful of cauliflower florets, 1½ cups canned chickpeas, and a few sliced ladies fingers. Simmer gently for 20 minutes. Uncover. Simmer for an additional 10 minutes to thicken. Taste and season. Finish with a large handful of fresh cilantro, 1 tablespoon lemon juice, and 1 teaspoon garam masala and serve with rice.

STICKY RICE WITH THAI VEGETABLE CURRY

FEEDS 3

INGREDIENTS

1¼ cups Thai sticky rice/jasmine rice
7 ounces eggplant
1 medium onion, peeled
5 ounces new potatoes, scrubbed
7 ounces butternut squash, peeled and
    seeds removed
3 ounces fine green beans
3½ ounces carrot, peeled
5 ounces mushrooms
4 ounces tofu and 1 tablespoon soy
    (optional)
1 tablespoon peanut oil
2 x 14-ounces cans of lowfat coconut
    milk
a small handful of cashews (optional)
a squeeze of lime juice
a handful of fresh cilantro/torn basil
    leaves (optional)
1 lime, cut into wedges

CURRY PASTE

10 small green chiles
5 fat garlic cloves, peeled
peanut oil
2 lemongrass stalks
2 shallots, peeled and chopped
a thumb-sized piece of fresh ginger,
    peeled and grated
3 ounces cilantro (leaves and stalks)
3–4 dried kaffir lime leaves/
    1½ tablespoons lime juice
grated zest of ½–1 lime
1 teaspoon salt
2 teaspoons ground coriander
½ teaspoon ground cumin

········ TIME SAVER ········

If you find yourself tight for time you can always sub in 2 tablespoons of a good store-bought curry paste instead—just add 4 dried kaffir lime leaves to the pan at the same time as the onion to boost the flavor.

Sticky rice is my favorite; I go for its glutinous texture and the way it works with a sauce. For this gorgeous meat-free curry, you can easily make your own paste (not by hand—you'll need a blitzer or grinder).

PREP

Soak the rice ahead: Measure into a bowl and cover with cold water. Leave overnight or for as long as you've got (even 20 minutes makes a difference).

Make the paste: Wash, dry and trim the tips of the chiles. Blitz in a food processor with the garlic and a tablespoon of peanut oil. Sit the lemongrass on a board. Bash with a rolling pin to bruise then chop as finely as you can. Add and blitz. Add the shallot and ginger. Blitz again. Add the remaining ingredients and enough groundnut oil to blitz into a thick paste.

Sort the rest: Slice the aubergine and thinly slice the onion. Cut the potatoes and butternut squash into bite-sized chunks. Trim the beans and cut in thirds. Thinly slice the carrot and mushrooms. Cube the tofu, if using, and toss in the soy. Set aside. Drain the rice and tip into a saucepan with 350ml cold water.

COOK

Heat the oil in a wok or large pan. Add the onion. Cook very gently, stirring, to soften without coloring. Add 2 tablespoons of the curry paste and continue to cook, stirring, for a minute or two as it releases its fragrance. Add the carrot and eggplant. Cook and stir for 5 minutes or until the eggplant is softening. Add the coconut milk and increase the heat until it almost boils. Reduce to low, add the squash and potato, and simmer for 10 minutes, or until the squash is tender.

Meantime, cook the rice. Bring to a boil, cover, and simmer for 10 to 15 minutes. It's done when the water is absorbed fully. Check it regularly.

Finish the curry: Add the mushrooms, beans, and a few of the cashews, if using. Cook for another 10 minutes or until tender. If the sauce looks like reducing too much, add a splash of water or vegetable stock. Stir frequently. Just before serving, squeeze in a bit of lime and stir through a little chopped cilantro or basil if you like. Taste and adjust the seasoning. Add the tofu, if using, to a pan with a little oil and fry for 3 to 4 minutes, turning, until well browned.

PLATE

Tip the curry into a large bowl. Top with cilantro, cashews, and tofu. Serve on your sticky rice with bits of lime for squeezing.

BONUS BITES

EGG FRIED RICE AND BACON

Add 1 tablespoon peanut oil and ¼ tablespoon sesame oil to a heated wok with a handful of frozen peas and cook for 1 to 2 minutes. Add a handful of cubed pancetta or char siu pork (p187) and cook until it's hot and crisping up. Beat 2 eggs and pour into the dish with 1¼ cups cold cooked basmati rice and 2 sliced scallions, stirring. Cook until piping hot. Season and serve with a bit of cilantro and a finishing sauce of a little hoisin sauce mixed with water.

COUSCOUS, ORANGE, FETA,
AND BEET SALAD

FEEDS 2 to 3

INGREDIENTS

4 beet
2 tbsp olive oil
salt and pepper
generous 1 cup instant couscous
3¼ cups boiling water
1 large orange
a handful of pine nuts
a small handful of fresh parsley
a small handful of fresh mint
1 x honey mustard dressing (p26)
4 ounces feta cheese
ZUCCHINI TZATZIKI
4–6 tablespoons Greek yogurt
1 garlic clove, peeled
½ a small zucchini, grated
a small handful of chopped mint
1 teaspoon sugar
a squeeze of lemon juice
a pinch of salt
½ tablespoon olive oil

—— CHANGE IT UP ——

Substitute a good Cheddar, goat, or simple salad cheese for the feta. Replace the tzatziki with hummus.

—— BONUS BITE ——

LAMB TAGINE WITH COUSCOUS

Cube 7 ounces lamb steaks. Fry off until browned in olive oil. Remove. Fry a sliced onion and 2 crushed garlic cloves until soft. Add a pinch of cayenne and 1 teaspoon each of cumin, coriander, ground ginger, and cinnamon. Stir for 2 minutes. Return the lamb. Add 16-ounce can of chopped tomatoes, scant 1 cup canned chickpeas, 1 tablespoon tomato paste, 4 chopped dried apricots, salt, pepper, and a little honey. Simmer for 30 to 40 minutes. Pile onto hot couscous and top with lots of chopped cilantro and a few chopped almonds.

Here's a tasty bit of salad to take your couscous places. This precooked grain can be rather dull, so treat it to lots of herbs, spices, fruit, and strong flavors. This combination will set your palate alight.

PREP Preheat the oven to 425°F. Peel and chop the beet into large chunks. Roll them in half the oil on a baking sheet and season with salt and pepper. Cook for 20 minutes, or until tender.

Meantime, cook the couscous. Tip the grain into a heatproof dish, pour over the boiling water and remaining oil, and cover with a dish towel. Leave for at least 5 minutes. Uncover and fluff it up with a fork to lighten and separate the grains a bit.

Segment the orange: sit it on a board. Using a paring or small serrated knife, slice the top and base away. Now, holding it firmly, cut down each of the segment lines toward the middle of the fruit to release the wedges of flesh from the membrane. Remove and leave them whole or chop them. Lightly toast the pine nuts in a dry pan for a minute or until just brown. Chop the herbs. Make up the dressing. Mix the tzatziki ingredients together in a bowl.

Cut the beet into bite-size pieces. Stir a bit of dressing, the pine nuts, and herbs into your couscous and season with salt and pepper.

PLATE Bang the couscous into a handsome bowl. Top with the orange segments and beet. Crumble over the cheese and drizzle over the rest of the dressing. Serve with the tzatziki, a bit of good brown bread and butter, or some warm pita.

BEET
RISOTTO

FEEDS 2

INGREDIENTS

8–10 ounces whole beet
2 shallots, peeled
2 fat garlic cloves, peeled
3¾ cups chicken/vegetable stock
    (p49/p15)
2 heaping tablespoons butter
a splash of olive oil
scant 1 cup vialone nano/carnaroli/
    arborio risotto rice
¾ small glass of white wine
a little fresh thyme (optional)
salt and black pepper
juice of ½ a lemon
scant ½ cup freshly grated Parmesan
a little bit of butter
STIR-INS
generous ⅓ cup crumbled blue cheese
1 tablespoon mascarpone, cream, or
    crème fraîche
a few baby spinach or arugula leaves
TOPPINGS
blue cheese and herb croquettes
    (see overleaf)
a handful of freshly grated Parmesan/
    crumbled Cheddar/goat cheese
2 tablespoons sour cream/plain yogurt
a few caramelized walnuts
½ tablespoon horseradish cream

With its shocking color and sound flavor, this one's quite the exhibitionist. I love the layers of flavor and texture that the stir-ins and toppings give the risotto here, but keep it nice and simple if that's how you like it. Serve as a main course, an appetizer, or as a lovely extra alongside a nice bit of beef or oily fish like salmon or mackerel.

PREP
Cut any leaves away from the beet, wash them, pop them in a pan, and cover with cold water. Boil until tender and easily pierced with a knife—allow 20 minutes for smaller beet. Set aside to cool.

Dice the shallots and garlic with a small sharp knife. Pour the chicken/vegetable stock into a pan, bring it to a boil then lower to a simmer.

Peel the beet. Chop and blitz in a processor with 4 tablespoons of hot stock or use a stick blender to make a thick, smooth puree. Prep your choice of stir-ins/toppings.

COOK
Put a second pan onto heat. Add the butter and oil. Once hot, add the shallot and garlic, stirring with a wooden spoon. Reduce the heat to low and cook very gently for 5 minutes, until the onion softens.

Tip the unwashed rice into the pan and stir well to coat it. Cook for a minute, stirring. Increase the heat. Add the wine and stir until it's almost absorbed, then add a large ladle full of hot stock immediately. Add the thyme, if using. Reduce the heat to medium so the mix keeps bubbling a bit but doesn't cook too fiercely as it absorbs the new liquid. Once absorbed, add another ladle of stock and keep stirring. Repeat until the stock is just about used and the rice is just about cooked (test a grain—the end result wants to be soft but with a tiny bit of texture and the risotto itself should neither be stiff and dry nor wet and soupy), about 15 to 20 minutes. Add salt, pepper, and lemon juice.

Stir in two-thirds of the beet puree. Taste and adjust the seasoning. Add the rest of the puree now (or add later as a topping) plus your choice of stir-ins and half the Parmesan. Stir in the butter to make it glossy. Taste and adjust. Turn off the heat, put the lid on the pan, and let rest for 3 minutes.

PLATE
Spoon the risotto into warm shallow bowls and finish with the remaining Parmesan and your choice of toppings.

TO GO WITH
CARAMELIZED WALNUTS
Heat ½ teaspoon butter in a skillet. Throw in a handful of walnut halves. Toss to sauté for 1 to 2 mins until lightly brown and toasted. Tip onto paper towels. Sprinkle with a bit of fine salt and superfine sugar.

ONION RISOTTO

FEEDS 3

INGREDIENTS

3 large mild/white onions, peeled
4 ounces Parmesan, plus extra to serve
4 tablespoons butter, plus extra to
    serve
2 fat garlic cloves, peeled and crushed
5 cups chicken/vegetable stock
    (p49/p15)
generous 1⅓ cups risotto rice
⅔ cup Noilly Prat (or other vermouth/
    dry white wine)
scant ½ cup heavy cream
salt and black pepper
a squeeze of lemon juice
a few grains of vanilla salt (optional)
a little fresh thyme

—— CHANGE IT UP ——

For a delicious cappuccino effect, add a
teaspoon or two of coffee before serving.
Or soak a couple of crumbled Amaretti
cookies in coffee and scatter at the bottom
of the bowls.

It's a contradiction, this dish—delicate, yet fully flavored. In a word, yummy. Using milder white onions makes it nice and sweet.

PREP Slice the onions thinly. Grate the Parmesan so you can chuck it in later without abandoning your stirring.

COOK Heat a large heavy-bottom pan. Add the butter. Throw in the onions and garlic. Stir to coat in butter then cook very gently on low/medium heat for up to 10 minutes until very soft and translucent. Don't let them color or it will spoil the flavor.

Put the pan of stock onto boil then reduce to a simmer. Half-cover with a lid.

Once the onions are soft, increase the heat slightly. Add the unwashed rice. Stir to coat the grains for 2 minutes. Increase the heat. Add the Noilly Prat and stir until absorbed. Add a single ladle of hot stock. Stir continuously until absorbed, then add another ladle and repeat. Continue to add stock, stirring until absorbed before repeating, for 15 to 20 minutes until the grains of rice swell and the mix is creamy. You may need all, more or a bit less liquid (if you need more, add a bit of hot water or a splash more wine).

When it looks and feels done (still a bit soupy with the rice softened, but not mushy) add the Parmesan and two-thirds of the cream, black pepper, and a little salt to taste. Add a little more cream or a squeeze of lemon juice if you feel it needs it. Cover and let settle for 2 minutes.

PLATE Spoon into warm bowls. Sprinkle with vanilla salt, if using, thyme, Parmesan, and dot each with a dab of butter. Serve with extra Parmesan for grating at the table.

TO GO WITH

BLUE CHEESE AND HERB CROQUETTES

Mix a bit of fried shallot, a pinch of dried sage or diced fresh, and some crumbled blue cheese like dolcelatte/Stilton. Roll into 4 mini-logs, about 1 inches. Roll in flour, dip in beaten egg, and coat in bread crumbs. While the risotto is resting, fry the croquettes in peanut, vegetable, or sunflower oil for a minute or so per side until golden outside, melting inside. Drain on paper towels and serve on top of the risotto.

A POST-ROAST CHICKEN RISOTTO

FEEDS 2

INGREDIENTS

meat stripped from your post-roast
* chicken (p54)*
2½ cups chicken stock (p49)
2 ounces Parmesan, plus extra to serve
a small/medium onion, peeled
2 tablespoons butter
1–2 garlic cloves, peeled
scant 1 cup risotto rice
1 small glass white wine (or more
* stock)*
a bit of chopped tarragon/thyme/
* rosemary/sage, to taste*
juice of ½ a lemon
a little bit of butter, plus extra for
* serving*
1 tablespoon cream/mascarpone/
* crème fraîche*
salt and black pepper

Can a roast bird be as good the second time around? Yes it can with this one...

PREP On roast chicken day: Enjoy your meal. Strip off the extra meat. Cover and chill. Make up your chicken stock using the carcass following the instructions on page 49.

On risotto day: Remove the meat from the refrigerator to get to room temperature. Bring the stock to a simmer in a pan. Grate the Parmesan and chop the onion.

COOK Melt the butter in a larger, heavy-bottom pan on gentle heat. Add the onion and crush in the garlic. Cook for 5 minutes or until soft and translucent. Fling the unwashed rice in and stir well to coat. Add the wine, increase the heat, and cook until it evaporates.

Add the first ladle of hot stock, stirring until it's absorbed, then add another without ever flooding the rice. Continue to add stock in this way—adding any chopped herbs as and when you like—until the risotto is almost done (the grains of rice should be creamy and the mix a bit soupy). Add most of your chicken, a bit of lemon juice, and the Parmesan. Stir in extra butter, cream/mascarpone/crème fraîche. Season, taste, and adjust the balance.

PLATE Spoon the risotto into warm bowls. Top with the remaining bits of chicken, some extra grated Parmesan, and a few extra fresh herbs.

BREAD AND CAKES

Baking's where it all began for me: the smell of fresh bread, the licking of the bowl, the general mess of it all. I was a hooked virgin cook. But then it got serious. Baking's an exact science. So you've got to treat it with respect. It's all about the relationship between fat, sugars, flour, baking powder or yeast; the shape and size of the pan or the spoon, the temperature of the eggs, measuring liquids exactly, and the heat of the oven. Get these things right and you're on your way to cookie heaven and other good places. Something as simple as a loaf of fresh bread with a crisp crust and a soft sweet crumb will stun the most discerning of palates. As for the cakes and the pizzas—I've included some classics … so you be the judge.

★ BAKING HEROES ★

✶ ✶ ✶ ✶ ✶ ✶ ✶ ✶ FLOURS ✶ ✶ ✶ ✶ ✶ ✶ ✶ ✶

ALL-PURPOSE FLOUR: Use for cookies, scones, cakes, a few quick breads, pie dough, and alternative pizza dough. It has no raising agent of its own. Plain whole wheat flour can be substituted for white where specified in a recipe. It tends to produce a heavier texture but the husk of the grain is there so there are health benefits.

SELF-RISING FLOUR: Comes in white and whole wheat. Already contains a raising agent. Don't confuse with all-purpose flour!

STRONG BREAD FLOUR: Contains a much higher level of gluten than standard white flour. This is activated by the kneading process and lets the bread rise. Use for loaves and pizzas. Strong brown/whole wheat bread flour has a stronger taste and makes a denser but healthier loaf.

MULTIGRAIN FLOUR: Mixes up the grains for a varied taste and texture. Has no raising agent.

CORNMEAL, OATS AND OATMEAL, **SPELT**, *Buckwheat*, **RYE FLOUR**, KAMUT, *Bulgur,* and other grains all provide their own different tastes and textures. Once you know your flours and recipes try combining different types of whites and browns.

✶ ✶ ✶ ✶ ✶ ✶ ✶ ✶ RAISING AGENTS ✶ ✶ ✶ ✶ ✶ ✶ ✶ ✶

YEAST For bread, buns, pizzas, and dough. It comes in three guises (see below). Use whichever's convenient. If substituting dried for fresh, use half the amount (e.g. for ⅓ ounce fresh yeast use ¼ ounce active dry).

FRESH YEAST: A living organism. Get it from health food stores and some bakers/grocery stores. It can be rubbed straight into the flour, though it is usually activated before use. To activate, sit it in a small bowl. Cream it with a spoon. Add a bit of the warm (not hot) water specified in your recipe. Cover and leave for 10 minutes until it produces a frothy head. If the water is too hot (over 85°F) you will kill the yeast.

DRIED YEAST: Needs activating before use. Add the specified amount to a bit of measured water with ½ easpoon sugar or honey. Stir, cover, and let froth.

ACTIVE DRY YEAST: Although sometimes I activate it first, this can be added directly to your dry ingredients. If in doubt, read the package directions. Check the expiration date. Always have some in.

AIR: Introduced by SIFTING FLOUR, WHISKING EGGS, RUBBING IN, and CREAMING. It's preserved by careful FOLDING IN and OPENING AND CLOSING THE OVEN DOOR GENTLY.

BAKING POWDER: A mix of acid and alkali and the most common raising agent. It works by interacting with the liquid in your dough or batter, producing carbon dioxide which fills the air pockets you've created when beating/creaming your mix. It reacts again when it meets the heat of your oven so you get a double-rising effect. Check the expiration date. It loses potency after a year; store in a dry place.

BAKING SODA: (AKA bicarbonate of soda or bread soda) an alkali which reacts with the acid ingredients in your batter/mix/eggs/molasses/lemon juice to create gases. These in turn react with the gluten in your flour which expands and your baking rises. Don't confuse it with baking powder.

★ ★ ★ ★ ★ ★ ★ ★ ★ ★ SUGARS ★ ★ ★ ★ ★ ★ ★ ★ ★ ★

SUPERFINE: Finer than granulated so perfect for baking.

RAW BROWN: A crunchy sugar useful in cookies and for topping cakes.

LIGHT BROWN: Useful in cookies and fruit cakes.

DARK BROWN: A strong dense flavor good for ginger cake and strong fruit cakes.

CONFECTIONERS': Use for some cookies and for frostings, buttercreams, dusting. Needs sifting to remove lumps.

HONEY: A distinctive flavor so use judiciously.

BLACKSTRAP MOLASSES: Great for gingerbreads, ginger cookies, and breads.

★ ★ ★ ★ ★ ★ ★ ★ ★ ★ EGGS ★ ★ ★ ★ ★ ★ ★ ★ ★ ★

SIZE MATTERS. Get it right. If you use a small egg when large is specified your proportions are wrong.

ALWAYS Bake with eggs at room temperature. Use the best you can: a good egg will flavor and color your baking.

★ ★ ★ ★ ★ ★ ★ ★ ★ ★ FATS ★ ★ ★ ★ ★ ★ ★ ★ ★ ★

BUTTER: Great for taste and color and natural. Unsalted is best. Use at room temperature for ease and speed unless cold is specified in the recipe (as in most pie dough).

MARGARINE: Use instead of butter if you must.

OILS: Use tasteless oils in cakes/muffin—save olive oil for bread and pizza.

★ ★ ★ ★ ★ WATER (AND OTHER LIQUIDS) ★ ★ ★ ★ ★

MEASURE these absolutely accurately. If you get it wrong your cake or bread won't rise properly or have the right texture. **THE CLUE'S IN THE RECIPE.** Some cakes want to be **"SOFT DROPPING"** (falling off the end of your spoon) and you'll need to judge that by adding more liquid until it does. Water is equally important for dough. Don't just slosh it in. **BE ACCURATE.** However, flours vary in their absorption rate so you may need to add more or less to get the right consistency.

QUICK
Flaky pastry

Wrap ¾ CUP (1½ STICKS) BUTTER in foil and stick in the freezer for an hour. Chill a mug of WATER. Sift scant 1⅔ CUPS FLOUR and a PINCH OF SALT into a bowl. Grate the butter coarsely into the flour, peeling the foil back as you go. Mix them lightly with a fork. Now add 2 TABLESPOONS WATER, mixing until you get a smooth firm dough. Add more water if needed. Pull it into a smooth ball and wrap in foil/wrap. Chill for 30 minutes before using.

DOCTOR BAKER

ALL FLOUR CONTAINS

PROTEIN
CARBOHYDRATE

AND EASILY ABSORBED

Calcium

for healthy teeth and bones.
WHOLE WHEAT FLOUR IS HIGH IN

VITAMIN B1 IRON
MAGNESIUM
ZINC & FIBER

WHICH HELPS
PROTECT AGAINST

both heart and bowel diseases
and in controlling weight.
MULTIGRAIN AND WHOLE WHEAT
FLOURS CONTAIN ESSENTIAL

FOLATE

Oats are full of slow-release energy
and will keep you going for longer,
while seeds and nuts are rich in

PROTEIN IRON
Phosphorus ZINC
CALCIUM, NIACIN
AND B VITAMINS

DATES, DRIED FIGS, AND
APRICOTS ARE ALL HIGH IN

FIBER & slow-release
energy, while
CHOCOLATE IS FULL OF

IRON

WHICH HELPS FIGHT ANEMIA
AND BOOSTS FEEL-GOOD FACTOR.

── TAKE THE HEAT ──

Never put your baking into a cold
oven or one that hasn't reached
the right temperature. Preheat
means just that. Inaccurate oven
temperature is the main cause of
a cake sinking.

── THE KNEAD TO KNOW ──
BREAD TECHNIQUES

MixINg You could use a spoon but why not use your hand? Get in touch with the dough and utilize your hand heat. Mix everything in a large bowl or sift the flour and salt onto a clean counter. Make a well in the center. Add the yeast and liquid. Draw the flour in and mix until you have a ball of dough.

KNEADING A workout for the gluten in the flour which makes it elastic so the gases can stretch it and the dough will rise. Do it by hand or machine. By machine: You need a freestanding mixer. Bang the dough in and mix for 8 minutes or until its elastic. By hand: Roll the dough into a rough ball. Slap it onto a floured counter. Flour your hands. Push and stretch the dough away from you. Then flip the just stretched portion back onto the main ball and press down. Rotate the ball around. Repeat the process for 10 minutes or until it feels smooth and elastic.

RISING Shape the dough into a ball. Brush lightly with oil. Sit it in a large bowl. Cover with a damp dish towel. Sit it in a warm draft-free place until it doubles in size (1 hour plus, temperature dependent). Poke it. If your finger leaves a hole, it's ready. You can leave it, covered, in the refrigerator for 8 hours if it suits. The longer the rise the better the flavor.

KNOCK IT BACK Scoop the risen dough onto a counter. Knead and punch it for 2 minutes to redistribute the air and for best-textured bread.

SHAPE Shape the bread to fit your oiled loaf pan or bang on a baking sheet.

SECOND RISE Most loaves need another rise once shaped. Consult your recipe.

Finishing Shiny glaze—brush with egg wash before baking and again 5 minutes before the bread is done. Natural look—dust with a bit of flour. Buttery—brush with melted butter when it's hot out of the oven. Olive oil—brush with oil before baking and 5 minutes before it's done.

TESTING FOR DONENESS Test every loaf. Take it out of the pan with a dish towel. Tap the bottom. It should sound hollow and feel light. Put it back, without the pan, if it needs longer/sounds dull and feels doughy. Cool on a rack.

STORING In a tin. It gets stale fast if you chill it. Freeze fresh as soon as it cools.

SHELF *Life*

Store your dry ingredients in sealed containers in dry cupboards.

Sugar lasts indefinitely.

Flour has limited shelf-life.

Check the pack if you don't bake often.

Watch out for wildlife. Weevils breed in flour, sugar, oats, etc. so check; they're tiny but visible.

CREAMING Beat soft butter and sugar into a light, white, airy cream. Use a wooden spoon or mixer but finish with the spoon. Beat for 5 minutes to aerate.

RUB IN Literally rub the butter into the flour using your thumbs and fingertips. Hold your hands high over the bowl as you do to add air.

FOLD IN Develop a cutting and folding action with a large metal spoon as you incorporate new ingredients into a delicate mix. Think figure of eight.

SIFTING Putting flour/cocoa/confectioners' sugar/raising agents through a strainer to aerate.

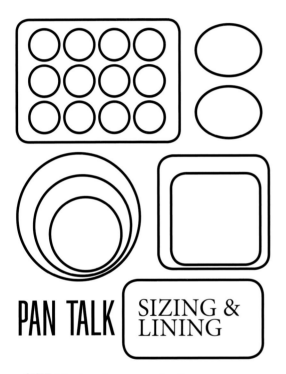

DONE YET?

SPONGES
Look for a golden brown cake that's risen well and shrinking away from the sides of the pan slightly. If you press lightly in the middle the sponge springs back.

OTHER CAKES
Test by piercing the center with a toothpick/wooden skewer. It should come out clean.

TURNING OUT

RUN a sharp thin knife smoothly between the edge of the pan and the cake. SIT a rack on top of the cake. PROTECT your hands with a dish towel. Holding cake and rack, INVERT so the cake shifts to the rack. REMOVE the pan. PEEL the paper off. TURN it upside down to cool and so it doesn't mark too much. COOL on the rack and store in an airtight container.

PAN TALK   SIZING & LINING

SIZE Match recipe to pan size if you want your cake to work.

GREASE Rub with soft butter or flavorless oil (vegetable/peanut).

LINE To protect from heat and prevent sticking. For the bottom, sit pan on wax paper/baking parchment. Draw around it with a pencil. Cut and lay in. For the sides, fold paper in half lengthwise. Wrap around the pan. Mark the length plus a bit. Cut and fit in. For a loaf pan all-in-one: cut paper to twice the size of the bottom. Put pan in the center. Cut diagonal lines to each corner. Tuck paper into the pan to fit and line completely.

BREAD CRUMBS

SOFT & FRESH: Slap stale bread in a processor or tear and blitz with a stick blender—blitz to the texture you want. **DRIED:** Preheat the oven to 350°F. Spread bread crumbs on a sheet and cook until golden brown/dried out. **PANKO STYLE:** lay slices out on a sheet overnight or until dried out. Bash or crumble to crumbs. **FRIED:** Put fresh crumbs into a pan on very low heat with a bit of oil/butter (crushed garlic and herbs if you want) and cook until crisp. Use to sprinkle on pasta instead of Parmesan and to top gratins.

CLASSIC
WHITE LOAF

INGREDIENTS

scant 3¼ cups strong white bread flour
2 teaspoons fine salt
1 x ¼-ounce pack active dry yeast
4 tablespoons butter, in cubes, plus
    extra for greasing
generous 1 cup milk
1 teaspoon thin honey
1 large egg (at room temperature)
peanut oil, for brushing
a little flour/beaten egg, for finishing
    (optional)

─── **CHANGE IT UP** ───

1. Nip off good plum-sized bits of dough
and shape into rolls. Let rise. Brush with egg
wash, sprinkle over poppy/sesame seeds,
and bake for 10 to 15 minutes. **2.** For a pesto
and olive loaf, add 1 teaspoon pesto with the
liquid, a few chopped green olives before
you finish kneading, and brush with olive oil
or an olive oil/pesto mix before baking.

─── **BONUS BITES** ───

• *Add the following to half the bread mix.*
• *Cook in a 1-pound loaf pan.*
HERB, CHEESE, AND BACON LOAF
By hand: Add ½ teaspoon mustard powder,
½ teaspoon dried oregano, and scant ½ cup
grated Cheddar to the flour before you add
the liquid. Add 4 slices of cooked, crumbled
American bacon to the dough just before
you finish kneading. By machine: Add all
the extras as you begin kneading. Brush
the loaf with thinned marmite/vegemite or
grated Cheddar/Gruyère and bake as before.
SIMPLE WHOLE WHEAT LOAF
Mix 4¼ cups whole wheat flour with 2 x
¼-ounce sachets active dry yeast, 1 teaspoon
fine salt, 1 teaspoon sugar or honey, scant 2
cups warm water, and 1 tablespoon olive oil.
Proceed as for white loaf. Bake in 2 greased
1-pound pans for 20 to 30 minutes at 450°F.

Unless you've got an artisan bakery nearby you won't be finding bread like this very easily. It's sweet, flavorsome, has an unbeatable texture and accommodates a range of great flavors. Ok, it takes a while to get to the table but most of that is actually downtime, when you can be getting on with other things…

PREP Sift the flour and salt into a bowl. Add the yeast and butter. Rub everything together between your fingers and thumbs until the fat and yeast are incorporated. Warm the milk in a small pan. Add the honey. Keep it lukewarm. Make a hollow in the flour. Beat then add the egg. Pour in generous ¾ cup of the milk and mix with your hands or a wooden spoon for dough that's soft, warm, and not too sticky. Add more milk if you need it. Pull it into a warm ball and sit it on a floured board.

Knead it by machine: Put the dough in the bowl of a mixer and knead with the dough hook for 8 minutes until it's smooth and elastic. Or do it by hand: pressing, stretching, folding, turning, and slapping it roughly for 10 minutes (p200) until glossy and pliable.

Let it rise: Roll the dough into a ball and brush it with a little peanut oil. Slap it into a large bowl. Cover with a damp dish towel. Leave it in a warm, draft-free place until it doubles in volume (about 1 hour).

Knock it back: Once risen, bang the dough back on the board. Knead and punch it for 2 minutes. Grease a 2-pound loaf pan. Use your hands to shape your dough into a rectangle the length of the pan but a bit wider. Fold the two sides under to create a seam and to a size that will fit the pan. Cover and let rise for another 20 minutes.

Use a sharp knife to make a 1¼-inch-deep cut down the center of the loaf for the split effect. Leave it for a final rise, about 10 minutes. Meantime, preheat the oven to 450°F.

Finish the loaf: Either sprinkle with flour, brush with egg, or keep it plain.

COOK Bake for 20 to 30 minutes. Turn it out of the pan. Tap the bottom to test for doneness. It should feel crisp and sound hollow. Put it back if it needs extra time. Cool on a rack.

PLATE This loaf slices beautifully. Cut it up and use for sandwiches or toasting. Enjoy with soup, or cut up into thin strips for boiled eggs.

HEALTHY SEED MULTIGRAIN

MAKES 1 LARGE LOAF

Multigrain and multidimensional—this one packs flavor and nutrition.

INGREDIENTS

2¾–3 cups multigrain brown flour
½ teaspoon salt
1 x ¼-ounce package active dry yeast
1 teaspoon superfine sugar or honey
1¼ cups warm (not hot) water
*1 tablespoon olive oil, or sunflower/
    canola/flaxseed*
*a small handful of mixed seeds
    (pumpkin/sunflower)*

PREP Tip the flour, salt, yeast, and sugar into a large bowl. If using honey, stir it into the warm water to dissolve. Add the water to the flour mix. Stir with your hand or a wooden spoon to form a rough dough. Add the oil and knead it into the mix for a minute.

To knead by machine: Slap the dough into your mixer bowl. Knead with the dough hook for 8 minutes. If the mix seems too sticky, add extra flour at the start, but don't make it too dry/stiff. By hand: Slap the dough onto a lightly floured board and knead for 10 minutes, until smooth and elastic.

Rise the dough: roll it into a ball and brush with a little oil. Put it into a bowl to rise; it should double in volume. Cover with plastic wrap or a damp dish towel. Leave it somewhere warm for an hour and check its progress occasionally.

Knock it back: slap the dough back onto the board. Knead for 2 minutes. Bang it into a very well-greased nonstick pan. Scatter the seeds on top. Cover and leave for 20 minutes.

COOK Meantime, preheat the oven to 425°F. Bake for 30 to 40 minutes. Remove from the pan and tap the bottom to test for doneness. It should sound hollow. Cool on a rack.

PLATE Slice for toast or sandwiches. It makes for a good high-energy breakfast bread and travels well for a picnic or lunch box.

—— **CHANGE IT UP** ——

For cinnamon toast, toast and spread with a mix of soft butter, superfine suga, and cinnamon.

—— **BONUS BITE** ——

FAST BLACKSTRAP MOLASSES BREAD
Grease 2 x 2-pound loaf pans. Mix 2 x ¼-ounce sachets active dry yeast with ⅔ cup warm water, 1 tablespoon blackstrap molasses, and 1 tablespoon honey. Cover and leave for 10 minutes until frothy. Mix together 2¾ cups whole wheat bread flour, scant 3¼ cups white flour, and 1 teaspoon salt in a bowl. Add the frothed liquid plus 3 cups warm water and stir to make a soft, loose dough. Spoon it into the pans. Cover with a dish towel. Let rise above the surface of the pan. Bake at 400°F for 30 to 40 minutes or until the bottom sounds hollow when tapped. Cool. Makes great toast and lasts well.

BANG-IT-TOGETHER SODA BREAD (OR MUFFINS)

MAKES 1 LARGE LOAF
OR 8 MUFFINS

INGREDIENTS

3½ cups all-purpose flour (not bread flour), plus extra for the sheet
scant 2 cups buttermilk
1 teaspoon salt
1 heaping teaspoon baking soda
1 teaspoon thin honey

TIP

If you don't have any buttermilk to hand, squeeze 1½ tablespoons lemon juice into the same quantity of milk and leave for 15 minutes out in the kitchen before using in its place. Alternatively, use plain yogurt soured with 2 teaspoons lemon juice.

—— CHANGE IT UP——

1. For brown soda bread, use 3 cups plain whole wheat flour or half white, half plain. Add a beaten egg and a glug of sunflower or light oil to the mix too.
2. Customize your breads. Add raisins or golden raisins, chocolate chips, dried or fresh blueberries,s or savory extras like olives and herbs to white soda breads—oatmeal, oats, seeds, or any dried fruits to brown breads.

So fast, so simple. Slice or split open and get lavish with the butter.

PREP Preheat the oven to 450°F. Sprinkle a little extra flour on a baking sheet.

Sift the flour, salt, and baking soda into a bowl. Make a well in the center.

Add the buttermilk and honey. Beat it together with a wooden spoon or use your hand, starting from the well and working outwards drawing the flour in.

The dough should be soft, not stiff (or you'll get a dry, heavy bread), nor should it be too sticky. Add more milk/flour as you judge it. Pull it into a ball.

Sit it on a lightly floured board. Pat it gently into a 2-inch-wide circular loaf. Use a sharp knife to cut a deep cross (2 inches) over the loaf so it marks into 4 quarters. Sit it on the sheet. For muffins: Grease and flour the holes of a large muffin pan. Cut and shape the dough to fit and fill 8 holes.

COOK Bake the loaf for 15 minutes. Reduce the heat to 400°F for another 20 to 30 minutes. Tap the bottom to test for doneness. It should sound hollow. Turn it upside down to cook for another few minutes if it doesn't. Cool on a rack. Cook the muffins for 5 minutes at 450°F, then reduce to 400°F and cook for another 10 to 15 minutes. Test as for the bread.

PLATE Eat on the same day smothered in butter, with cheese, cold meats, soup, honey, cream cheese, or jam.

BONUS BITES

BANG IT IN THE PAN BREAD
Using half the quantity above, make up the soda bread into a dough as before. Pat out to fit a large skillet (about 9 inches). Heat the pan. Fry for 10 to 15 minutes per side until crusty and the crumb is cooked.

LAGER LOAF
Sift generous 1¾ cups all-purpose flour, 1 level tablespoons baking powder, and 1 teaspoon salt into a bowl. Add 1 level tablespoon granulated sugar, 1 cup finely grated strong Cheddar, and 2 teaspoons dried herbs of your choice. Pour scant 1½ cups lager in slowly, beating as you go. Spoon into a well-greased 1-pound loaf pan and bake in a preheated oven at 375°F for 40 minutes or until cooked through. Eat warm or cold.

PIZZA

MAKES 4 REGULAR PIZZAS

INGREDIENTS

2¾ cups strong white bread flour
1 teaspoon fine salt
2 x ¼-ounce sachets active dry yeast
1 teaspoon superfine sugar
1¼ cups warm water
2 tablespoons olive oil, plus extra for
  greasing
TOMATO SAUCE (OPTIONAL)
1 tablespoon olive oil
4 garlic cloves, peeled and diced
1 x 14-ounce can of chopped tomatoes
1½ teaspoons sugar
1 tablespoon tomato paste
salt and pepper

·········· **TIME SAVER** ··········

Make more dough than you need, roll out as
bases, and freeze on sheets. Remove. Store in
freezer bags until needed. Top and bang in
the oven, giving them an extra 2 minutes.

——— **BONUS BITES** ———

PISSALADIÈRE

Make quadruple amounts of caramelized
onion (p80) adding 4 crushed garlic cloves,
2 teaspoons brown sugar, and ½ teaspoon
balsamic vinegar. Roll the dough out to fit
a large rectangular baking sheet. Top with
the onion, 2 pinches of oregano/thyme,
a handful of black olives, and 12 drained
anchovies. Cook for 15 to 20 minutes.

LOW-FAT CRISPY DOUGH

Sift scant 214 cups all-purpose flour, ⅓ cup
white bread flour, and ¾ teaspoon fine salt
into a large bowl. Add ½ teaspoon superfine
sugar. Measure ½ cup lowfat milk and ¾
cup hot water into a separate bowl. Add 2 x
¼-ounce sachets of active dry yeast to the
liquid. Cover with a dish towel. Let froth
for 10 to 15 minutes. Pour into the flour
mix, add 3 tablespoons extra all-purpose
flour and mix for a very soft, slightly sticky
dough. Knead, rise, knock back, and roll as
before. Top with lighter toppings.

*Pizza's all about getting the simple things right: you want quality
dough, an excellent tomato sauce (or other tasty base), a delectable
topping, and a very hot oven. Find the dough and the sauce on this
page—turn over for toppings. This quantity makes 4 regular, 6 small,
or 1 large tray bake pizza. Vary it to suit the occasion.*

PREP
Sift the flour and salt into a bowl. Add the yeast and sugar. Boil scant
½ cup of the water and mix with the generous ¾ cup of cold. Check
the temperature—it should be comfortable to the finger. Add to the flour with
the olive oil. Mix everything with your hands or a wooden spoon to get a soft
smooth dough that's neither too wet nor dry. Add extra flour or water if you
need to.

Pull the dough into a ball and knead by either throwing it into the bowl of
a mixer and processing with the dough hook for 8 minutes or sitting it on a
lightly floured board and kneading by hand (p200) until smooth and elastic.

Place the ball of dough in a large bowl and brush it lightly with olive oil. Leave
in a warm place covered with a damp dish towel or plastic wrap until it doubles
in size—approximately 1 hour.

Meantime, make your tomato sauce, if using. Heat the olive oil in a pan on very
low heat. Add the garlic, sweat, and stir for a minute without browning. Add
the tomatoes, sugar, and tomato paste and season to taste. Increase the heat
to medium. Simmer for 10 to 15 minutes, stirring occasionally. Taste to judge
acidity, adding more sugar and adjusting seasoning if needed. Set aside.

Knock the risen dough back and knead for another 2 minutes on the floured
board. Divide into four pieces. Sit one piece on the board, covering the rest
with a dish towel so they don't dry out. Flatten it with the palm of your hand.
Make indentations with your finger ½ inch from the outside to create a rim
all the way around. Flip the dough over. Put one hand in the middle. With
the other, gently stretch the dough out, rotating the pizza as you go. Now get
a rolling pin and roll out, turning it 45 degrees between each roll to keep it
circular. Get it as thin as you can. Repeat with the remaining pieces. Let the
pizza bases rise again for another 5 minutes.

COOK
Preheat the oven to its highest temperature. Place your pizza bases
on oiled baking sheets. Spread tomato sauce thinly over each, if
using, leaving a ½–¾-inch rim. Cover with your topping of choice (see overleaf
for inspiration). Shove your baking sheet into the oven. Cook until golden and
crisp (about 8 minutes, depending on the thickness of the dough and your
choice of topping).

PLATE
Finish with any extras such as grated Parmesan, arugula leaves,
olive oil, or as dictated by your chosen recipe.

GARLIC

FETA AND CARAMELISED ONION

FUNGHI

SALAMI AND FIG

PIZZA TOPPINGS

GARLIC AND TOMATO

Make up some garlic butter by creaming together scant ⅓ cup soft butter in a bowl with 1–2 crushed garlic cloves. Spread thinly over two-thirds of each base using the back of a spoon. Spread tomato sauce over the remaining thirds. Drizzle with a little oil and scatter over a little sea salt. Bake for 4 to 6 minutes or until cooked.

FETA AND CARAMELIZED ONION

Make up some caramelized onion (p80). Smudge the base with mascarpone then the tomato sauce. Dot over the caramelized onion, add some crumbled feta, a bit of oregano, a few dabs of garlic butter (see right), and a drizzle of olive oil. Cook for 6 to 8 minutes or until golden and bubbling.

ZUCCHINI AND GOAT CHEESE

Smear your pizza bases with a layer of mascarpone. Grate 1 medium zucchini and scatter over the bases with cubes of goat cheese to taste, sea salt, and black pepper, dabs of garlic butter, and a drizzling of olive oil. Add Parmesan shavings when cooked.

CHERRY TOMATO

Scatter 6 sliced cherry tomatoes over each pizza base. Drizzle over olive oil. Sprinkle over a little sea salt. Bake for 6 minutes. Add more salt, a drizzle of oil, and a little arugula or basil before serving.

MARGHERITA

Cover your pizza bases with tomato sauce. Sprinkle over 5–7 ounces diced mozzarella and a pinch each of dried thyme and oregano. Dot with a handful of olives and drizzle lightly with olive oil. Bake. Add grated Parmesan.

FUNGHI

Heat a little olive oil and a little bit of butter in a pan. Cook 2 diced garlic cloves for a minute without browning. Add 2 handfuls of thinly sliced white/cremini mushrooms. Cook for a minute. Add a glug of white wine, season, and cook for another minute. Top your bases with either a smudge of tomato sauce or a smeared covering of mascarpone. Cover thinly with the mushrooms. Scatter with diced mozzarella, a good pinch of oregano, and a drizzle of olive oil. Finish with a few strands of caramelized onion. Sprinkle with sea salt. Cook for 6 to 8 minutes until bubbling.

SALAMI AND FIG

Smear the bases with the tomato sauce. Place as many torn pieces of salami as you like evenly over the top. Place blobs of fig relish or a few slices of fresh fig. Scatter each pizza with a few ½-inch cubes of mozzarella, a few red pepper flakes, and a handful of torn basil. Drizzle with olive oil. Cook for 6 to 8 minutes or until golden and bubbling.

POLLO

Slice and shred a good handful of cold roast chicken. Smear your bases lightly with tomato sauce and top evenly with a good scattering of diced mozzarella, crumbled blue cheese, and the chicken. Sprinkle over a few leaves of torn tarragon, season, and drizzle with olive oil, making sure the chicken has some coverage so it doesn't dry out in the scorching heat. Slap the tray in the oven for 6 to 8 minutes or until crisp and golden. Remove. Top with a few arugula leaves and shavings of Parmesan.

DOUBLE CHOC CHIP GINGERS AND CHOC CHERRY SOUR COOKIES

MAKES 12 COOKIES

INGREDIENTS

6 tablespoons butter, softened
1 cup all-purpose flour
¾ cup superfine sugar
1 teaspoon vanilla extract
grated zest of ½ a small orange
1 medium egg
2 ounces semisweet chocolate

DOUBLE CHOC CHIP
1 level tablespoon unsweetened cocoa

CHOC GINGERS
1 ounce candied ginger, diced

CHOC CHERRY SOURS
1 ounce dried sour cherries, halved

So many cookies are just so-so—these cookies are just so good. Thinner than most, they make a beautiful base for more daring flavors. So, make the batter, add your option.

PREP Preheat the oven to 350°F. Grease 2 large baking sheets.

Tip the butter into a bowl. Break it up with the wooden spoon. Sift in the flour. Add the sugar, vanilla extract, and orange zest. Beat the egg. Bang it in. Beat everything together using a wooden spoon until smooth.

Sit the chocolate on a board. Use a long sharp chef's knife to dice it into small bits. Add it all to the batter. Now prep and add your chosen extra, sifting the cocoa over the batter if making the double choc chip option.

Work into the base batter with a metal spoon or fork.

COOK Drop heaping teaspoons of batter well apart on the sheets to allow for spreading (you may need to cook in batches). Bake for 8 minutes or until they are crisping at the edges. Remove. Leave on the sheets for 3 minutes. Run a metal spatula very carefully underneath to loosen them. Leave for another 4 minutes before removing to a rack to cool.

PLATE Enjoy with a cup of coffee.

BONUS BITE

CHOCOLATE FLORENTINES
Preheat the oven to 350°F. Grease two large baking sheets. Lightly toast ½ cup slivered almonds in a dry skillet on very low heat for a minute, stirring, until very pale brown. Remove. Melt 4 tablespoons butter in a pan and combine with ¼ cup superfine sugar, 2 teaspoons thin honey, and 1 teaspoon grated lemon or orange zest in a pan on low heat. Cool in a bowl for 5 minutes. Add generous ⅓ cup sifted all-purpose flour, ⅓ ounce chopped raisins, 1¼ ounces finely chopped mixed peel, and 1½ ounces roughly chopped candied cherries and stir lightly until well combined. Using your fingers, shape and squeeze the mix into 12 blobs. Space them well apart on the baking sheets, flattening them slightly with your fingers, and bake for 8 to 10 minutes, until golden-edged but not dark. Rest on sheets for 2 minutes. Slide a metal spatula underneath. Remove to cool on a rack. Melt 4 ounces milk/white/semisweet chocolate in a bowl over a pan of water (p226). Spoon a little of the melted chocolate onto the flat side of each cooled cookie. Leave for 5 minutes. Repeat, using a fork to make wavy lines in the chocolate for effect if you want to. Let set.

VANILLA CUSTARDS

MAKES 12 COOKIES
(OR 6 AS CUSTARD CREAMS)

INGREDIENTS
¾ cup (1½ sticks) butter, softened
⅔ cup confectioners' sugar
½–1 teaspoon vanilla extract
1¼ cups all-purpose flour
2 ounces custard powder
**CUSTARD CREAM FILLING
(OPTIONAL)**
4 tablespoons butter, softened
1 cup confectioners' sugar, sifted
3 drops vanilla extract
1–2 tablespoon raspberry jam (or
    whatever jam you fancy)

—— CHANGE IT UP ——
For lime custards, make a lime buttercream
by adding the finely grated zest and juice
of ½ lime and a squeeze of lemon
to the custard cream filling.

—— BONUS BITE ——
SHORTBREAD CIRCLES OR HEARTS
Cream ¾ cup (1½ sticks) butter and ¼ cup
superfine sugar as above. Sift in 1 generous
1 cup all-purpose flour and 1 ounce custard
powder. Beat together, adding 1 teaspoon
vanilla extract. Pull into a firm dough with
your hands. Roll out to ¼ inch thick on a
floured board. Cut out 12 x 2½-inch circles
or hearts, rerolling between. Sit them on a
greased baking sheet, prick lightly all over
with a fork, and sprinkle with superfine
sugar. Bake as above until pale gold. Cool
on sheet for 5 minutes. Add more sugar.
Sandwich as above or with whipped cream,
jam, and raspberries. Or enjoy plain.

*An alternative take on one of the UK's favorite cookie; it's kind of chic
but it takes you back in time and puts a smile on your face...*

PREP Preheat the oven to 350°F. Grease a large baking sheet.

Cream the mix: Tip the butter into a large bowl. Break it up with a
wooden spoon. Beat for a few seconds. Sift in the confectioners' sugar and beat
for a good few minutes until soft and creamy white. Beat in the vanilla extract.
Sift in the flour and custard powder.

Mix with a fork until integrated. Draw into a ball with your fingers. Divide into
12. Roll each bit lightly between your hands to shape into a ball. Sit them well
apart on the baking sheet. Use a fork to press down very lightly into each one,
first one way, then the other to flatten slightly and cross-hatch the surface.

COOK Bake for 10 to 15 minutes or until pale golden. Don't let them
brown.

Cool for 2 minutes then run a metal spatula under and transfer to a rack. Cool
completely. Store in an airtight container until needed.

For custard creams: Beat the butter in a bowl. Add the confectioners' sugar and
vanilla extract and mix until soft. Spread 6 cookies with the jam, then cover
with the frosting. Sandwich with the remaining cookies.

PLATE Pile them up and get stuck in...

GINGER CHILI LIMES

MAKES 12 COOKIES

INGREDIENTS

10 tablespoons butter, softened
1 cup superfine sugar
¼ cup raw brown sugar
1 tablespoons dark corn syrup
1 small egg, beaten
generous 1 cup all-purpose flour
1 teaspoon baking powder
½ teaspoon baking soda
3 teaspoons ground ginger
a pinch of cinnamon (optional)
a small pinch of red pepper flakes
½ teaspoon salt
grated zest of ½ a lime

—— CHANGE IT UP ——

For chocolate ginger chili limes, melt
4 ounces semisweet or milk chocolate
very slowly in a bowl over a pan of barely
simmering water. Spread a little over
the base of the cooled gingers. Let set
before eating.

TIP
Store ginger cookies separately as other cookies can pick up their flavor.

A delicious ginger cookie with an exotic twist … great with a cup of tea or coffee.

PREP Preheat the oven to 350°F. Grease 2 large baking sheets.

Tip the butter into a bowl. Beat it for a few seconds with a wooden spoon. Add the sugars and cream together until the mixture is soft and very pale. Add the dark corn syrup. Add the egg and beat furiously. Sift the flour, baking powder, baking soda, ginger, and cinnamon into the bowl.

Add the red pepper flakes, salt, and lime zest. Using a large metal spoon, fold the mix together, cutting down into it then folding gently in figure-of-eight movements until it amalgamates.

Roll the mix into 12 walnut-sized balls. Place well apart on the sheets to allow for spreading (you may need to cook in batches).

COOK Bake for 15 to 20 minutes or until golden brown. Remove. Leave on the sheets for 2 minutes. Slide a metal spatula carefully under to loosen them and transfer to a rack. Letcool. Store in an airtight container until needed.

PLATE Pile onto a plate.

BONUS BITES

GINGER SNAPJACKS
Preheat the oven to 375°F. Melt ½ cup (1 stick) butter gently in a pan. Remove. Mix in generous 1¼ cups oats, ¾ teaspoon ground ginger, ¼ cup +2 tablespoons soft light brown sugar, and 1 tablespoon semolina. Spoon into a well-greased 11 by 7-inch shallow pan, pressing the mix to fit. Bake for 15 minutes. Cut into 12 with a sharp knife after a few minutes and let cool in the pan. These cookies are thin and delicate, so lift them carefully with a metal spatula.

GINGER BRANDY SNAPS
Preheat the oven to 325°F. Melt ¼ cup granulated sugar, 4 tablespoons butter, and scant ¼ cup dark corn syrup in a pan. Remove. Mix in generous ⅓ cup sifted all-purpose flour, 2 level teaspoons ground ginger, 1 teaspoon lemon juice. Space 4 teaspoons of mix well apart on a very well greased baking sheet and bake for 8 minutes or until golden. Remove. After 1 minute run a spatula underneath. Roll each one around a wooden spoon handle. Remove after a minute. Cook and roll remaining mix. Cool. Enjoy as they are or roll in melted chocolate.

BUTTERMILK
SCONES

MAKES 8

INGREDIENTS

scant 1⅔ cups self-rising flour
½ teaspoon baking powder
½ teaspoon salt
4 tablespoons soft butter
¼ cup superfine sugar
⅔ cup buttermilk, plus extra for
  brushing
granulated sugar, for finishing

TIP
Use a wine glass if you don't have a cutter. Reflour the cutter every time for a cleaner cut and a better rise.

········· TIME SAVER ·········
Freeze cooked scones on a baking sheet for 20 minutes. Seal in freezer bags. Thaw and reheat for 10 minutes at 350°F for 8 to 10 minutes. Freeze uncooked scones as above. To cook, thaw as long as it takes the oven to preheat. Bake for the regular time plus another minute or two.

Using buttermilk in your scones raises their game—team them with jam and Devonshire cream for a classic cream tea.

PREP Preheat the oven to 425°F. Grease a baking sheet. Sift the flour, baking powder, and salt into a large bowl. Add the butter. Rub it into the flour between your fingers and thumbs, lifting the mix high over the bowl as you do so, until it looks like fine sand. Keep it light (overhandling scones makes them heavy). Add the sugar and two-thirds of the buttermilk. Mix with a fork. Add more buttermilk until you have a soft (not wet) dough. Draw it together with your fingers and knead it very lightly for a second until you get a smooth ball.

Sit the dough on a floured board. Pat it out very lightly into a rough circle approximately 1 inch thick. Cut out the scones using a floured 2½-inch cutter, pressing down sharply without twisting. Lift the scones out cleanly and place on a baking sheet. Reroll the scraps and repeat, reflouring the cutter. Brush the scones with extra buttermilk and sprinkle with sugar.

COOK Bake for 15 minutes until risen and golden. Cool on a rack.

PLATE Split in two when warm or cold. Serve butter, jam, or fruit curd and Devonshire or whipped heavy or whipping cream.

BONUS BITES

ORANGE, LEMON, AND GOLDEN RAISIN CUTAWAY SCONES
Preheat the oven to 425°F. Grease a large baking sheet. Sift 3½ cups self-rising flour, a pinch of baking powder, and a pinch of salt into a large bowl. Rub ¾ cup (1½ sticks) butter into the flour, then mix in the grated zest of ½ a lemon and ¼ orange, 2½ tablespoons superfine sugar, and scant ½ cup golden raisins/dried fruit, with a fork. Add as much of 2 large beaten eggs as you need to form a soft smooth dough. If too dry, add a splash of milk. Sit on a lightly floured counter, pat out as above, and cut into triangular scones with a sharp, floured knife. Sit them on a baking sheet. Brush the tops with a little milk and a sprinkle of sugar. Bake for 10 to 12 minutes.

MULTITOP CHEESE, ONION, AND OLIVE SCONES
Fry a minced onion gently in olive oil until golden. Cool. Preheat the oven to 400°F. Grease 2 baking sheets. Sift scant 1⅔ cups all-purpose flour, 2 heaping tablespoons baking powder, a pinch of salt, ¾ teaspoon cayenne, and 1 teaspoon mustard powder into a bowl. Rub 2 tablespoons butter into the mix with your fingers. Add the onion, a few chopped black olives, 1 cup grated strong Cheddar cheese, and a beaten egg. Mix together with a fork. Add 6 tablespoons milk to the mix gradually. Pull the dough into a soft ball, pat out lightly on a lightly floured board until 1 inch thick, and cut out as above. Brush the tops of the scones with a little egg/grated Cheddar/pesto, or a spreading of mustard, and bake in the oven for 15 to 20 minutes. These are good warm, split, spread with cream cheese or butter. Make and serve with soup for a good lunch.

VICTORIA SPONGE CAKE WITH LEMON AND PASSIONFRUIT CURD & CREAM

FEEDS 8

INGREDIENTS

1 cup (2 sticks) soft butter, plus extra
    for greasing
4 medium eggs
scant 1⅔ cups self-rising flour
generous 1 cup superfine sugar
2 teaspoons vanilla extract
a pinch of salt
1–2 tablespoons milk (if required)
a little sifted confectioners' sugar or
    superfine sugar for finishing
CURD
juice and grated zest of 2 large lemons
½ cup superfine sugar
4 tablespoons butter
2 large eggs, beaten
2–3 passionfruit, halved
CHANTILLY CREAM
generous ¾ cup heavy cream
1 tablespoon confectioners' sugar
a few drops of vanilla extract

········· **TIME SAVER** ·········

Save on your prep time by adding 1
teaspoon baking powder to the sponge
batter. Bang it all into a bowl/mixer. Beat for
5 minutes or until creamy. Bake as above.

——— **CHANGE IT UP** ———

1. Fill with your choice of jam/whipped
cream/sliced strawberries/peaches/
raspberries.
2. For a gluten-free Victoria sponge, preheat
the oven to 325°F. Whisk 6 medium eggs
and ¾ cup superfine sugar together until
pale and fluffy, then fold in
1 cup sifted rice flour, 1 teaspoon xanthum
gum, and 3 drops of vanilla extract. Divide
between two greased and lined sandwich
pans and bake for 20 to 30 minutes.

This old girl still has it: keep her classic or be bold with a more unusual filling. Start with all the ingredients at room temperature, and it's always light and gorgeous.

PREP Preheat the oven to 350°F. Grease two 7-inch sandwich pans. Line their bottoms. Beat the eggs together in a small bowl. Sift the flour onto a plate.

Cream the mix: Slap the butter into a large bowl and break it up with a wooden spoon. Add the sugar. Beat them together furiously for 4 to 5 minutes until creamy, white, and airy. Now add the egg, a little at a time, beating continuously (too fast and it may curdle). If it starts to look grainy, beat even harder, adding 2 teaspoons of flour. Add the vanilla extract. Hold a strainer high over the mix. Sift the flour and salt into the bowl a bit at a time.

Fold it in lightly: use a large metal spoon to cut into the ingredients and fold them together with a few gentle scooping figure-of-eight movements. Once amalgamated, the batter should drop softly off the end of the spoon (fold in a little milk if it looks too thick). Divide between the pans, smoothing to the edges very lightly but not pressing down. Keep the air in there.

COOK Bake for 20 to 25 minutes. The cakes are done when they're high, golden, and spring back when touched in the middle (don't test too soon). Open and close the oven door carefully. Remove and run a knife around the edges to loosen and take them out of the pans (p201). Peel the lining paper away in strips and very carefully. Let cool on a rack before filling.

Meanwhile, make the curd filling. Sit a large bowl over the top of a pan of barely simmering water. Add the lemon juice, zest, sugar, and butter. Melt slowly. Stir to dissolve the sugar. Add the beaten eggs. Stir constantly with a wooden spoon on low heat for a few minutes until it thickens and coats the back of the spoon. (If it starts to split, sit the bowl in cold water and beat wildly). Remove from the heat. Scoop out the pulpy insides of the passionfruit and stir into the mixture. Let cool.

Just before filling, make the chantilly cream: Whip the cream in a cold bowl until it starts to thicken. Sift the confectioners' sugar and add with the vanilla. Whip until light and airy, not stiff or grainy. Taste and adjust until you like it.

Using a metal spatula, spread the flat side of one of the sponges with curd. Cover with chantilly cream and sit the second sponge on top. Sprinkle with superfine or confectioners' sugar.

PLATE Sit the cake on a large plate. Cut into slices … enjoy.

BONUS BITES

CHOCOLATE VICTORIA

Replace 1 tablespoon of the cake flour with unsweetend cocoa.
Make a chocolate frosting by melting 2 ounces chocolate (p226)
and adding to ½ cup (1 stick) creamed butter mixed with 2 cups
confectioners' sugar and 2 teaspoons milk. Use to cover.

FRUIT VICTORIA

Add 2 teaspoons grated lemon/orange zest to the batter with
1 tablespoon lemon/orange juice. Frost with lime buttercream
(p212).

COFFEE VICTORIA

Add ⅓ cup finely chopped walnuts and 1–2 tablespoons cold
coffee to the cake batter instead of milk. Frost with coffee
buttercream (p219).

SPONGE DROPS

MAKES 12 TO 16

INGREDIENTS

4 medium eggs (at room temperature)
½ cup superfine sugar
scant 1 cup self-rising flour
generous ⅓ cup cornstarch
3 drops of vanilla extract
confectioners' sugar, to serve

FILLING

3–4 tablespoons jam or lemon curd
1 x chantilly cream (p216)
a carton of raspberries or strawberries

·········· **TIME SAVER** ··········

To speed up the whisking process, sit the
eggs and sugar in a heatproof bowl over a
pan of very gently simmering water.

────── **BONUS BITE** ──────

JELLY ROLL

Grease and line a jelly roll pan/2 sandwich
pans, bringing the paper up over the edges.
Sprinkle well with superfine sugar. Whisk
½ cup superfine sugar with 4 eggs as above
until stiff and foamy. Very gently fold in
½ teaspoon vanilla extract, 2 tablespoons
warm water, grated zest of 1 lemon, and
generous ¾ cup sifted all-purpose flour.
Pour into the pan. Bake for 12 to 15 minutes
at 375°F; it should be high, golden, and
just firm. Sprinkle sugar over another piece
of paper. Remove the cake from the oven.
Loosen the edges. Invert onto the sugared
paper. Remove the pan and the paper.
Spread with lemon curd. Use the paper to
roll it up.

*Think jelly roll but in a much neater package. These whisked baby
sponge cakes are great piled with jam, cream, and fruit for a sweet tea.
Sort out your technique before moving onto the real deal—jelly roll is
an impressive favorite.*

PREP Preheat the oven to 350°F. Grease and line 2 baking sheets with
baking parchment.

Crack the eggs into a large bowl. Add the sugar. Whisk them into a
mousse with an electric hand whisk or in a mixer until pale, thick, stiff,
and voluminous. Once the beaters leave a thick trail on top of the mix it's
done. This could take about 8 minutes.

Sift over the flours and add the vanilla extract. Using a large metal spoon, fold
them together very gently in figure-of-eight movements until combined. Take
care to keep it light and airy.

Spoon tablespoons of the mix onto the sheets, keeping them well apart to allow
for spreading. Slice the strawberries, if using.

COOK Bake for 9 to 10 minutes or until the drops are risen and have
crispy golden brown tops. Let cool on the sheets. Make and chill
the chantilly cream.

PLATE Spread the jam or curd onto the flat sides of half the drops. Top
with cream and raspberries or sliced strawberries. Sandwich with
the remaining drops and dust with confectioners' sugar. Alternatively, top
every one of them. Pile onto a plate with extra whole berries.

SINFUL CHOCOLATE COFFEE CAKE AND FROSTINGS

FEEDS 8

INGREDIENTS

5 ounces semisweet chocolate (70% is
  best), broken into squares
1 teaspoon instant coffee granules
9 tablespoons butter, softened
½ cup + 2 tablespoons superfine sugar
5 eggs, separated
  (at room temperature)
½ cup self-rising flour
1½ teaspoons baking powder
a pinch of baking soda
2 tablespoons unsweetened cocoa
finely grated zest of ½ a medium orange
1 tablespoon brandy/rum/amaretto
1 teaspoon vanilla extract
1 tablespoon water

—— CHANGE IT UP ——

1. Decorate further to suit any event. Add your choice of candles/fresh cherries/crumbled chocolate flake/chocolate curls/pick 'n' mix candies/grated chocolate. **2.** For a simple finish, sift 2–3 tablespoons confectioners' sugar over your naked cake. **3.** For a chocolate chili cake, add 1 tablespoon red pepper flakes to the batter.

—— BONUS BITE ——

CHOCOLATE TORTE

Make the cake up as above. Melt 2 tablespoons apricot jam or marmalade gently in a pan. Brush it over the top and sides as it comes out of the oven. Cool. Just before frosting, melt 6½ ounces semisweet chocolate, 9 tablespoons unsalted butter, and 1 tablespoon dark corn syrup in a bowl over a pan of water, stirring as it melts. Pour over the cake for a smooth finish.

Rich, decadent, and blissfully tempting. Adapt with your choice of gorgeous frostings, cloak it in chocolate or leave plain. Dress it up or keep it tasteful. To fill and cover your cake, just double up the frosting.

PREP Preheat the oven to 325°F. Grease and line the bottom and sides of a 8½-inch loose-bottom/springform pan with baking parchment.

Put a small pan a third full of water on very low heat. Sit an ovenproof bowl on the top, leaving the bottom clear of water. Add the chocolate pieces and coffee granules and leave until the chocolate has melted (do not stir). Once it's liquid, remove from the heat and stir to dissolve the granules. Let it cool.

Meantime, tip the butter into a large bowl and break it up with a wooden spoon. Add the sugar. Beat for 5 minutes or until the mix is pale, light, and fluffy.

Beat the egg yolks. Add them to the mix with the cooled chocolate. Stir well. Sift in the flour, baking powder, baking soda, and cocoa. Add the orange zest. Fold the mix together very lightly with a large metal spoon until incorporated. Stir in the brandy, vanilla extract, and water.

Whisk the egg whites in a large clean bowl until stiff, then stir 1 tablespoon into the chocolate mix to loosen it. Add the rest, folding lightly and gently to incorporate. It will resist at first but it will come together. Don't overwork it. Pour into the pan and tip to spread it evenly.

COOK Bake for 45 minutes. Test for doneness—a skewer/toothpick inserted into the middle should come out clean. Remove from the oven and cool on a wire rack for 10 minutes in the pan. Don't worry if the top cracks. Run a blunt knife around the edge of the cake to loosen, release the spring, and place a rack or plate over the cake. Invert it. Remove the bottom. Peel off the lining. Reinvert onto a rack and let cool completely.

PLATE Cut the cake in half with a serrated knife. Lift the top half away and lay on the rack. Fill and top with a frosting. Slice and eat.

FROSTINGS

1 COFFEE BUTTERCREAM
Cream 8 tablespoons softened butter until smooth. Sift 1½ cups confectioners' sugar and beat into the butter gradually unti light. Beat in 2–3 teaspoons cold strong black coffee. Spoon and smooth a third of the frosting over the cut side of one half. Dollop the rest of the frosting on the top. Smooth and swirl to peak and pattern extravagantly.

2 CHOCOLATE FUDGE
Melt 8 tablespoons butter with 1 tablespoon strong black coffee and 3 tablespoons water. Let it cool a bit. Sift generous 2⅓ cups confectioners' sugar and ¼ cup unsweetened cocoa into a bowl. Beat in the butter mix until thick and smooth. If it starts to look odd, add a bit of cold water. Divide between the middle and top as above.

LIME, LEMON, AND ELDERFLOWER DRIZZLE CAKE

FEEDS 6

INGREDIENTS

scant 1¼ cups self-rising flour
a pinch of baking powder
2 teaspoons ground almonds
¾ cup (1½ sticks) butter, softened
generous ¾ cup superfine sugar
2 large eggs (at room temperature)
    beaten
grated zest of 1 large lemon
grated zest of 1 large lime
a splash of elderflower cordial
2 tablespoons lime juice
1 tablespoon lemon juice
3 tablespoons milk
DRIZZLE
3 tablespoons confectioners' sugar
juice of 2 fat limes
juice of ½ a lemon

TIP
If the cake is browning ahead of time, cover lightly with baking parchment (open and close the oven door slowly as you do so).

——— CHANGE IT UP ———
To make lemon and lime poppy seed cake, follow the main recipe, using 1¼ cups self-rising flour and omitting the ground almonds. Add 3–4 tablespoons poppy seeds at the final folding in.

This is a much zingier version of a typical lemon drizzle cake, and much better for it. Make sure to taste both mix and the drizzle and adjust for a good strong bright flavor. Use granulated instead of confectioners' sugar if you like your topping a bit crunchier.

PREP Preheat the oven to 325°F. Grease and line the bottom and sides of a 2-pound loaf pan. Sift the flour and baking powder into a bowl. Add the almonds and set aside.

Tip the butter into a separate bowl and break it up with a wooden spoon. Add the sugar and beat furiously for 5 minutes or until pale, light, and very creamy. Dribble the beaten egg bit by bit into the mix, beating wildly to incorporate. If it looks like it is splitting, add a bit of flour and keep going.

Sift the flour/almonds into the bowl (tip in any bits which stay in the strainer).

Add the zests. Using a large metal spoon, cut and fold the mixture together with large, light figure-of-eight movements until just combined. Fold in the cordial, juices, and milk very gently. Check you have a soft dropping (off the end of the spoon) consistency. Taste the batter. Add a little more juice or milk as appropriate.

COOK Ease the batter gently into the pan. Bake for 50 minutes or until well risen, golden brown, and springy to the touch. Test for doneness—a skewer/toothpick inserted into the middle should come out clean. Remove from the oven. The cake will probably lose height but don't worry.

Have the drizzle ready to go. Sift the confectioners' sugar into a bowl, add the juice, and mix. Taste to check that it's very zingy, adding more of either citrus juice if it isn't. Prick the hot cake all over with a toothpick/thin skewer. Pour the drizzle evenly over the top. After 10 minutes, use the paper to lift the cake out of the pan. Sit it on a rack. Peel the paper away. Let cool.

PLATE Enjoy on the same day with a cup of coffee or tea. It lasts for 3 days in an airtight container and freezes well.

YORKSHIRE TEA LOAF

FEEDS 12

INGREDIENTS

scant 2 cups boiling water
2 Yorkshire or ordinary tea bags
scant 1¼ cups raisins
⅔ cup currants or generous ½ cup
    golden raisins
generous ⅓ cup superfine sugar
1¼ ounces candied ginger, diced
grated zest of ½ a small orange
grated zest of ½ a lemon
2¼ ounces candied cherries
scant ⅓ cup walnuts, roughly chopped
2 medium eggs, beaten
scant 2 cups all-purpose flour
½ teaspoon pumpkin pie spice

—— CHANGE IT UP ——

1. For an earl grey and fig loaf, switch the Yorkshire tea bags for earl grey tea bags and add 6 chopped dried figs to the raisins and golden raisins before proceeding as above.

2. For a rum and orange loaf, omit the tea. Mix 1½ cups boiling water with scant ¼ cup orange juice and 2 tablespoons dark rum and use this to soak the golden raisins and raisins. Add the 2 ounces chopped dates to the tea mixture when adding the remaining fruit and proceed as before.

3. For a tea, prune, date & walnut loaf, add 2 ounces chopped dates to the soaking fruit before adding 1¼ ounces each of chopped dates and walnuts when adding the remaining flavorings.

I love Yorkshire tea. I love cake. The relationship was inevitable. This one's so easy and delightfully fruity. Get it going the night before.

PREP Pour the boiling water into a measuring cup. Add the tea bags. Let it brew for 5 minutes. Discard the bags. Pour the hot tea into a heatproof bowl with the raisins and currants or golden raisins and let cool, covered, overnight or for at least 6 hours.

Preheat the oven to 300°F.

Grease and line a large loaf pan (8 by 4 by 2¾ inches). Add the sugar, ginger, zest, a mix of halved and whole candied cherries, and the walnuts to the tea mixture. Stir well, mixing in the beaten eggs.

Sift the flour and mixed spice into the mix. Beat everything together and pour into the pan.

COOK Bake for about 1½ hours, until risen and golden brown. Stick in a toothpick/skewer to test—it should come out clean (doublecheck. It might have just hit a cherry). Give it longer if it needs it. Let it rest on a rack for 15 minutes. Remove from the pan to cool. Peel off the lining paper.

PLATE Slice when cold using a serrated knife. Eat as it is or spread with butter and top with slices of Cheddar or a semihard cheese. Have it plain with coffee or tea, or enjoy as part of a picnic lunch with celery, cheese, bread, and pickles.

GINGER APPLE LOAF WITH BUTTERSCOTCH FROSTING

FEEDS 8

INGREDIENTS

1¼ cups self-rising flour
3–4 teaspoons ground ginger
a pinch of cinnamon
½–1 teaspoon pumpkin pie spice
¼ cup soft brown sugar
4 tablespoons soft butter
2 medium eggs
½ tablespoon blackstrap molasses
1½ tablespoon dark corn syrup
1 large eating apple, diced into ½-inch
  cubes
½ ounce candied ginger, diced
  (optional)
⅔ cup milk
1 teaspoon baking soda
BUTTERSCOTCH FROSTING
6 tablespoons butter
½ cup brown sugar
¼ cup cream
generous 1 cup confectioners' sugar
½ teaspoon vanilla extract
a few pieces of candied ginger
  (optional)

—— CHANGE IT UP ——

1. Add 1¼ ounces whole candied cherries to the batter. **2.** Grate in half a carrot and add together with scant ¼ cup finely chopped walnuts.

Unashamedly attention-seeking; you've got sweet butterscotch fudge and a moist gingery cake with just a hint of lovely healthy apple.

PREP Preheat the oven to 350°F. Grease and line the bottom of a large loaf pan (8 by 4 by 2¾ inches).

Sift the flour, ginger, cinnamon, and pumpkin pie spice into a large bowl. Add the sugar. Add the butter in bits then incorporate by rubbing it in between your fingertips. Beat in the eggs, molasses, and dark corn syrup using a wooden spoon to make a smooth batter. Stir in two-thirds of the apple and the candied ginger, if using.

Heat the milk in a pan until just boiling. Remove from the heat and pour slowly into the batter, stirring as you go. Stir in the baking soda.

Pour the batter into the pan and scatter the remaining apple over the top.

COOK Bake the cake for 40 to 60 minutes or until a toothpick/skewer comes out clean. Cool it in the pan for 15 minutes and then turn it out. Strip away the lining paper. Let cool on a rack completely.

Meanwhile, make the frosting by melting the butter and sugar over low heat, stirring until the sugar has dissolved. Slowly add the cream, stirring, and continue to cook until the mix is thick and glossy. It will spit but that's fine. Remove from the heat. Let cool then sift over the confectioners' sugar and add the vanilla. Beat well until smooth.

Once the cake is completely cooled, smother it with the frosting. Smooth it out with a spatula for a polished look or keep it rough and rustic. Decorate with a few extra pieces of ginger sliced on the diagonal, if you're using it.

PLATE Serve as a whole and slice in front of guests, or just nick a slice every now and then for a perfect complement to a cup of coffee.

BONUS BITE

CHOCOLATE APPLE MUFFINS
Sift scant 1½ cups all-purpose flour, 2 teaspoons baking powder, ½ tsp baking soda, and ¼ cup unsweetened cocoa into a bowl. In a separate bowl beat together 2 eggs, generous ⅓ cup superfine sugar, 2 tablespoons sunflower oil, the grated zest and juice of ½ orange, and ⅔ cup cold milk. Add this mixture to the flour, whisking together with a fork, until you have a lumpy batter. Add 2 ounces broken chocolate buttons and half an eating apple, cut into chunks. Spoon into 8 muffin cases and bake for 15 minutes at 400°F until risen and firm. Let cool on a rack.

RASPBERRY RIPPLE
CHEESECAKE

FEEDS 12

INGREDIENTS

BASE
8 ounces ginger cookies
4 tablespoons butter
RIPPLE
scant 1¼ cups raspberries
2 teaspoons superfine sugar
FILLING
4 cups soft cream cheese
  (at room temperature)
generous 1 cup superfine sugar
2 teaspoons vanilla extract
generous ¾ cup sour cream
½ cup heavy cream
4 tablespoons all-purpose flour
1 tablespoon cornstarch
4 eggs (at room temperature)
juice of 4 limes, plus grated zest of 2
juice of 1 lemon
8 ounces white chocolate, melted

✶✶✶✶ CASH SAVER ✶✶✶✶
Use frozen raspberries; or buy cheap in
summer and freeze your own.

⋯⋯⋯ TIME SAVER ⋯⋯⋯
The base and puree can be made a day
ahead. Just refrigerate until needed.

TIP
For a clean edge to your cheesecake slices, cut with a sharp knife you've dipped in hot water then dried.

Here's your traditional New York Cheesecake, but the raspberry ripple takes it somewhere else. Watch out for cracks … enjoy!

PREP Base: Break the cookies up a bit then pulse/blitz them in a food processor until fine, or tip into a freezer bag and bash them with a rolling pin. Melt the butter gently in a pan. Remove from the heat, add the fine crumbs, and stir well. Press the mix down over the bottom of an 8-inch loose-bottomed cake pan. Chill.

RIPPLE: Tip the raspberries and sugar into a small pan. Heat very gently, stirring until the fruits fully release their juices. Tip the mix into a strainer over a bowl. Push the fruit through with the back of a wooden spoon, discarding the seeds left in the strainer. Scrape any extra puree left on the other side of the strainer. Set aside.

Preheat the oven to 340°F (low heat means less chance of cracking).

FILLING: Get a big mixing bowl. Add the cream cheese and stir to loosen it up with a wooden spoon. Stir in the sugar, vanilla extract, sour and heavy cream, then sift the flour and cornstarch over the mix. Stir together using a metal spoon. Don't beat it.

Crack the eggs into a bowl and beat well with a fork. Dribble them into the mix gradually, stirring rapidly with the wooden spoon until fully absorbed. Add the lime zest and lemon and lime juice.

Break the chocolate into bits, tip into a heatproof bowl, sit over a pan of barely simmering water (with the bottom clear), and leave until melted. Remove from the heat and stir until smooth. Cool for a minute, then stir into the egg mix.

Get the pan from the refrigerator. Pour in half to two-thirds of the mix. Smooth to the edges of the pan using a spatula or back of a metal spoon. Drizzle the raspberry puree over the top in irregular lines or swirls. Spoon over the remaining mix and smooth it gently to the edges.

COOK Bake in the oven for 35 to 40 minutes until firm-ish at the edges but only just set and still wobbly in the center when the pan is shaken a bit. Turn off the oven, leaving the cake in there for an hour as it cools down. (Take it out now and it will crack and won't firm up enough.) Remove from the cooled oven and place on a rack for 10 minutes to rest. Carefully run a thin blunt knife between cake and pan to loosen, then pop the cake back in the oven with the door open and leave for another hour. Take the cheesecake from the oven and let cool before removing the sides of the pan and chilling in the refrigerator for 2 hours.

PLATE Serve plain, or dot with a layer of raspberries or summer berries.

Desserts

The "dessert"—a word normally followed by the phrases "oh I shouldn't," "oh go on then," "why not?" and, finally, "mmmmm." The world of the dessert tends to divide people. Some have savory palates while so many others have sweet. It's much the same in the kitchen. There are some people out there who go crazy for making desserts and others who could do without. In this section,

I promise you that whatever your taste and preference, you'll find some absolutely gorgeous treats. From the humble crumble to a sinful triple chocolate tart this section ain't light on the skill set. So pick up your fork, your spoon, your whisk, and rolling pin. Wherever your palate is coming from, this chapter will sort you out with some classic techniques.

THE DESSERT ROOM
BASIC INGREDIENTS

You need the proper stuff to make a proper dessert; from your grocery store or your farmer's market it's all out there and easy to get hold of.

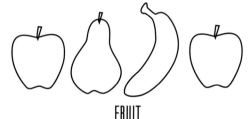

FRUIT

Get in season and locally if you can. Select by touch, smell, and looks (though this final test can be deceptive—it's often the prettiest fruit that don't taste as good). Get loose rather than bagged so you can check the state of it. Get berries off-season in frozen packs for purees, ice cream, and sorbets. Look out for other fruit in the freezer cabinet or freeze your own if that's what you're into.

CHOCOLATE

70% cocoa solids are best for cooking. Shop around for a brand you trust. Go orgnaic/fairtrade.

•••• *Melting* CHOCOLATE ••••

Break chocolate into a bowl. Sit it into the top of pan which is a third full of gently simmering water. Don't let the bottom touch the water. Chocolate melts at a low temperature so will seize and solidify if too hot. Contact with a single drop of cold liquid has the same effect. Let it melt. Stir with a chopstick to avoid wasting it. If you're adding liquids to chocolate to melt, they must be warm.

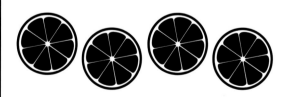

LEMONS

Buy unwaxed if you need to zest them. Always have some in.

CREAM

Get one that's fit for purpose. **LIGHT**: for pouring only. It splits if boiled and won't whip. Swirl into soups and pour on desserts.

HEAVY: here's your best cooking cream as it boils without splitting; downside is it's fattier. It whips well. **WHIPPING** cream does what it says on the can and tastes less fatty (it is). You can substitute for heavy cream in some cooking. **CRÈME FRAÎCHE**: has a slightly sour taste. Serve it with tarts and fresh fruit—it won't split when heated. **DEVONSHIRE CREAM**: rich and thick and can transform the simplest dessert.

EGGS & SUGAR
see p198

BUTTER

Comes in salted and unsalted form. Chefs swear by unsalted butter for baking. It's got a fresher taste, is healthier and affects the quality of your pie dough.

FLOUR

Grocery stores sell a whole range of different flours and with different blends of grain and organic options. Experiment and find a good one.

SYRUPS

Honey, maple, dark corn. They're all useful sources of sugar, particularly in English traditional desserts.

VANILLA

Comes in different guises. Buy natural vanilla extract for ease and value—find a brand you love. Vanilla paste contains seeds. A vanilla bean is the real deal. Keep one in for special occasions. Split and scrape for ice creams and desserts.

• • • • • • • *Dark Corn Syrup* • • • • • • • •

Weighing out dark corn syrup can be a challenge. To be accurate, spoon the syrup out into a clear glass or plastic measuring cup put on the counter until the required amount, then bend down and check at eye level.

• • • • • • • *Make Your Own* • • • • • • • •
VANILLA SUGAR

Keep used vanilla beans. Wash and dry them well. Store in a jar of superfine sugar.

GELATIN

A must for jelly makers. It comes in powder or sometimes leaf form. Vegetarians can use agar-agar instead.

CINNAMON
Use sticks for flavoring compotes. Ground is convenient.

CARDAMOM
Keep a stock for partnering with fruit and sweet things.

PASTRY

PHYLLO Too epic to make at home so buy it in packs—it comes in long rectangular or square sheets.

PUFF Keep a good all-butter puff pastry in the freezer for when you feel a pie coming on.

DESSERT NUTRITION

Let's not pretend this is the healthiest chapter but there's valuable stuff in here still. YOGURT PACKS LOADS OF *Calcuim* FOR BONE BUILDING AND MAINTENANCE. BLUEBERRIES ARE PACKED WITH VITAMIN C WHICH STRENGTHENS THE IMMUNE SYSTEM APPLES ARE RICH IN FIBER which lowers cholesterol and are a good source of CHROMIUM & QUERCITIN PISTACHIOS & ALMONDS ARE A GOOD SOURCE OF COPPER which is good for skin, hair, eyes, WHILE RASPBERRIES ARE LOADED WITH CALCIUM AND SULFUR which helps regulate blood sugar levels and boosts hair and skin and nail health. GRAPEFRUIT CONTAINS FOLIC ACID, VITAMIN C, AND HIGH LEVELS OF *Bioflavonoids* which boost the immune system.

STORE IT

BUTTER UNSALTED lasts 3 months and SALTED lasts 6 months chilled.

SPICES Keep them in the dark with the tops firmly on or they lose strength.

CHOCOLATE Has a shelf life in theory although that's never an issue in my house...

FRUIT BERRIES have a very short shelf life. Get them straight into the refrigerator. BLUEBERRIES last longer than others. BANANAS emit ethylene gas which causes other fruit and vegetables to rot quickly so store them separately. APPLES Best kept in the refrigerator. PEARS Best bought under-ripe and stored chilled. GROCERY STORE FRUIT Often seems to be on the edge so check it frequently and throw rotten stuff away before it contaminates anything else.

PUFF PASTRY Keep some in the freezer.

OWN PIE DOUGH Freeze it uncooked wrapped in freezer bags for a month or store uncooked but wrapped in the refrigerator for 1 day. BAKED TARTS can be stored in airtight containers for 3 days.

CREAM—*Whip it*

Some people overwhip cream and it goes grainy. Or it won't thicken at all. Check this out: keep cream refrigerated always. Even a few minutes at room temperature or near a heat source can inhibit it. Whisk it in a large wide bowl so it's got air to feed on. Do it with a metal balloon whisk so you can sense the feel of your cream as it thickens and you'll know when to stop (not possible with an electric machine). Hold the bowl at an angle as you whip. Softly whipped cream holds in a soft peak. Use this for spooning onto your desserts. Stiffly whipped cream is better for piping.

PLUMS CONTAIN POTASSIUM helping control blood pressure and regulating fluid in the body WHILE CHOCOLATE RELEASES MOOD-ENHANCING ENDORPHINS with the dark stuff high in IRON and ANTIOXIDANTS

SUGAR SYRUP
FOR FRUIT SALAD

Use this simple little sugar syrup to jazz up a fruit salad.

Put 1¼ cups sugar and generous 2 cups of water in a heavy-bottom pan. Heat very slowly, stirring, so the sugar dissolves completely. Only then let it boil. Stop stirring. Boil for 2 minutes. Let cool. Chill it and pour over your fruit. If you like you can add aromatics.

MAKING PIE DOUGH
COOL TIPS *(for hot hands)*

COOL your hands in very cold water

AVOID making pie dough on a hot day or close to a heat source

FLOUR everything in sight

Use **CHILLED** butter

MEASURE the ingredients accurately—proportions matter

Work **QUICKLY** and gently or the pie dough will toughen up as you stimulate the gluten

Use the right **SIZE** pan

ROTATE the pie dough as you roll it

RUN a floured spatula under it if it sticks to the pastry board

To transport, **ROLL** over your rolling pin and gently lay it down

PATCH it up with extra dough or the filling may leak

Use a bit of **EXCESS** dough to press the rest into the sides of the tart pan

Leave a dough **OVERHANG** so if the dough shrinks a bit you're safe

PRICK the bottom so it doesn't rise

CHILL your pie dough for the required time so it cooks properly

Buy some **PIE WEIGHTS** (or use dried beans)

Check out the recipes for how to bake **BLIND**

Get your oven **TEMPERATURE** right—too low and it may slide down the pan and flatten, too hot and it may catch

DOUGH *secrets*

To calculate the size of dough needed to line a pan, use the string test. Lay a piece of string down into and across the widest part of your pan. Measure it. Add extra for the overhang. There's your dimension.

GELATIN *Handler*

Gelatin is a tricky beast to master. It comes in granule form (see package directions) and leaf form—my choice. To tame it, use 4 gelatin leaves to set 2½ cups of liquid (use 5 sheets for fruit terrine or a firmer set). Snip each leaf with scissors and put it into a bowl with 3 tablespoons of your cool liquid. Let it soak for 10 minutes. Sit the bowl over a pan of simmering water. Let it melt. Add it to the rest of your liquid. For jelly: pour it into wetted molds (for turning out) or into glasses. Cool. Chill until set.

LOOKING SWEET
A FEW POINTERS FOR ARTISTIC PRESENTATION

Serve simple things in **PRETTY DISHES**

FROST GLASSES: chill in the refrigerator or quickly in the freezer. Cool for ice cream

STEAM GLASSES upside down over a kettle or an of boiling water. Dust with sifted confectioners' sugar

DUNK STEMMED BERRIES strawberries and cape gooseberries into melted chocolate

GRATE CHOCOLATE or crumble chocolate flake over an ice cream, meringue, or creamy dessert

DUST THE DESSERT world in confectioners' sugar

MAKE SHATTERED CARAMEL
Melt ¼ cup sugar slowly, no stirring, in a heavy pan until a light caramel color. Remove. Cool for a minute. Pour onto silicone baking parchment. Let it set. Shatter it. Use over ice cream, sundaes, or meringues.

BLUEBERRY, BLACKBERRY, AND STRAWBERRY CRUMBLE

FEEDS 4 TO 6

INGREDIENTS

CRUMBLE MASTER TOPPING
¾ cup (1½ sticks) butter
scant 1¼ cups self-rising flour
a pinch of salt
generous ¾ cup ground almonds
scant ⅓ cup superfine sugar
scant ¼ cup raw brown sugar
a few drops of water to finish
FILLING
generous 3 cups strawberries
scant 2¾ cups blueberries
generous 2 cups blackberries
3–4 teaspoons superfine sugar

········· **TIME SAVER** ·········

1. Make crumble topping up to a day ahead and chill. Add the water before adding to the dish.
2. Use the normal rubbing in method with cold butter rather than frozen.

—— **BONUS BITE** ——

BAKED FRUIT MERINGUE
Make up a batch of basic white meringue (p240). Pack 4 small greased dishes with your choice of fruit base and pipe or dot the meringue over the top. Bake at 350°F for 20 to 30 minutes until the fruit is cooked (test with a skewer in the center) and the meringue top has crisped up.

A lovely buttery summery crumble; this one's perfect for a crowd. Give it a go then try out the other seasonal options. For crumble for one: make and freeze a batch of topping. Prep an individual dish of any fruit combination you fancy. Throw on as much crumble as you need. Bake for 15 to 20 minutes. Always make custard….

PREP

For the topping: Wrap the butter in foil and put it in the freezer at least an hour before you want to cook (or the night before) so you can grate it easily. Sift the flour, salt, and ground almonds into a large bowl. Add any nutty sediment left in the strainer. Grate the frozen butter coarsely onto the mix in big loose curls. Add the sugars. Mix everything together very lightly with a fork. Set aside.

Preheat the oven to 400°F. Grease a large rectangular ovenproof dish (19 by 7½ inches). Wash and dry the fruit. Hull the strawberries. Halve any large ones. Tip the fruit into the dish and mix it up. Sprinkle with sugar.

Finish the topping: Flick just a few drops of very cold water over the mix and run a fork through it to make it even crumblier. Top the fruit: scatter the mix lightly and evenly over the top without pressing it down.

COOK

Bake in the oven for 30 minutes, reducing the heat to 375°F halfway through cooking. The crumble should be golden-topped with hot fruit bubbling at the edges—cover with baking parchment/foil if it starts to darken. Stick a metal skewer into the center for 5 seconds then hold it against your wrist to check it's properly hot in the middle.

PLATE

Remove from the oven and let settle for 5 minutes. Sit the dish on the table. Spoon out onto plates. Serve with custard (p236), Devonshire, Chantilly, or cinnamon-spiced whipped cream, vanilla ice cream (p236), or thick Greek yogurt with vanilla and honey.

▬ CHANGE IT UP ▬

1 APPLE AND BLACKBERRY CRUMBLE
Peel, core and roughly chop 1½ pounds sharp eating apples. Tip them into an ovenproof dish with ¾ cup blackberries. Sprinkle with sugar. Top and bake as above for 30 to 40 minutes.

2 PLUM, PEACH, AND RASPBERRY CRUMBLE
Grease an ovenproof dish. Cut 6 peaches and 6 plums around their centers down to the pit. Twist the halves in opposite directions to separate. Remove the pits. Chop the flesh roughly. Throw into the dish with generous 1½ cups raspberries. Sprinkle with 3 teaspoons sugar. Top and bake as above.

3 RHUBARB AND GINGER CRUMBLE
Grease an ovenproof dish. Trim the ends off 1 pound 10 ounces rhubarb. Wash, dry, and slice into 1-inch lengths. Tip into a large pan with 4 tablespoons water and 3–4 teaspoons sugar. Cook gently on low heat for 3 to 4 minutes until it just begins to soften. Taste for sweetness, adding a bit more sugar if you need to. Tip fruit and liquid into your dish. Add 10–20 pieces of chopped candied ginger, ¾ cup halved strawberries, and a squeeze of lemon juice. Add topping. Bake as above.

BAKED BLACKBERRY STUFFED APPLES WITH MERINGUE TOPPING

FEEDS 2

Deliciously soft and flavorsome baked fruit with a soft crispy topping; also try this with big halved peaches.

INGREDIENTS

2 eating apples
a little butter for greasing and topping
a squeeze of lemon juice
4 large blackberries
6 tablespoons cider/apple juice/diluted elderflower cordial/white wine
MERINGUE TOPPING
1 egg white
¼ cup superfine sugar

—— CHANGE IT UP ——

1. Fill each apple with your choice of the following: maple syrup and butter/1 tablespoon lemon curd/a small piece of marzipan, and a dab of butter.
2. Stuff with a mix of scant ¼ cup finely chopped walnuts, 2 chopped dates, 2 tablespoons soft butter, ¼ ounce diced candied ginger, and ½ tablespoon brown sugar. Top with butter.

········· TIME SAVER ·········

Leave off the meringue and make plain stuffed baked apples.

PREP Preheat the oven to 350°F. Butter a shallow ovenproof dish.

Core the apples but leave the base intact so the filling doesn't leak out. Score a thin line around the center of each fruit so it won't burst during cooking. Squeeze a few drops of lemon juice into each cavity. Add 2 blackberries to each and top with butter.

COOK Sit the apples, open-end upward, in the dish. Spoon in the cider or other liquid. Bake for 20 minutes or until the fruit is well on its way to being tender (squeeze to get an idea). Baste them once or twice, spooning over any juices.

Make the meringue topping ten minutes into cooking. Whisk the egg white in a grease-free bowl for a few seconds until white and frothy. Add a teaspoon of sugar. Whisk to amalgamate. Add another. Repeat. When it's all in, whisk for about 4 minutes until the mixture is glossy, thick, and stands in stiff peaks.

Remove the apples from the oven. Heap meringue onto the top of each one like a hat or pipe it from a pastry bag fitted with a large tube into a stylish swirl. Bake for another 15 minutes plus or until the fruit is tender inside, crisp, and browning on top.

PLATE Eat straight from the dish to enjoy the lovely juices. These are great with chilled Greek yogurt and honey or low-fat crème fraîche whipped with confectioners' sugar.

BONUS BITES

BAKED CINNAMON APPLE
Stew 4 peeled chopped apples with a good pinch of cinnamon, 2 teaspoons superfine sugar, 2 teaspoons lemon juice, 1 teaspoon butter, and 2 tablespoons water (you may need a bit more). Stir over low heat to get a thick puree. Pour into an ovenproof dish and let cool. Make up meringue as above and cover. Bake in a preheated oven at 350°F for 15 minutes.

FIGS ON FRENCH TOAST
Cut 4 large or 8 small figs in two lengthwise. Beat 2 small eggs in a wide shallow bowl with 2 tablespoons sour cream, ½ teaspoon vanilla extract, a pinch of cinnamon, and ½ tablespoon sugar. Sit 4 brioche slices in the mix for 1 to 2 minutes a side. Put them on a rack. Heat a little butter in a small skillet on gentle heat. Add the figs to heat through for 1 to 2 minutes. Set aside. Increase the heat a bit and add the brioche. Fry for 2 to 3 minutes a side until hot and golden brown. Dust with a little sifted confectioners' sugar, top with the figs and drizzle with a little honey or maple syrup.

SUMMER ROAST PEACHES

FEEDS 1

INGREDIENTS

a little butter for greasing
1 large peach per person (size and
*   appetite dependent)*
a squeeze of lemon juice
4 tablespoons white wine/fruit juice/
*   amaretto*
TOPPING 1
½ teaspoon cinnamon
1 teaspoon superfine sugar
1 teaspoon butter
TOPPING 2
1 teaspoon maple syrup or thin honey
1 teaspoon butter
TOPPING 3
1 teaspoon raw brown/vanilla sugar
1 teaspoon butter

—— CHANGE IT UP ——

Use raspberries to make up a fresh berry
sauce (p239). Pour over the warm peaches.

—— BONUS BITES ——

BAKED PEACH MERINGUE

Sit a fresh or frozen raspberry in each peach
cavity. Make up a white meringue topping
(p240) and use this to cover the fruit. Bake
for 20 minutes or until the fruit is cooked
and meringue crisp. Serve surrounded by a
raspberry fresh berry sauce (p239).

SKILLET BAKED PEARS

Preheat the oven to 350°F. Melt 1 tablespoon
butter in a metal handled pan. Add 2
teaspoons superfine sugar, a pinch of
cinnamon, and a good squeeze of lemon
juice. Stir. Halve 4 small pears lengthwise.
Sit them, cut-side down in the pan. After
3 minutes, transfer to the oven to cook for
another 15 minutes or until tender.

Slap these in the oven for a luscious summer dessert. When peaches
aren't about, use apricots or nectarines instead. Plums are usually
around through the winter. The quantities given below are for 1 peach
so adjust accordingly.

PREP
Preheat the oven to 350°F. Lightly butter a shallow ovenproof dish
or pan.

Cut the peaches in half lengthwise. Twist to separate the halves. Remove
the pits. Sit them cut side up in the dish/pan. Squeeze a little lemon juice over
each one.

Topping 1: Mix the cinnamon and sugar with the butter. Stuff into the cavity
and coat the top. Topping 2: Fill the cavity with maple syrup or honey. Top
with butter. Topping 3: Dredge with brown or vanilla sugar. Top with butter.

Add your choice of liquid to the dish or use a bit more butter on your fruit.

COOK
Roast the fruit until soft, bubbling and slightly caramelized (20 to
40 minutes, size and ripeness dependent). Check and baste with
their juices every so often.

PLATE
Rest the fruit for a minute or two before eating. Sprinkle with
slivered almonds or pistachios if you want. Eat as they are with
their juices or top with Devonshire cream or vanilla ice cream. Alternatively,
enjoy with French toast (p231). Good warm or cold.

RHUBARB JELLY

FEEDS 4

INGREDIENTS

2 pounds rhubarb, cut into 2-inch
   lengths
½ cup superfine sugar
½ tablespoon elderflower cordial
2-inch piece of fresh ginger, sliced
5 cups water
6 sheets gelatin
1¼ cups chilled sparkling white wine/
   pear cider/elderflower pressé/
   champagne

✶✶✶✶ CASH SAVER ✶✶✶✶
Use the poached fruit as the base for a
crumble or mix it up with yogurt and muesli
and banana for a healthy breakfast. Use any
leftover juice in cocktails or smoothies.

⋯⋯⋯ TIME SAVER ⋯⋯⋯
Make the rhubarb juice the day ahead.

Who would have thought this would work? Sticks of ordinary rhubarb transformed into an elegant dessert. Get your gelatin skills sorted and team it with custardy vanilla ice cream for a reworking of a traditional English childhood classic.

PREP Preheat the oven to 400°F. Cut the rhubarb into 2-inch lengths, cutting off and discarding any leaves. Bang it into a roasting pan with the sugar, cordial, ginger, and water. Cook for 20 minutes until tender. Or put it all in a pan and bring to a boil. Reduce the heat to a minimum and barely simmer until the fruit is soft and the flavors infused. Remove and let cool.

Sit a fine strainer over a bowl. Line it with cheesecloth if you have some. Pour the cold fruit and its juice in and let it drip through. Don't mess with it or press the fruit—a pure drip means a clear jelly. Measure out 2½ cups of the liquid. Recycle the poached fruit/jelly (see left).

Cut the gelatin sheets into large, rough bits. Sit them in a dish and cover with cold water. Let soak and soften up for 10 minutes, or as the pack directs.

COOK Put a third of the juice into a pan on very low heat. Pour the water away from the soaked gelatin and squeeze out any excess. Add the softened gelatin to the warm liquid in the pan, stirring with a wooden spoon as it dissolves. It should take a few seconds only and you'll see it's suddenly clear. Remove from the heat and add to the remaining two-thirds of the juice immediately. Let cool for 10 minutes.

Add your bubbles of choice. Rinse a serving bowl or jelly mold with cold water. Pour the jelly in. Shake it. Or pour it into individual glasses. Chill for a few hours or overnight.

PLATE Serve the glasses as they are or top with vanilla ice cream. To unmold a jelly, run a blunt knife down one side to release the air. Invert it onto a plate and shake to release. Remove the mold. This jelly's good with a crisp tuiles cookie (p251) or brandy snap (p213).

VANILLA
ICE CREAM

MAKES 1½ POUNDS

INGREDIENTS

generous 1 cup milk
1 vanilla bean or 4 drops of natural
    vanilla extract
4 egg yolks
½ cup superfine sugar
generous 1 cup whipping/heavy cream

—— BONUS BITE ——
HONEYCOMB ICE CREAM

Make the basic vanilla ice cream as right.
Put it into your machine to churn or into
the freezer if making by hand. Chop 1–2
chocolate-coated honeycomb bars into
smallish bits. By machine: Stop the ice-
cream maker just as the mix has set, add the
honeycomb pieces, and churn for another 30
seconds to distribute. Transfer to a chilled
plastic container and freeze. By hand: Stir
the honeycomb pieces into the ice cream
after the final beating process.

—— CHANGE IT UP ——

1. Add chunks of homemade or
store-bought meringue or bits of your
favorite chopped chocolate bars to the ice
cream before freezing.
2. Fold in ripples of lemon curd,
butterscotch, or fresh berry sauce just
before freezing
3. For fruity ice creams, blitz up generous
1 cup thick mango/raspberry/banana/
blackcurrant puree and add to the basic
custard before churning.

TIP

The base you make here (before cooling)
is the classic custard sauce in its own right.
Enjoy with everything from apple pie to
crumble to Bakewell tart.

*Where would the world be without ice cream? I'm guessing a much
sadder place. Desserts would be incomplete. Wafer cones would be
redundant. Ok it may be easier to pick up a tub from the store but it's
nowhere near as special. This vanilla is the mother of them all. But feel
free to add other bits and pieces, and purees.*

PREP
Pour the milk into a heavy-bottom pan. Split the vanilla bean
lengthwise down the center. Scrape out the seeds with the blade of a
knife. Add to the milk with the bean. Or use extract. Bring the milk almost to
boiling point, watching, so it doesn't boil over. Remove from the heat. Leave it
for 20 minutes so the flavor can infuse.

Pour some cold water into a bowl or a sink for cooling the custard later.

To make the custard: Tip the egg yolks and sugar into a large bowl. Beat with a
balloon whisk until the mix is frothy enough to leave a trail on the surface.

Reheat the milk until almost boiling. Remove from the stove and pour over
the sugar and egg mix in the bowl, beating continuously with a wooden
spoon. Pour it back into the pan and return to very low heat. Stir continuously
until the sauce is thick enough to coat the back of a wooden spoon. Don't be
tempted to rush this process or the mix may split. Beat hard and dunk the pan
in your cold water if this happens.

Sit the pan in the cold water to cool. Stir occasionally. When it's cold, add the
cream. Put a freezer-proof plastic container into the freezer to prechill.

FREEZE
If you're using an ice-cream machine, pour the mix in and
churn as per your machine's guidelines (usually 20 minutes).
Once set, spoon it into the chilled container and freeze. By hand: chill your
shallow container in the freezer for an hour. Add the cold mix and freeze for
3 hours. Remove. Bang the ice cream into a bowl or processor and beat to
break down the ice crystals. Return to the container and freeze for another
hour. Repeat this process twice or even 3 times, beating each hour, until the ice
cream is wonderfully creamy. Store to freeze until you need it.

PLATE
Remove from the freezer 10 minutes before you need it. Use an
ice-cream scoop or tablespoon dunked in very hot water to scoop
it out into neat balls. Sit alongside a piece of hot fruit tart or crumble. Use in
meringue sundaes. Or drizzle with fresh berry, hot chocolate, or salted caramel
sauces (p238–9) and enjoy.

GRAPEFRUIT WATER ICE

Cut 4–5 fat juicy grapefruits in half on a board. Save any stray juice. Juice them with a juicer or by hand, squeezing out every bit. Measure out generous 2 cups grapefruit juice and strain through a fine strainer into a bowl. Add ½ cup superfine sugar and stir to dissolve. By machine: Churn for 30 minutes or until set. Transfer it to a prechilled plastic container. Freeze until needed. By hand: pour into a shallow container and freeze. Remove every 30 minutes over a 2-hour period and break the ice crystals up with a fork. Once smooth, leave it frozen. Let the ice relax for 5 to 10 minutes before serving. Shape into balls with an ice-cream scoop to serve in a dish or scrape it out and serve in shot glasses with a spoon—this is strong stuff!

RASPBERRY VODKA SORBET

Tip 1 cup superfine sugar and generous ¾ cup cold water into a small heavy-bottom pan. Heat slowly to dissolve the sugar, stirring a couple of times until it looks clear. Increase the heat and bring to a boil. Simmer for 1 minute then remove from the heat and let cool. Tip 3⅔ cups raspberries, 2 tablespoons lemon juice, and 2 tablespoons vodka into a processor and blitz to a smooth puree. Push the puree through a strainer into a bowl with a wooden spoon. By machine: Add 2 beaten egg whites to the puree and cold sugar syrup and churn until frozen. Transfer to the freezer in a prechilled plastic box. By hand: Mix together the fruit and cold syrup and pour into a shallow freezerproof container. Freeze it for an hour plus or until large crystals are forming. Tip it into a processor or bowl and beat until it breaks up. Add the beaten egg whites to the mix and return to the freezer. Remove every 30 minutes over a 2-hour period and break the ice crystals up with a fork. Freeze until needed.

HONEY, LIME, AND LEMON FROZEN YOGURT

Wash, dry, and grate 3 large unwaxed lemons and 1–2 limes. Tip the zest and squeeze the juice into a large bowl with 1 tablespoon honey, a few drops of vanilla extract, and ½ cup sifted sugar. Spoon 1¼ cups plain Greek yogurt, ¾ cup whipping cream, and 2 tablespoons ice cold water into another bowl. Whisk until it starts to thicken. Add to the juices and stir in gently. Pour the mix into a shallow plastic freezerproof box. Freeze until needed.

CHOCOLATE SAUCE

Fit a heatproof bowl into the top of a pan that's a quarter full of water. Check that the bottom of the bowl doesn't touch the liquid. Break 9 ounces good-quality semisweet chocolate into squares. Drop them into the bowl with 1 teaspoon vanilla extract, 6 tablespoons water, and ½ cup dark corn syrup. Put the pan onto very gentle heat. Let the contents melt slowly, stirring sometimes until the mix is liquid and smooth. Take the bowl off the pan and let it cool completely. Stir in ⅔ cup light cream. Use now or store in a clean jam jar and chill until needed. The sauce will solidify, so reheat it very gently to return to pouring consistency.

SALTED CARAMEL SAUCE

Put 2 tablespoons butter, 2 tablespoons dark corn syrup, scant 1 cup soft brown sugar, 1 teaspoon vanilla extract, and a pinch of vanilla or sea salt into a pan. Bring to a boil for 30 seconds. Remove from the heat and stir in 4 tablespoons light cream. Use straightaway or store in a jar until needed.

FRESH BERRY SAUCE

Tip scant 2 cups raspberries/1½ cups strawberries/
blackberries into a processor with a squeeze of lemon
and a splash of water. Strain over ¾ tablespoons
confectioners' sugar, then blitz in the food processor
or with a stick blender until smooth. Tip the puree into
a strainer over a bowl and push it through with the
back of a spoon. Taste and adjust the sweet/
sour balance. A tablespoon of crème
de cassis adds a nice note, if you've got
any about. Chill until needed.

SAUCES

BOUTIQUE
MERINGUES

MAKES UP TO 50 MINI-MERINGUES OR 12 SHELLS

INGREDIENTS
WHITE MERINGUE MIX
4 eggs
generous 1 cup superfine sugar
BROWN MERINGUE MIX
4 eggs
½ cup light soft brown sugar
½ cup superfine sugar

1 x chantilly cream (p216, optional)

—— CHANGE IT UP——

1. For glazed meringues, sprinkle a little superfine sugar over the meringues before cooking. **2.** For chocolate meringues, coarsely grate 8 ounces semisweet chocolate and fold gently into the white meringue mix before shaping into large shells. **3.** For mocha meringues, whisk 1 teaspoon coffee granules into the white sugar mix. Dip the cooled cooked meringues in melted chocolate to finish.

Style it up or style it down—meringue's got everything going for it: taste, looks, and wow factor. Go for the classic white option or the brown alternative.

PREP Start by degreasing your equipment. Dunk a large bowl (glass or metal preferably) and the beaters from your whisk into boiling water. Dry them well. Preheat the oven to 300°F. Separate your eggs with grease-free hands (p153) putting the whites into the dry bowl. If any yolk escapes into it, start again. For white meringues: Measure the superfine sugar out into a cup. For brown: Mix the two sugars together.

Whisk the egg whites for a few seconds. As soon as they've reached the white and foamy stage, add a teaspoon of your chosen sugar. Whisk it in for a minute. Add another spoonful. Whisk it in. Repeat. Once it's all in, continue to whisk until the mix is glossy, thick, and stands in stiff peaks when flicked. It could take 5 minutes.

Line 2 large baking sheets with greaseproof or silicone-coated baking parchment. Dab a bit of meringue in each corner and center to stick down. For big shells: Spoon one or two heaping tablespoons of mix onto the sheets, keeping it smooth or teasing it into peaks. Leave space between each. For mini-meringues: Dot teaspoons of mix onto the sheets or fit a pastry bag with a large/medium tube. Pipe it in small rounds. Reduce the oven to 275°F.

COOK Bake the white or brown meringues for 1½ hours for larger shells, 45 minutes to 1 hour for small ones. If they lift easily off the baking parchment they are done. For chewy centered meringues, remove and sit the sheet on a rack (not a cold counter—they crack). For crisper meringues, turn the oven off and let them dry inside for 1 hour or until they're cold. Sit them on a rack to cool completely. Make up your chantilly cream, if using, and use to sandwich the cooled meringue shells together (below).

PLATE Pile your single or sandwiched white or brown meringue shells onto a plate and serve as they are or with fruit soup.

TO GO WITH
FRUIT SOUP

Make 6 hours before eating. Tip 3 cups water into a pan, add scant 1 cup superfine sugar and a 2-inch strip lemon zest. Stir over low heat until the sugar dissolves. Add a sprig of rosemary and 1 large glass of rosé/beaujolais/perry. Increase the heat and simmer for 3 minutes. Remove. Chill. Just before eating, mix ¾ cup each of hulled quartered strawberries/raspberries/blueberries/diced nectarine into the syrup. Ladle into 6 soup plates. Scoop out the zest and rosemary.

WHITE MERINGUE BASKETS WITH MANGO PASSIONFRUIT SAUCE

MAKES 4 TO 6 MERINGUE BASKETS

INGREDIENTS

1 x white meringue mix (opposite)
generous ¾ cup heavy cream
SAUCE
1 mango
juice of 1 plump lime
1 tablespoon superfine sugar
3 large passionfruit

—— CHANGE IT UP ——

1. Fill the baskets with a handful of mixed sliced and whole fruit (raspberries/ blueberries/sliced strawberries). Dust with confectioners' sugar to finish. **2.** Fill with lemon passionfruit curd. **3.** Make a big basket by piping or spooning half the mix into a flat, circular basket base (8 inches). Build the rest around the sides to make a steep wall. Cook as before for 1½ to 2 hours. Turn off the oven and let cool inside.

—— BONUS BITES ——

PAVLOVA For a softer-centered basket follow the recipe above to the point where half the sugar has been whisked into the egg whites. Fold the remaining sugar in, adding 1 teaspoon each of lemon juice, vanilla extract, and sifted cornstarch. Pipe or shape into one large basket as above. Cook at 275°F for an hour or until hard outside. Turn the oven off but let cool inside. Fill with your choice of fresh fruit, whipped cream, and fresh berry sauce (p239).

A classic white meringue WLTM exotic fruity flavors for friendship … maybe more.

PREP Preheat the oven to 150°C/Gas 2. Line 2 baking sheets with baking parchment.

Make the sauce: peel the mango over a bowl to catch the juices. Slice the flesh off and scrape it from the seed. Blitz the flesh and juices to a puree in a processor or blender. Tip it back into the bowl. Add the lime juice and sugar. Halve the passionfruit. Scoop the seeds and pulp into the mix. If it's very sweet, add a little extra lime juice. Chill it.

Make a quantity of white meringue following the basic method opposite. Spoon or pipe it onto the prepared sheets to make baskets. To spoon: Heap 2–3 tablespoons of mix per basket. Using the back of a spoon, flatten each one out a little in the center to make a space to hold the fruit. Tease the mix up steeply around the sides. The meringue may rise as it cooks so make a distinct shape. To pipe: Draw 6 x 3¼-inch circles on the parchment. Fit a thin or star tube to a pastry bag. Pipe a base, working from the center outward in a continuous spiral until complete. Pipe a wall around the edges. Or pipe a few big blobs onto the circle. Spread them flat with a palette knife. Pipe blobs around the outside to make a wall to hold the filling in later.

COOK Bake for at least an hour or until crisp. Turn off the oven and let the baskets dry out. Peel them off the paper. Sit them on a rack to cool. Pour the cream into a cold bowl. Whip it until it just holds its shape and before it hardens up.

PLATE Spoon a little sauce into the baskets. Pile in the whipped cream and spoon over more sauce to finish.

CINNAMON BROWN SUGAR SHELLS WITH PISTACHIOS AND RASPBERRIES

MAKES 12 MERINGUE SHELLS

INGREDIENTS

1 x brown meringue mix (p240)
1–2 teaspoons ground cinnamon (to taste)
12 shelled pistachios
generous ¾ cup heavy cream
1 teaspoon confectioners' sugar, sifted
a small pinch of ground ginger (optional)
scant 2½ cups fresh raspberries

—— CHANGE IT UP ——

1. For hazelnut shells, add chopped hazelnuts instead of pistachios and don't include the spices. **2.** For chocolate shells, sift a bit of unsweetened cocoa into the mix with the cinnamon.

—— BONUS BITE ——

BLACKBERRY STACKS

Make the meringue mix as above without the spice. Pipe into individual disks on wax paper (tracing circles onto the paper then piping from the center in an outward spiral). Cook as above then pile with whipped cream and fresh blackberries. Leave open or top with another disk. Make a fresh berry sauce with blackberries (p239) and drizzle over to finish.

A decadent mix of spice, nuts, and brown sugar with a fresh lift of tangy raspberry.

PREP Preheat the oven to 225°F. Line 2 baking sheets with parchment.

Make up the brown sugar meringue following the method on p240, whisking in the cinnamon at the end or folding it in lightly with a large metal spoon.

Spoon or pipe the mix into shells/large blobs. Spoon it: Use 2 tablespoons. Scoop the mix up in one spoon and use the other to ease it off onto the sheet. Keep the surface smooth for a neat look or rough it up a bit. They will expand, so leave space between them. Pipe it: Fix a plain or medium tube onto a pastry bag. Hold the bag in one hand. Fold the sides down over your hand then spoon the mix into the bag. Pull the sides up then twist it to close at the top, squeezing the meringue down to the tube. Point it at the paper and squeeze to release as much as you need for each meringue.

Chop the nuts roughly. Sprinkle sparingly over the meringues.

COOK Bake for 2 hours for a crisp result or 1 hour for chewy meringue. Carefully peel the paper away from one or two to check the base is crisp. Give them extra time if needed.

Peel the paper off the bases. Cool on a rack (not a cold counter) to avoid cracking.

Whip the cream in a cold bowl with a hand or balloon whisk so you can feel how it's thickening up. Add the confectioners' sugar to taste and a little ground ginger, if you like.

PLATE Pile the meringues up on a big plate. Bang the cream into a dish and raspberries into another. Serve at the table so people can help themselves. Alternatively, sandwich the raspberries and cream between the meringues for neat eating.

A PROPER ENGLISH APPLE PIE

FEEDS 4

INGREDIENTS

PIE DOUGH
2½ cups all-purpose flour
a pinch of salt
¾ cup (1½ sticks) cold butter, plus extra for greasing
scant ⅓ cup superfine sugar
½ teaspoon grated lemon zest
1 large egg

FILLING
1½ pounds tasty eating or cooking apples (peeled, cored weight)
1 tablespoon butter
a squeeze of lemon juice
1 teaspoon lemon rind
3 cardamom pods/3 cloves/a pinch of cinnamon
scant ⅓ cup superfine sugar
generous ¾ cup water

FINISH
1 small egg, beaten with 1 teaspoon water
superfine sugar to sprinkle

CHANGE IT UP

For a tutti frutti pie, add small chunks of summer fruit such as peach, apricot, nectarine, plum to the softened apple just before filling and omit the spices.

BONUS BITE

APPLE PLUM PUDDING CAKE
Prep the apples as above. Chop 2 plums. Cream together scant 1 cup superfine sugar and 6 tablespoons soft butter until light. Gradually beat in 2 beaten eggs. Sift in scant 1⅔ cups all-purpose flour, 2 teaspoons baking powder, and 1½ teaspoons ground cinnamon. Add the grated zest of 1 lemon and fold the mix lightly together. Stir in the fruit plus 1–2 tablespoons milk until the mix is soft enough to drop off a spoon. Put into a lined 8-inch round pan and bake in a preheated oven at 350°F for 1 hour.

Here's a very relaxed apple pie and an easy introduction to a sweet basic pie dough: it's great with cheese, cream, or ice cream.

PREP Make the pie dough By hand: Sift the flour and salt into a bowl. Cut the butter into small cubes. Drop them into the bowl. Rub the fat and flour between your fingers until they amalgamate. Add the sugar and lemon zest. Beat the egg then dribble it in gradually, mixing with a fork as you go, until you have a pliable dough that's neither sticky nor dry (you might not need it all). Roll it lightly into a ball and wrap in plastic wrap. Chill for 30 minutes. By machine: Pulse everything except the egg in a processor. Pour the egg gradually through the funnel. Pulse until it comes together. Wrap and chill.

For the filling: Peel the apples. Core or quarter then cut out the seeds with a sharp knife. Slice or chop them roughly then throw into a pan with the butter, lemon juice and zest, spice, and a splash of water. Cook and stir on very gentle heat until almost tender but holding shape. (Smaller pieces of watery apple will take 5 minutes, others will take longer). Set aside to cool. Taste; if the apple is very tart add a bit more sugar.

Preheat the oven to 340°F. Grease a shallow circular 7-inch enamel pie dish or similar.

Sit your chilled dough on a lightly floured board. Cut one third off to make the lid. Roll the larger two-thirds out using a floured rolling pin, turning it 45 degrees after each roll to keep a regular shape. Create a large thin circle wide enough to line your dish, with some left over. Do this by eye or use the string test for accuracy (p229). Roll the pin under the dough. Lift it over and into the pan then manipulate it to fit, pasting any cracks or holes as you go. Now, roll out the other piece in a circle big enough to cover the top of the pie plus a bit. Don't worry if you need to reroll during any part of the process. It's normal. Roll any extra bits out and cut out leaves for decoration, if you like.

Spoon the cooled filling into the dish. Lift the pie dough lid over it using the pin, lay it down, and pinch/crimp the edges together to seal them. Brush it lightly with the beaten egg/water to give it shine. Cut a couple of slits in the center. Stick your leaves on top if using. Sprinkle with sugar.

COOK Bake the pie for 30 minutes or until the crust is golden, crisp, and buttery. Remove and sit it on a wire rack. Leave it in its pan.

PLATE Bang the pie on the table. Serve with a wedge of strong or crumbly cheese, (like Cheddar) a pitcher of cream, yogurt, or ice cream. It reheats well. Take it into work to warm in the microwave or take it out in the pan for a picnic.

PLUM, PEACH, BANANA, AND APPLE TARTE TATIN

FEEDS 4

INGREDIENTS

1 x 1-pound 2-ounce pack puff pastry
2 plums
2 apricots
1 large cooking apple
3–4 eating apples
1 banana
4 cardamom pods
½ cup superfine sugar
scant ½ cup pear cider (perry)
3 tablespoons soft butter

—— **BONUS BITES** ——

FAST APPLE BUTTER TART FOR 2.
Roll 4 ounces puff pastry out very thinly. Rest it in the refrigerator. Cut into 2 x 7-inch circles. Peel, core, quarter, and thinly slice 2 apples. Arrange the slices concentrically on each tart, overlapping slightly. Dot with a few little bits of butter, sprinkle with a little superfine sugar, then bake at 450°F for 10 to 15 minutes. Melt 2 tablespoons apricot jam with a little water and brush over the hot tarts. Eat with vanilla ice cream.

Here's one of the great French classics made simple; crisp pastry, gorgeous soft fruit, sticky caramel. Make it upside down in the pan then bang it in the oven. It looks and tastes ridiculously gorgeous.

PREP Sit the puff pastry on a lightly floured board. Roll it out until it's about ¼ inch thick and big enough to cover the top of a 8 by 10-inch iron-handled skillet with 1¼ inches extra all around the sides. Invert the pan onto the pastry and cut around it, allowing for the extra 1¼ inches, using a sharp knife. Lift it onto a plate. Chill it.

Prepare the fruit: Cut the plums and apricots in two. Twist the halves to separate. Remove the pits. Peel and core the apples. Cut one of the eating apples in two horizontally. Retain one of the halves to make a centerpiece. Quarter the other half and cut the remaining apples into eighths. Slice the banana. Toss the fruit in a little lemon juice. Preheat the oven to 375°F.

Make the caramel sauce. Bash the cardamom pods lightly to expose the seeds. Fling them into the center of your skillet. Add the sugar and cider. Stir a couple of times. Boil for 2 minutes or until it turns golden brown. Don't burn it. Add the butter, stirring. Remove from the heat as soon as it melts.

Working with care, place the halved apple, cut side down, in the center of the skillet. Arrange the other fruit around it, either randomly or in a pattern, fitting pieces tightly together. Return the skillet to very low heat for 4 minutes so the fruit starts to cook and the sauce to caramelize. Remove from the heat.

Cover the fruit with the pastry. Slip your rolling pin under the circle. Lift it over the skillet then lower it down. Using a wooden spoon or fork handle, gently tuck the edges down the sides of the skillet.

COOK Shift the tart to the oven. Bake for 30 minutes or until puffed, crisp, and golden. Remove and let rest for 5 minutes (the pastry will sink but that's fine). To turn it out: place a large plate (wider than the skillet) over the pastry. Holding skillet and plate firmly, invert the skillet so the tart and any extra juice will slip out.

PLATE Serve this impressive looking tart at the table. Enjoy it warm or cold with whipped cream, yogurt, Devonshire cream, or good thin custard (p236).

DELICIOUS APPLE AND PISTACHIO STRUDEL WITH SPICED CREAM

FEEDS 4

Fall embodied in a delicious apple-packed crisp phyllo package; beat the spiced fruit juices into some softly whipped cream for the perfect accompaniment.

INGREDIENTS

9 tablespoons butter
½ cup raisins
2 tablespoons rum
2 large cooking apples
1 tablespoon lemon juice
¼ cup superfine sugar
1 teaspoon ground cinnamon
4 large sheets phyllo dough
½ cup dried white bread crumbs
   (p201)
scant ¼ cup pistachios, shelled weight
1¼ cups heavy cream
a bit of superfine sugar, sifted

PREP Melt the butter gently in a small pan on low heat. Brush a little over a large baking sheet with a pastry brush. Set the rest aside.

For the filling: Tip the raisins and rum into a small bowl to soak. Peel and core and slice the apples thinly. Chuck them into a larger bowl with the lemon juice, sugar, and cinnamon, stirring to coat the fruit so it doesn't brown.

Sort the phyllo dough: Lay a large sheet of wax paper or a dish towel on your counter. Unwrap the pack of phyllo dough. With great care (it's delicate), peel away the first sheet. Lay it flat on the wax paper. Cover the rest.

Quickly brush the sheet of phyllo all over with butter so it doesn't dry out. Scatter a third of the bread crumbs over it. Lay a second sheet of phyllo directly on top. Brush all over with butter again and scatter over another third of the bread crumbs. Repeat until you have 4 layers of phyllo together. Finish with more butter (no crumbs).

Mix the rum, raisins, pistachios, and apples. Drain off and save their juices. Spoon/pile the filling onto the edge of the phyllo dough nearest to you, leaving a bit of space at the end and on the two long sides for folding. To roll: Pull the edges of the long sides of phyllo up onto the filling then fold the close end up and over the apples, pushing gently as you go and using the paper to help. Roll up, keeping the long edges tucked up so it's enclosed well. Place seam down on the baking sheet.

COOK Brush the strudel with more butter and bake for 25 to 30 minutes until golden brown. Test for doneness with a skewer. It should be hot inside. Remove and brush with more butter. Cool on the sheet for 5 minutes. Transfer to a serving dish for eating hot or at room temperature. Meanwhile, whip the cream, adding the reserved rum and spice juice.

PLATE Dust the strudel with confectioners' sugar. Slice and enjoy with your whipped cream, or serve with vanilla ice cream or honey with yogurt.

SINFUL TRIPLE CHOCOLATE TART

FEEDS 6 TO 8

INGREDIENTS
PIE DOUGH
scant 1⅔ cups all-purpose flour
2½ tablespoons confectioners' sugar
a pinch of salt
scant 3 tablespoons superfine sugar
8 tablespoons cold butter, cubed
1 small egg, beaten
FILLING
3½ ounces milk chocolate
5 ounces semisweet chocolate (70%)
5 ounces white chocolate
7 tablespoons butter
3 whole eggs, plus 4 extra egg yolks
½ cup superfine sugar

TIPS
1 When rolling out your dough to fit the pan, either judge the size by eye or use the string technique (p229) to be really accurate.
2 If your tart starts to turn a darker brown while cooking, cover the top with some baking parchment.

Here's my favorite chocolate tart of all time. It's more subtle than most, smoothly intense, yummy. Put it out there with a sorbet.

PREP Make the pie dough. By hand: Sift the flour, confectioners' sugar, and salt into a bowl. Stir in the superfine sugar, add the butter and rub together between your fingertips until the mix resembles fine bread crumbs. Add the beaten egg gradually, mixing it with a fork until you get firm dough which is neither too dry nor sticky. (Add a drop of cold water if you need to or a little extra flour). Roll it into a smooth ball. By machine: Put the flour, sugar, butter, and salt into a processor. Pulse until it amalgamates. Add the egg a little at a time, pulsing, until the dough is right. Roll it into a ball. Flatten it slightly. Wrap it in plastic wrap. Chill for 30 minutes.

Roll the dough out on a lightly floured board as thinly as you can to fit the bottom and sides of a 9-inch tart pan, allowing a bit extra for overhang. Set aside any extra dough. Line the pan: Run a metal spatula under the dough. Lift it up on the pin and lower into the pan. Ease it down to fit the sides and bottom, leaving a wide overhang. Mold and mend any cracks with the extra dough. Chill for 30 minutes. Preheat the oven to 350°F.

Bake it blind: Prick the bottom lightly with a fork and lay a large piece of baking parchment into the shell. Fill with a layer of pie weights or dried beans. Bake for 15 to 20 minutes until pale and firm. Remove. Lift the parchment and weights/beans out. Return it to the oven for a few minutes. Remove. Once it's cooled slightly, take a sharp knife and remove the overhang.

Make the filling: chop the milk chocolate randomly into fine and larger dice. Scatter them evenly over the baked cooled tart base. Break the dark and white chocolate into a heatproof bowl. Add the butter. Sit the bowl over a pan of gently simmering water, keeping the bottom of the bowl clear. Once the chocolate has melted, remove from the heat, stir until smooth, and let cool.

Increase the oven temperature to 425°F. Put the eggs and sugar into a large bowl. Whisk for a few minutes using a balloon or electric handheld whisk until you get a white fluffy mousse. Pour the cooled chocolate onto the mousse. Using a large metal spoon, cut into the mix and lightly fold it together with figure-of-eight movements until just amalgamated. Pour into the pastry shell.

COOK Bake for 7 to 10 minutes until the chocolate is just set and is a bit firmer than a mousse. The skill is to know when it's done—shuffle the pan to check that it's firm in the center. If there's a gap between filling and pie dough, it's very well done. Remove. Sit it on a rack for 5 minutes. Lift it out of the pan. Let cool.

PLATE Sit the tart on a serving plate to slice at the table. Dust with a bit of cocoa or confectioners' sugar if you like and serve with shot glasses filled with grapefruit water ice or raspberry vodka sorbet (p237).

BAKEWELL TART

FEEDS 6 TO 8

INGREDIENTS

PIE DOUGH

scant 1⅔ cups all-purpose flour
a pinch of salt
8 tablespoons cold butter, cubed
scant 3 tablespoons superfine sugar
1 medium egg, beaten

FILLING

3–4 tablespoons raspberry jam
9 tablespoons soft butter
½ cup + 2 tablespoons superfine sugar
3 eggs plus 1 extra yolk (at room temperature)
1¾ cups ground almonds
1 teaspoon almond extract
1 teaspoon amaretto (optional)
a few slivered almonds

—— CHANGE IT UP ——

Switch the raspberry jam for strawberry, plum or black cherry jam instead.

—— BONUS BITE ——

CUSTARD TART

Make up a batch of sweet pie dough as above, adding a pinch of nutmeg with the flour. Chill for an hour. Preheat the oven to 350°F. Roll the dough out thinly and use to line a 8½-inch tart pan and blind bake as above. (This is a very wet filling, so be sure to repair any cracks or holes in the base and sides before cooking). Make the filling by putting ¼ cup superfine sugar and ½ teaspoon vanilla extract into a bowl. Add 4 eggs and beat until mixed. Add 1¾ cups milk and mix again. Strain the mix through a strainer and pour into the tart shell. Sprinkle over lots of freshly grated/ground nutmeg and carry very carefully to the oven. Bake for 15 minutes or until the custard sets. Judge it by the amount of wobble (shuffle the pan); it should look set. Remove and let cool before eating.

An easy-to-make traditional English dessert; this may look a bit safe on taste but trust me, it's not. It's soft, jammy, heavy on the almond frangipane, absolutely gorgeous.

PREP Make the pie dough: Sift the flour and salt into a bowl. Add the butter. Rub them together between your fingertips until the mix resembles fine bread crumbs. Stir in the sugar. Add the beaten egg gradually, mixing with a fork until you get a firm dough which is neither dry not sticky. Add a drop of cold water or flour if you need. Pull it into a smooth ball.

By machine: Pulse the flour, salt, and sugar. Add the butter. Pulse. Add the egg gradually until the dough is right. Roll into a ball. Flatten it. Wrap it in plastic wrap. Chill for 30 minutes. Preheat the oven to 350°F.

Roll the dough out on a lightly floured board to ⅛ inch thickness. Line the sides and bottom of an 8½-inch tart pan, allowing extra for an overhang.

Line with baking parchment and fill with pie weights. Bake the shell blind for 20 minutes. The sides should feel crisp and start to look a pale brown. Remove. Lift out the paper and pie weights. If the bottom is very pale and soft give it a few extra minutes. Remove. Carefully cut away the pie dough overhang after a few seconds.

For the filling: Spoon the jam into the partcooked shell and spread it evenly to cover. Tip the butter and sugar into a bowl and cream the mix together by beating hard with a wooden spoon for a few minutes until it's light, white, and smooth. Beat the eggs and yolk together in a bowl and add to the creamed mix a little at a time, beating constantly to stop the mixture curdling. Add the ground almonds, almond extract, and amaretto, if using, folding everything together very gently with a large metal spoon.

Spoon the mix into the tart in large blobs, then join them up so you don't disturb the jam. Scatter slivered almonds over the top.

COOK Bake for 25 to 30 minutes. It's done when the center looks firm but springy and it's a lovely golden brown. If it browns up early, cover with baking parchment. Remove.

Let cool on a rack. Remove the sides of the pan after 5 minutes.

PLATE Slice your tart at the table. Eat on its own or serve with vanilla ice cream or custard (p236), fromage frais or whipped cream. It's also great with a cup of coffee or tea and keeps well.

LEMON POSSET
AND CRISP TUILES COOKIES

FEEDS 4

INGREDIENTS

1¾ cups heavy cream
scant ½ cup superfine sugar
2 lemons

The Elizabethans got it right with this one; just the three ingredients, very little effort, and a beautiful thick creamy lemon outcome. Make it a day ahead or several hours before serving.

PREP Get your containers organized (small cocktail or wine glasses, cups, small dishes). Zest one lemon and juice two. Tip the zest and juice into a small bowl.

Pour the cream and sugar into a large pan (the mix will boil up).

COOK Put the pan onto very gentle heat. Stir to dissolve the sugar. Let it come to a boil very slowly. Regulate the heat so it won't boil over.

Boil the mix for just 3 minutes. Remove. Stir in the zest and juice. If it starts to look a bit lumpy, that's ok. Taste and if it's not sharp enough (don't let the cream or sugar dominate) add a bit more juice. It should taste like a really good cheesecake.

Let cool. Pour into your glasses of choice. Put them into the refrigerator to set. Chill for at least 4 hours.

PLATE Serve topped with a handful of sliced berries and accompanied by crisp tuiles cookies (below).

TO GO WITH
TUILES COOKIES

Preheat the oven to 375°F. Grease and line 2 large baking sheets. Melt scant ¼ cup butter in a pan over low heat. Tip it into a bowl to cool. Put 2 egg whites and ½ cup superfine sugar into a clean bowl. Beat with a fork for 3 minutes. When the mix is thick and frothy, sift over and beat in generous ⅓ cup flour and 4 drops of vanilla extract. Once the batter is smooth, slowly beat in the cooled butter. Use a teaspoon to put 4 blobs of mix well apart on each sheet (they expand). Using a metal spatula, spread them into very thin circles. Bake for 5 to 6 minutes until pale tan in the middle and browned at the margins (check after 4 minutes). Remove from the oven. Leave for 5 seconds only. Slide a spatula under each one to loosen then lift them off. Mold them into large curls over a rolling pin or back of a wooden spoon, holding them there for 5 seconds. Rest on a rack to crisp up. Repeat with the rest of the mix. Store in an airtight tin.

INDEX

A HUGE THANK YOU TO ALL THESE LOVELY PEOPLE ...

My editor Simon Davis for all his superhuman efforts, patience, and making things fit; Claire Peters for making it look beautiful; Chris Terry for the amazing photographs; Emily Jonzen for great support; Jane O'Shea for believing in me; Felicity Blunt for being a brilliant agent; my brother Tom and sister Polly for always being there for me; the rest of the family; Louise for helping out; Dad for being chief taster and always supporting; Mickey (who always picks up the scraps) and Mom—for being her usual perfect self, for all her help and inspiration, and for putting up with me.

Editorial Director Jane O'Shea
Creative Director Helen Lewis
Project Editor Simon Davis
Designer Claire Peters
Design Assistant Jim Smith
Photographer Chris Terry
Food Stylist Emily Jonzen
Stylist Iris Bromet
Illustrator Claire Peters
Editorial Assistant Louise McKeever
Production Director Vincent Smith
Production Controller Leonie Kellman

First published in 2012 by
Quadrille Publishing Limited
Alhambra House
27-31 Charing Cross Road
London WC2H 0LS
www.quadrille.co.uk

Text © 2012 Sam Stern
Photographs © 2012 Chris Terry
Design and layout © 2012
Quadrille Publishing Limited
This Lyons Press edition first published in 2013

Lyons Press is an imprint of Globe Pequot Press.

Library of Congress Cataloging-in-Publication Data is available on file.

ISBN 978-0-7627-8802-6

Printed in China

10 9 8 7 6 5 4 3 2 1